D0803506

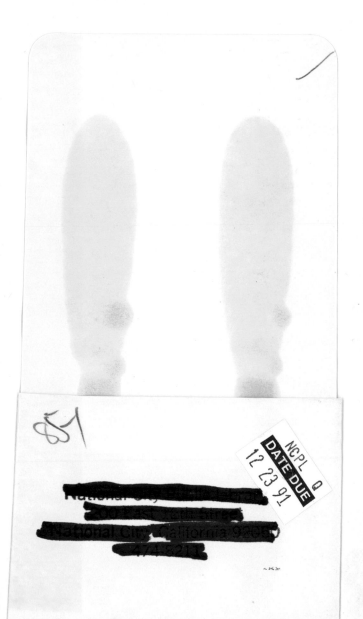

851

A Matter of Degree

Other books by Lucy Kavaler

Freezing Point: Cold As a Matter of Life and Death
Mushrooms, Molds, and Miracles
Noise, the New Menace
The Astors: A Family Chronicle of Pomp and Power
The Private World of High Society

For Young Readers:
Life Battles Cold
Cold Against Disease
The Dangers of Noise
Dangerous Air
The Wonders of Fungi
The Artificial World Around Us
The Wonders of Algae
The Astors: An American Legend

A MATTER OF DEGREE
Heat, Life, and Death

by Lucy Kavaler

1817

HARPER & ROW, PUBLISHERS, New York

Cambridge, Philadelphia, San Francisco,
London, Mexico City, São Paulo, Sydney

FIRST EDITION

Designer: Ruth Markiewicz

Library of Congress Cataloging in Publication Data

Kavaler, Lucy.
    A matter of degree.
    Bibliography: p.
    Includes index.
    1. Heat—Physiological effect.   2. Adaptation (Physiology)   3. Life (Biology)   4. Heat—Social aspects.
I. Title.
QP82.2.H4K38 1981   574.19′162   80-8789
ISBN 0-06-014854-3   AACR2

81 82 83 84 85 10 9 8 7 6 5 4 3 2 1

For my father, L. I. Estrin
in memory of the many good years

Contents

Acknowledgments

Heat has always held a fascination for me. It can kill, excite, bring comfort or misery, injure, or relieve. In this book it is my aim to show the effect of heat on living things. Humans, animals, plants, and microbes have adapted in ways so strange and extreme as to challenge the imagination.

My investigation of the many aspects of heat has ranged from police department crime reports, athletic records, emergency room heat-wave statistics, cancer research, and travelers' advisories to tales of survival in the desert. I should like to acknowledge here the many people who have helped me in the course of my research. I have received valuable information in person where possible, by telephone, and by mail, and have been given comments and expert opinion, reports, and papers, many unpublished.

I should like to express my thanks to those who provided me with data on human reactions, both physical and psychological, about the effects of the sun and of fire: Dr. Barbara L. Drinkwater, Institute of Environmental Stress, University of California, Santa Barbara; Dr. Lewis Goldfrank, Albert Einstein College of Medicine, and Director, Emergency Medical Services, North Central Bronx Hospital; Biostatistics and Vital Statistics, New York City Department of Health; New York City Police Department; Masako Momiyama-Sakamoto, Meteorological Research Institute, Tokyo; Dr. Anderson Spickard, Vanderbilt School of Medicine; Dr. Stanley H. Schuman, Medical University of South Carolina; Dr. Stephen L. Corson, Reproductive Endocrinologist, Philadelphia; Dr. Ralph F. Goldman, Director, Military Ergonomics

Division, U.S. Army Research Institute of Environmental Medicine; Dr. Michael Marmor, Institute of Environmental Medicine, New York University Medical Center and the Rockefeller Foundation; Dr. Frederick H. Rohles, Jr., Director, Institute for Environmental Research, Manhattan, Kansas; Dr. Gary Greenberg, Wichita State University; Dr. Robert A. Baron, Director, Social and Developmental Psychology, National Science Foundation; Dr. Hans E. Landsberg, University of Maryland; Dr. William C. Gentry, University of Minnesota Hospitals; Gordon Vickery, Administrator, Federal Emergency Management Agency, U.S. Fire Administration; Gerontology Research Center, National Institute on Aging; and Environmental Data and Information Service of National Climatic Center.

My research into fever, both as a phenomenon and as a therapy, was aided by Dr. Ivan Kochan, Miami University; Dr. Eugene D. Weinberg, Indiana University; Dr. George Crile, Jr., Cleveland Clinic; Dr. Kenneth Luk, Mt. Zion Hospital and Medical Center; Dr. Max L. M. Boone, University of Arizona; and Dr. C. M. Blatteis, University of Tennessee.

I appreciate the assistance of the many physicians who provided me with information about diseases of the tropics and their impact upon Americans: Dr. Myron G. Schultz, Director, Parasitic Diseases Division, Centers for Disease Control; Bureau of Epidemiology, Centers for Disease Control; Dr. Richard A. Finkelstein, University of Texas Southwest Medical School; Dr. Eleanor E. Storrs, Gulf Research Institute; Dr. Paul A. Blake, Deputy Chief, Enteric Diseases Branch, Centers for Disease Control; Kendall King, Research Corporation; Dr. Robert C. Hastings, Chief, Pharmacology Research Department, U.S. Public Health Service, Carville; Dr. Richard Carter, National Institute of Allergy and Infectious Diseases; Dr. Howard B. Shookhoff, New York City Department of Health; Dr. Peter Jordan, Director, Research and Control Department, St. Lucia, West Indies; Dr. M. G. Taylor, London School of Hygiene and Tropical Medicine; Dr. Donald E. Weidhaas, Director, Insects Affecting Man Research Laboratory, U.S. Department of Agriculture; Dr. N. Kent, Division of Malaria and Other Parasitic Diseases, World Health Organization, Geneva; Dr. Ernest Bueding, Johns Hopkins University School of Hygiene and Public Health; Dr. Vincent C. McCarthy, University of Maryland School of Medicine; Dr. Leonard J. Bruce-Chwatt, Royal Society of Medicine,

London; and Dr. Elizabeth Barrett-Connor, University of California San Diego School of Medicine.

Additional material on life in desert and tropics was furnished me by Marion O'Connor, United Nations Development Programme; Erik P. Eckholm, Worldwatch Institute; Yaacov Levy, Consul of Israel, New York; Jennifer Gillis, Peace Corps; and Dr. Garrett Hardin, University of California, Santa Barbara.

The sections dealing with the effects of high temperature on animals from dinosaur to present day, in desert and jungle, were aided by Dr. Eugene S. Morton, National Zoological Park, Smithsonian Institution; Dr. Neil Greenberg, University of Tennessee; Dr. Nicholas Hotton, Research Curator, Smithsonian Institution; Dr. J. J. Bull, Laboratory of Genetics, University of Wisconsin; Dr. Stephen M. Russell, University of Arizona; C. D. Bramwell, University of Reading, U.K.; Dr. Alan M. Beck, Director, Bureau of Animal Affairs, New York City Department of Health; José Torre-Bueno, Rockefeller University; Dr. Alfred P. Fishman, Hospital of the University of Pennsylvania; Dr. Ira Rubinoff, Director, Smithsonian Tropical Research Institute, Canal Zone; Dr. E. B. Edney, University of California, Riverside; and Dr. Walter G. Whitford, New Mexico State University.

Information on the ability of microorganisms to endure high temperatures and the effect on food safety was furnished me by Dr. Thomas D. Brock, University of Indiana; Dr. Eugene E. Staffeldt, New Mexico State University; R. V. Lechovich, Head, Food Science and Technology, Virginia Polytechnic Institute and State University; and Edmund A. Zottola, University of Minnesota Agricultural Extension Service.

My studies of the effects of heat on plant life were aided by Dr. Lowell Hardin, Agricultural Specialist, Ford Foundation; J. Remenyi, Ford Foundation; Dr. John H. Lonnquist, University of Wisconsin; Thomas R. Hargrave, International Rice Research Institute, Manila; Dr. Ariel E. Lugo, University of Florida; Francesca Sherwood, Centre for Overseas Pest Research, London; and Dr. Roderick H. Wagner, Director, Desert Biome, Ecology Center, Utah State University.

I should also like to add a word in memory of Marie Rodell, for her help and belief in this as in my other books and for her friendship. And I should like to thank Arthur for his encouragement and positive outlook.

A Matter of Degree

Of Riot, Murder, and the Heat of Passion

On a June Sunday in 1967, three young men broke into a photographic supply warehouse in Tampa, Florida. The temperature was in the mid-90s and the humidity was high; nonetheless, both citizens and police gave chase. One of the robbers, stripped to the waist to better endure the heat, was stopped in his run by a high cyclone fence, and there he was shot by a policeman. As the bullet struck, the young man reached up, grabbed at the fence, and hung on. He was in this position, with his hands over his head, when other pursuers rushed up. The scene was prolonged, because the ambulance called by a bystander was lost on its way. The young man was black and the policeman was white. All the criteria for a riot were present. And by nightfall, despite police guarantees of an investigation of the shooting, crowds had gathered and police cars were being stoned, stores looted, and power lines knocked down.

Similar scenes of violence took place that year in Newark, Cincinnati, Atlanta, and many other cities. By the end of September, 164 riots had broken out in 128 cities, five of them in New York and four in Chicago. The largest number took place in July, the National Advisory Commission on Civil Disorders learned, after studying the records month by month. There had been just one minor disorder in January, none in February.

The temperature records of the cities in which riots occurred gave high readings for the day preceding the incident that precipitated the violence. It was 90 degrees Fahrenheit or higher in Atlanta, Newark, Cincinnati, Phoenix, Tucson, Dayton, Paterson, Cambridge, and Tampa and was in the 80s before riots in Rockford, Illinois; Detroit and Grand Rapids, Michigan; and Elizabeth, Englewood, New Brunswick, and Jersey City, New Jersey. And so it has become customary to blame the long hot summer for riots.

Heat alone, to be sure, does not bring on a riot; poverty, unemployment, economic and social injustices, and real or fancied antagonisms are basic causes. But summertime temperatures make the lives of the city poor increasingly miserable. Brick and concrete retain much more heat than do soil and grass; even after sundown the buildings and streets remain hotter than the air, while grass by then is cooler. Winds that might bring relief are blocked by buildings. At night the inner city is an island of heat.

The discomfort of their crowded airless rooms drives city residents out onto the streets in the evenings in numbers sufficient to be dangerous should a provocative incident occur. Most riots begin between 7 P.M. and 1:30 A.M., before exhaustion sends people back inside to bed.

New York City has had two major power blackouts, one on a November night and the other in July. There was little looting in November. During the July blackout, stores were emptied to the bare walls, and furniture, television sets, large appliances and small, clothing, and anything else that could be carried away was taken. Estimated losses of storekeepers ranged from $150 to $300 million, and 3,076 people were arrested.

When the lights came on again, the November blackout was recalled. A comparison between the two is not truly valid, because the July blackout lasted much longer; however, it seems logical to attribute some of the lawlessness to the high summer temperatures. Many New Yorkers, weary after a day of readings over 90 degrees, were out on the streets. A city plunged in darkness was provocation for plunder, and it was warm enough for looters to stay outside and go from one store to another, taking more each time.

Tempers explode when it is hot. In cool weather, discontent may be expressed with less violence. Astronomers of an earlier day used to say that inhabitants of Mercury had to be very hot-tempered, because that is the planet closest to the sun. At the end of a ten-day heat wave, a newspaper reported that a knife fight broke out when one man asked another, "Hot enough for you?"

On the night of August 4, 1892, murder took place in the town of Fall River, Massachusetts, and Lizzie Borden was accused of having hacked her father and stepmother to death with an ax. Although she was acquitted after a sensational trial, many went on believing in her guilt.

Few of the hundreds of thousands of words that have been written about the murder mentioned the great heat wave in Fall River that August. But all those living in the Borden house must have been at a high level of irritability because of the heat. Was Lizzie the most affected, or might it have been the maid in her stifling attic room? Some witnesses did later claim to have seen the maid commit the act, but their words were discounted.

What really happened in Fall River long ago may never be known, but deaths by violence are indeed a feature of heat waves. Both New York and St. Louis sweltered in July 1966. Thirty-one homicides and 23 suicides took place that month, compared to 13 homicides and 38 suicides during a period of moderate temperatures.

The New York City Police Department Crime Comparison Reports reveal that 157 murders and non-negligent manslaughters occurred in July of 1977, compared to 117 in May. The total of felonies known to have been committed in July of the previous year amounted to 42,734, against 38,516 that May. August is a bad month too. In the summers of 1979 and 1980, the New York police department transferred men from headquarters duty and ordered overtime to increase the number of officers patrolling the streets. During the prolonged 1980 heat wave, the Texas Department of Human Resources found the number of cases of child abuse to be markedly higher than in previous summers, when heat was less intense.

To study the effects of heat on human behavior, a test was carried out at the Kansas Institute for Environmental Research in which high school dropouts, juvenile delinquents, and parolee volunteers were packed in a small, hot room. Arguments and fistfights broke out, and one young man threatened another with a knife. When the same volunteers were placed in less crowded conditions in a cooler room, nobody became aggressive.

Even normally calm people tend to become tense, irritable, and unreasonable, given to snapping over trivia at spouses, children, lovers, relatives, friends, and colleagues, when it is hot. Students crowded in a 90-degree room were hostile to a speaker, while those in a cooler room were prepared to give him a chance. The discomfort of heat could affect a personnel manager deciding whether to hire an applicant, a couple deciding whether to separate.

When heat is accompanied by humidity, irritability reaches a peak. In a study, "The Child and the Weather," reported in the *Pedagogical Seminary* in 1898, Edwin G. Dexter, a Denver teacher, related the frequency of corporal punishment in the schools to the weather. After analyzing 606 instances occurring from 1883 to 1897, he claimed that humidities of 80 to 90 percent, rare in Denver, were linked to an increase of 100 percent in disciplinary problems, compared to the days of low humidity. (Little attention was paid to the fact that the decision as to whether behavior deserved punishment was made by adults, equally irritable in the humidity.)

When heat is accompanied by hot winds, the effect is even more unsettling, particularly to the emotionally unstable. And some winds, like the chinook from the Rockies, can raise the temperature 40 degrees within hours. It has often been said that Italian judges are lenient about crimes of passion committed when the hot, dust-bearing sirocco blows up from the Sahara. "A society's treatment of crime may also be indicative of its emotional attitude—in Latin countries, for example, the law of murder differs considerably from that prevailing among the Teutonic people, and more allowance is made for the state of mind of the murderer." This statement from the *Encyclopedia Britannica* (1957 edition) presents a stereotype that probably does not stand careful scrutiny. But many Americans share the implied view that a person who commits a crime of passion in certain foreign countries will be acquitted or given a mild sentence. And it happens often enough to keep the stereotype alive.

Such a case began on a March day in 1972 when Ginette Vidal, a forty-one-year-old French medical secretary, and her handsome twenty-nine-year-old lover, Gerard Osselin, drew up a contract swearing to be faithful for life and stating that if either of them broke the contract, the other could kill the faithless one. Both lovers were married, but even sexual relations with spouses was considered breaking the contract. The lovers lived together, but Gerard, lonely for his wife, slipped away to see her every so often. One day Ginette came home when her lover was sleeping, went through his pockets, and found a shopping list in his wife's handwriting. Considering this sufficient proof of infidelity, she shot him where he lay.

At her trial, she cited the contract, surprised to learn it was not legal. Her defense attorney pleaded, "It is hard at this woman's age when you have heard the bells of perfect love ringing, suddenly to see all this taken away from you." The jury found her guilty, but the sentence was for only ten years. The emotion that had caused her to kill was taken as an extenuating circumstance. Although many criminals motivated by jealousy do not get off as lightly as Mme. Vidal, some sympathy is felt for them, and the "crime of passion" is seen as quite different from a murder in cold blood.

Our vocabulary reveals how, misery, riot, and murder notwithstanding, we are prejudiced in favor of heat and against cold. To be hot-blooded is to be human. Our deepest feelings are linked with heat, and even negative emotions are viewed as better than none at all. We burn with passion, or with rage or lust. We are consumed in the flame of love or, less happily, in the green flame of envy. Being human means being able to catch fire with excitement. Hot-tempered, we take action in the heat of anger, carry on heated arguments, and get hot under the collar. We may send a scorching letter without waiting to cool off. We glow, simmer, seethe, and boil. And when the passion of love or anger is spent, it leaves us burned out. We breathe fire when aroused and see fire in the eye of an angry opponent. Burned up, worked up to a white heat, we may be incited by the inflammatory words of a fiery speaker or firebrand, even a hothead. We may go into a red-hot or white-hot rage. Wishing to succeed, we become fired with ambition. We fall into a hotbed of iniquity, never a cold one. Many of us have a low boiling point. Those who are likable are warmhearted and warm in their manner.

Dogs, cats, and other animals who are given human attributes are warm-blooded. In contrast, cold-blooded creatures such as snakes or lizards are commonly viewed as emotionless.

To be a lukewarm lover is not good enough. We do not like the cold person, the cold-blooded, or the one whose heart is like ice while planning things coolly. A lack of sexual and/or emotional response is known as being frigid. We are repelled by anyone who is icy, glacial, chilly, chilling, frosty, frostbitten, or wintry in manner; who freezes us out or gives us the cold shoulder. The old slang expression for jail was the "cooler," where those who were hot-tempered were sent to cool off.

The practice of combining words involving heat with words connoting deep feeling has a kind of logic, based on the fact that the body's reactions to the sudden onset of rage, fear, lust, or intense anxiety are remarkably similar to those induced by sudden exposure to extreme heat. The heart beats faster in response both to emotion and to external heat, and breathing quickens. The blood vessels in the skin dilate, and there is an increase in blood flow, making the skin flush. If the blood vessels remain dilated for long, some liquid leaks into the tissues and the face looks swollen. This is the face we associate both with sexual passion and with rage. There is not much difference between the facial expressions for each of these very different emotions. The endocrine glands are activated by heat and hormone secretion is increased. There is a heightened feeling of excitement. Sweating is not only a response to heat but also to nervousness; it begins instantly when one is trapped in an elevator, threatened by a menacing person, or interviewed for a job.

While excessive heat produces many unpleasant results, warmth is the state that humans prefer to all others. Cold is dreaded and the feeling of being chilled detested. Despair is associated with low temperatures, and the negativism of coldness adds a nuance to F. Scott Fitzgerald's "In a real dark night of the soul, it is always three o'clock in the morning" ("The Crackup" [1936], *Esquire*). Three o'clock in the morning, standing for the low point of the day and of life, happens to be the time when body temperature drops to its lowest level, some 3 degrees below its daytime peak. Metabolism is slowed, and it is harder to take action.

When we remember childhood, it is always high noon in summer, the sun is shining with a golden light, and one clear beautiful warm day follows another. The Arctic and Antarctic are described as unfriendly and hostile, while the tropics are viewed as having a friendly warmth.

It is only when pleasing warmth turns into unpleasant hotness that negative emotional and physical characteristics appear. Some people are stimulated by the heat to perform at their peak. Well-motivated individuals compensate for their discomfort by trying harder and keep the quality of their endeavors high by more intense concentration. However, a drop in efficiency, accuracy, and judgment is so common that before air conditioning came into general use, many offices closed early on hot days.

The extent of the decline was investigated by the U.S. Army Research Institute of Environmental Medicine in order to determine how soldiers would perform in hot climates, but the results apply to civilians as well. Soldiers were required to exercise in heat of 103 degrees at high humidity, which caused a rise in body temperature. They were allowed to rest for a while and then, still overheated, were asked to detect light signals flashed in a random manner. A second group of men exercised at 75 degrees. More light flashes were reported by the men who were hotter, which at first seemed to indicate that this state increased their alertness and competence. But when their detection reports were compared with the true number of signals, it was found that the increase was in false reports. Their judgment was not as sound as that of cooler men. They had become more willing to take a risk and insist that they saw a signal when in fact there was none.

Purdue University students participating in a psychological test carried out in an oppressively hot room gave what they believed were electric shocks to a stranger who had written nasty things about them. However, another group of students, deliberately made angry *before* entering the overheated room, gave fewer shocks. When questioned by psychologists Robert A. Baron and Paul A. Bell, one spoke for all: "The only thing I thought about was getting the hell out of there." The less they reacted to the stranger and the fewer shocks they gave, the sooner they could leave the room. Similarly, outside of the psychology laboratory on many occasions a hot, angry person decides not to stay and argue or commit violence but simply to go home.

Have these reactions anything to do with riot behavior? Dwellers in the crowded, foul-smelling, noisy slums face the heat after having in all probability been angered by employers, shopkeepers, bus drivers, policemen, and members of their families. On very hot days, says Baron, they, like the college students, would probably prefer to escape, but they have no place to go, so they commit violent acts. While riot control depends in the long run on amelioration of basic economic and social problems, Baron sees the establishment of small neighborhood parks, swimming pools, baseball fields, basketball and handball courts, and air-conditioned community centers as a way of helping people cool off physically and emotionally.

The temperature that induces excitement, argument, riots, and aggression is very high, but there is an upper limit. Once heat goes beyond that, it is less rather than more stimulating. Studying mice so as to better understand human aggression, Kansas State University researcher Gary Greenberg conducted temperature experiments. To a point, the hotter it got, the more the mice bit one another. But when the temperature reached 95 degrees, the biting declined and the animals became placid, moved about slowly, trying to keep cool, and were indifferent to the other mice.

Animal bites of humans occur much more frequently in summer than the rest of the year, notes the New York City Department of Health, but this biting cannot just be blamed on heat-induced irritability. It is rather more in line with Noel Coward's old song about mad dogs and Englishmen going out in the midday sun. Pleasant summer weather brings dogs (mad and otherwise) and children out of doors in great numbers. Children between the ages of five and nine are the most often bitten. Once it gets really hot, stray dogs become less and less active and do less and less biting.

For people, too, when high temperatures are prolonged, no effort, no emotional upset, no physical activity is undertaken that will add to the burden of heat the body is enduring. A great indifference to other people and to situations that would normally be exciting or troublesome takes over. "Some loss in initiative is probably the most important single direct result of exposure to a hot environment," states Douglas H. K. Lee, formerly Associate Director of the National Institute of Environmental Health Sciences and an expert on adaptations to desert conditions.

"Who cares about the troop withdrawal? It's too hot to care about anything" was the frequent comment by inhabitants of Seoul, South Korea, when American troop cutbacks were being discussed in August of 1977. In temperatures of 95 to 100 degrees, the air over Seoul was a thick, brown smaze.

Similarly, the French Foreign Legionnaires, waiting to go home in 1977 from newly independent Djibouti in Africa, became lethargic. Until then they had recognized the importance of carrying out their duties in the strategic Red Sea port, even though they considered it a desolate hotbox. Motivation must be high if individuals are to overcome their inclination to heat-induced lassitude. Once that motivation was lost, groups of Legionnaires spent the afternoons in the stifling Café de Paris beneath ceiling fans circulating hot air. The ice in the whiskey melted so fast that the drinks were warm before they could be swallowed. Hour after hour the men sat without speaking. They were too enervated to do more than swat the flies. And so passed one long hot afternoon after another.

Whenever, as in cases like these, northerners in hot regions become inactive or are unable to function effectively in their jobs, it is taken as confirmation of a popular belief, nurtured by fiction: Americans and Europeans transported to the tropics, it is said, go to seed, failing in their efforts to run the rubber plantation or hold the job in the foreign department of the bank or export-import firm, often drinking too much. As alcohol makes the body hotter, they become even more uncomfortable and incapable of effective action. Scorpions run through their houses, wives return home or take lovers, servants cheat them, meals are inedible, and sleep impossible. In fact, however, far from going to seed, most immigrants do become acclimatized and manage to run the plantation and do their work in the office. But this does not make so good a story.

The stereotype of the native of Africa and the Far East is also that of a lazy person, lying in the shade and refusing to do a good day's work. The custom of the siesta seems to provide additional proof of local lassitude; surely only children and old people take naps in the daytime. Northern tourists are frustrated at finding themselves with no place to go during what they view as the peak hours of the day. The hours from 12 to 3 P.M., even in a capital city such as Asunción, Paraguay, are quiet, with shops and business offices closed and everyone gone home.

It is often suggested that civilizations in the tropics have lagged behind those of temperate zones in terms of scientific, industrial, literary, and artistic development, because the high temperatures make people lethargic. There is some truth in this, but not in the way it is commonly meant. Heat of itself does not prevent a high level of intellectual achievement. The great early civilizations arose in tropical and subtropical regions. High temperatures did not impede the ancient Egyptians and Babylonians. The massive temples and pyramids of Luxor, the great palace of Ashurbanipal in Assyria, are clearly the creations of highly civilized and striving peoples, not savages relaxing all day under a tree. Complex philosophies and sophisticated art forms have been developed by the hot-climate Indians and Chinese. The magnificent temple cities of Chichén Itzá and Uxmal in the torrid

Yucatán survive as evidence of an extremely advanced culture in the American tropics.

Even today, with these great civilizations long gone, many people, both native and foreign, are active and successful in tropical regions. The natives are physiologically well-adapted to their environment, and a good number vigorously exploit their opportunities in agriculture, industry, and government. They behave in ways that seem slow to Northerners but that are appropriate to the tropics. The high-powered individual who works at top speed is the most likely to fall victim to heat exhaustion. Those who do best in the heat yield to it to some degree. The scorned siesta is not childlike or lazy; it is advisable to work early and late in the day and avoid exertion during the hottest hours.

Still, there is no denying that progress toward industrial development is exceedingly slow in many countries of the tropics, especially where there seems little reason to achieve complex agricultural and manufac-turing systems. To take the most extreme example, in some remote tropical jungles people can live off the land well enough to remain at a Stone Age stage of development to this day. The Tasadays discovered only recently in the Philippines were so primitive as to be ignorant of the fact that any humans other than their small tribe existed in the world; exploration was not necessary when sufficient food was availa-ble in the area they inhabited.

But tribes able to survive in this way are increasingly rare. Gradually, population pressures in hot regions have been becoming so great as to demand a real effort to fulfill basic needs. But even this has not led to rapid industrialization. The failure can be attributed largely to indirect, rather than direct effects of heat. The natives of the tropics and deserts of the world are often weakened by famines resulting from drought, flood, or civil war and, even in better times, by a low-protein diet. Illness is rampant, causing millions upon millions to drag out their days. Thus heat contributes to a low standard of living among those best equipped by nature to endure it.

One might think that heat could not both quench ambition and stimulate passion, but it is so. Excitement and anger, lassitude and indolence are but a few of the many human responses to excessive heat.

How Hot Is Too Hot?

Every summer a mass migration takes place, with millions moving from hot to cool. The journey may take the traveler to Newport, Brighton, the Catskills, the Swiss Alps, Darjeeling, or Fire Island. Failing that, an almost equally good escape from the discomforts of July in New York, Rome, Athens, or Atlanta can be achieved by means of air conditioning, cooling a room to the temperature one would find at the seashore or in the mountains.

A commonly held belief is that we must be kept cool at home and at work in order to be healthy, happy, and efficient during the summer. It is fortunate at this time of energy crisis to be able to take the economically sound position that this is not true and that holding the air conditioning to 78 degrees is healthful and, for the majority of people, comfortable. Department store managers may find that women will not try on winter coats in August, and pizzerias lose customers to ice cream parlors; however, on the average, people are happier when warm, even a little too warm.

The American taste for heat is considerably higher than most of us believe, according to tests by the American Society of Radiation and Air-Conditioning Engineers and Kansas State University's Institute of Environmental Research. To the surprise of the testers, a great many participants liked being in a room at 82 degrees better than at any of the lower temperatures, and three of the volunteers were still content after spending three hours in a test chamber that was 98 degrees. Eight relative humidities were tried, but temperature was found to be the more important factor in the feeling of comfort. Men were more troubled by humidity than were women. For the men, temperature was seven times as important as humidity in terms of their comfort, while women considered it nine times as significant.

In these, and in other tests too, temperatures in the mid- to upper 70s at a relative humidity of 50 percent were repeatedly selected by people wearing clothes of average weight. A naked person lying quietly is comfortable only when the air temperature is between 85 and 88 degrees. We can remain in this environment for any length of time without getting too hot or too cold, without even sweating. When we leave the beach to enter a locker room only a few degrees lower than that, we shiver.

Why then are so many people uncomfortable at 78 degrees, the temperature selected by the Carter administration as a reasonable air conditioning limit? Individual responses to heat vary so much that some people really do suffer physiologically at temperatures quite unremarkable to the average. Others dislike the very idea of being hot and get edgy as soon as they start to perspire. The sharp, shivery sensation of going from too hot into too cold is pleasurable to many, and when this contrast is missing they feel deprived. Theater, store, and restaurant owners, therefore, like to use excessive air conditioning. To make things worse, it is difficult to provide a standard temperature throughout a large area. Those parts of a store, office, or restaurant where one is most likely to be are frequently the hottest, because of crowding, lights, or shape.

But even when the room really is 78 degrees, it can feel uncomfortable to those coming in from the sweltering out-of-doors. An overheated person entering a warm room will cool off slowly. It takes longer to become seriously overheated if one starts out cool. And so the individual who strolls to work through streets comparatively cool in the early morning will not object to a 78-degree office, whereas the one who rushes and comes in perspiring will find it unbearable.

The greatest single enemy of comfort in hot weather is clothing, and the people who express the greatest discomfort are usually overdressed. Many men, in particular, are burdened by clothes more suited to another season or climate. Australian aborigines describe the degree of cold according to how many dogs one needs to have huddled around in order to keep warm. A chilly night might thus be a three-dog night, a really cold one a six-dog night, while late spring might merely call for a dog or two. A more conventional measurement (by our standards) has been offered by the Chinese, who may describe a pleasant fall day as a one-suit day, a later fall day as a two-suit day, and a frigid winter one as a twelve-suit day.

Americans add or subtract "clos," the units in a system of measurements devised some forty years ago to provide a scientific way of determining the weight of clothing. One clo is the amount of insulation needed to keep a person comfortable in a 70-degree room. Thus, the typical business suit has the value of one clo, compared to .01 for a bikini. The man wearing a business suit will want a room temperature set 6 degrees lower than he would if he took off the jacket, rolled up his sleeves, took off his tie, and opened his shirt collar. The bikini wearer would prefer that the temperature be raised 10 degrees.

The other aspect of fuel conservation, reducing room heat, is harder to take. Even the Army used to give 71.6 degrees as the proper temperature for areas where soldiers were sitting or standing. Very few of the participants in the environmental research studies were comfortable at 66 degrees, although they were healthy college students, ranging in age from eighteen to twenty-four. When the temperature range was extended downward, not a single student found so short a period as three quarters of an hour at below 62 degrees to be tolerable.

Well, enjoyment is one thing, but what about health? The opinion is frequently expressed that it is not only healthier but also more virtuous to be cold, and that keeping a house well heated is a sign of poor moral character and an encouragement to all sorts of illnesses. It is unfortunate during a fuel crisis to have to point out that while it may be virtuous, even sensible, and certainly is economical to be cold, it is *not* healthier. The one health problem that can be blamed on steam heat is that it dries out the mucous membranes of the nose, which normally provide a barrier to the many cold viruses in the air. However, even here it is hard to show that people living in overheated homes have more colds than they would if they turned down the thermostat.

"The moderate curve of the death index [in the United States] is ascribed to the wider use of the effective room heating system: that is, protected by the artificial weather thus brought about, the American people do not appear to be affected by the seasonal changes so markedly as other nations." This is the way the situation appeared in 1967 to Masako Momiyama-Sakamoto of Tokyo's Meteorological Research Institute. As improved home heating became more common in Japan, signs of "deseasonality in mortality" could be observed there too; the high winter peak of infant mortality fell.

Momiyama's studies appear to place too much reliance on differences in heating without making a similarly exact comparison of medical care. Countries where central heating is universal are those with the best health systems. Still, the Scandinavians, who have well-heated houses, are not more prone to illness than the British, who traditionally do not—and both have good medical care.

Low room temperature is particularly hazardous to the elderly, with their declining metabolic rate and cardiovascular function. A study in Portsmouth, England, of pensioners trying to stretch their incomes by using as little fuel as possible showed that body temperatures as much as 4 to 5 degrees below normal—hypothermia—were common. Any accident, such as a fall or illness, that makes an elderly person briefly immobile can be catastrophic, as heat loss from an already cold body is rapid. Many deaths in England have been attributed to unintentional or "accidental" hypothermia (as opposed to medically induced hypothermia during hazardous surgery).

The problem is becoming more common in the United States too, and for much the same reasons. Although most victims of accidental hypothermia have been found in rooms between 50 and 60 degrees, some were as high as 65; even this temperature may be too low for those with atherosclerosis or other conditions impairing the circulation. Medications, including tranquilizers and diuretics, make the old more susceptible to hypothermia. (Aspirin does not have this effect; only above-normal temperatures are lowered.) Because many of the body's reactions are not as keen as in the past, old people may be quite unaware of being cold. Often it is the children or grandchildren on a visit who complain and as a result are considered weaklings by the older generation.

Among healthy older people, the decline in metabolic rate to a large extent is counteracted by a decrease in evaporative heat loss through the skin. Still, the danger to all elderly people is such that the National Institute on Aging suggests that the elderly, particularly those over seventy-five years maintain homes at 70 degrees and a number of physicians think temperatures should be higher than that for those with extremely poor circulation.

Most people will become acclimatized to whatever is their environment. Australian schoolchildren study best in classrooms at the 75 to 77 degrees they are used to, whereas English schoolchildren concentrate more easily when the room is 65. Even individuals who enjoy being hot do in time adapt to the low indoor temperatures maintained for fuel economy. Due to temporary acclimatization, most people prefer to have a room temperature 1 or 2 degrees lower in the winter than in the summer. Keeping a room a little warmer than one likes in the summer and a little cooler in the winter, makes it easier to adjust to the weather out of doors.

The temperature one likes has little to do with the temperature that can be endured. In mid-eighteenth-century France, thousands of bushels of corn had to be discarded when they became infested with insects. In an attempt to save some of the corn, two French scientists heated it in the public bakery ovens. They placed a thermometer inside so as to determine just how much heat was needed to kill the pests without burning up the corn. They pulled out the thermometer in gingerly fashion after a while, but by the time they were able to read it, they realized that it must have cooled down. A young girl who worked at the bakery offered to climb into the oven, check the corn, and read the thermometer for them. She stayed in there for twelve minutes and then, it is said, crawled out to report that the reading was slightly above 287 degrees Fahrenheit. (There is no record as to whether the corn pests were destroyed; perhaps the scientists were too startled to notice.)

Withstanding temperatures far above the boiling point would seem a trick or a unique knack, like being a fire-eater at a carnival, but since then many others have performed similar feats. During World War II in tests run by the U.S. Air Force Air Materiel Command, men in lightweight clothing endured 49 minutes at 179.6 degrees Fahrenheit and 24 minutes at 239 degrees when the air was dry. After all, as Ralph F. Goldman, Director of the Military Ergonomics Laboratory, pointed out, many individuals with no motive but pleasure will spend time in the dry heat room of a sauna bath, where temperatures range from 176 to 212 degrees. Wet heat is much harder to endure, and yet this does not stop people from going to steam rooms in a Turkish bath kept at 132 degrees.

But then why should not humans be able to endure such extreme heat for short periods of time when we have ranged all over the globe, finding no place too hot to tolerate? The desert air may be so overheated that objects seem to quiver in a haze. A bare foot will burn and blister if it touches the ground. The sun blazes mercilessly overhead, and there is seldom the relief of rain. In tropical jungles the limits of endurance are stretched by heat accompanied by humidity so high that sweat drips down the body into the shoes and onto the ground. Yet communities are established, farmlands expanded, oil wells drilled.

Humans evolved on earth in warm regions, and have a predilection toward warmth. For us heat is equivalent to life itself. In Ptolemaic Egypt the Books of the Dead contained a spell to keep heat in the body of the deceased until resurrection. Without heat nothing can happen to humans, animals, plants. The response of many animals and plants to excessive cold is a state of dormancy, the slowing or virtual cessation of body functions. As physician William Harvey put it in the seventeenth century, "Warmer things are more agile and colder things more lazy."

Regardless of the temperature around us, our body temperature is held close to its norm of 98.6 degrees (oral) or 99.6 degrees (rectal), the deep-body temperature, by a variety of physiological protective devices. When chilled, the body shivers. When overheated, the body sweats. Of the two, sweating is the more effective. Shivering can add only 350–400 calories an hour to the cold body, while just a little more than a quart of sweat rids the hot body of 580 calories, and this is a pretty typical amount produced during exercise on a hot day. Just sitting in the shade on a 100-degree day will make an average-sized man lose a cup of sweat in an hour. A healthy person who leads a sedentary life still needs to take in two to three quarts of water a day, either as liquid or in food, to replenish the water lost to keep temperature stable.

An elaborate temperature-regulating mechanism is located in the hypothalamus, a tiny bit of brain tissue that lies at the base of the midbrain and also regulates the appetite, water balance, and many sympathetic-nervous-system functions. The anterior portion of the hypothalamus controls heat responses, the posterior cold. Warm or cold receptors in the skin signal the sympathetic nervous system that the temperature is changing, and the impulse is passed along to the thermostat in the brain, arousing it to action. Possibly because environmental cold is so devastating to warm-blooded people, there are only one eighth as many warm receptors as there are cold, and they are farther from the surface. But they still are highly sensitive to the heat around them.

In order to get rid of body heat, warm blood is diverted from the internal organs and sent to the skin, where the heat can be lost to the atmosphere. The heart beats faster and more strongly so as to pump this blood out to the skin. Deep-body temperature then falls, and skin temperature rises. If it rises enough, sweating begins after a time lag of two to eight minutes.

Sweat pours from the eccrine glands—2.5 million of them in a man of average size. More of the glands are in the chest and abdomen than on the back. Half of all sweat pours from the trunk and one fourth from the lower limbs.

The heat beneath the armpits is so great that the Jibaro Indians of Ecuador tell how their ancestors warmed meat and edible roots by holding them there.

Men are better able to get rid of excess body heat than are women, because they start sweating sooner, having a body temperature slightly lower and a skin temperature higher to start with. And even when sweating, women usually produce less sweat, despite having more active sweat glands. Thin women have 100 sweat glands per square centimeter (0.155 square inch) of skin, compared to 59 in males. The slower onset of sweating gives women a greater rise in temperature when they start exercising or go out on a hot day.

Children may start sweating sooner and more heavily than adults of either sex, and in some tests girls had double the sweat rate of women. Yet physiologists have observed that this extra sweat does not cool the children's bodies any better than the lesser sweat does the adult.

Many people wake up on hot nights in a pool of sweat, although the night air is cooler than that of the day. Sweating begins at a lower skin and body temperature during sleep than when one is awake. During exercise, the sweating trigger is somewhat different. The body temperature rises, but skin temperature does not change or actually drops. In that case the rise in the temperature of the blood reaching the brain sets off the sweating mechanism.

The thinness of the body shell affects the ability to endure heat. The skinfold thickness of heat-tolerant Indonesians from tropical Surabaya is less than that of Japanese, who mind the heat more, reported Y. Toda of the Japanese Committee for International Biological Study.

Women usually complain of being cold before men do, which is at odds with their physiology. Women, even thin ones, have an extra layer of subcutaneous fat which provides warmth, the degree depending on the amount of fat. The insulating properties of fat are such that obese people of both sexes find heat intolerable and are susceptible to injury. An exception to the customary female distaste for cold is found among "shopping bag ladies," who become less active when it is hot, while the "street men" are more active, reports Dr. Alan M. Beck of New York City's Department of Health. These homeless individuals carry all their possessions with them and are at the mercy of the weather. The women move around the streets, scavenging most vigorously when the temperature is between 45 and 55 degrees. They appear to have a better ability to endure cold than do men. Possibly in the final analysis the subcutaneous fat makes the difference.

Women develop a higher heart rate and body temperature than will men in the same hot factory and therefore are at greater risk of injury. The National Institute of Occupational Safety and Health has recommended that the standard for maximum temperatures to be experienced during the workday be set several degrees lower for women than for men.

But for all their physiological disadvantages, women are happier in the heat nonetheless. This can probably be attributed to the fact that they dress more lightly than men and, even more important, like heat better. Age plays a part, with elderly women sometimes being very slightly warmer than younger women or men, possibly as a result of postmenopausal hormonal changes.

But although women start out by being colder than men, they adapt to the temperature around them more rapidly. The way this works out is that men are hot for longer than women are cold. And so consider a couple on a two-hour plane flight from New York to Chicago. At takeoff the man is too hot and takes off his jacket, while his female companion finds it too cold. The cabin temperature remains unchanged, but the woman soon becomes comfortable enough to take off her coat, and some time later the man ceases to complain of being overly warm.

A traveler who thrives on the hot desert air of an Arizona summer may be thoroughly uncomfortable in the humid Yucatán. Unless sweat is dissipated into the atmosphere, it will not be so effective in cooling the body. As the sweat drips, making the skin wet, a film forms there, reducing what little evaporation might occur. When you mop your brow on a hot, humid day, you are removing the film as well as the sweat and allowing more sweat to reach the surface. Should the skin remain wet for long periods of time, which happens most often in the tropics, the sweat glands can become stopped up by small horny plugs. The sweat is still being formed and is trying to force its way out. The red, itchy rash of prickly heat is caused by this friction. It appears during summer heat waves in temperate climates, too.

No matter what the climate or season, the metabolism of a person resting quietly creates as much heat as a 90- to 100-watt light bulb, as much heat as is needed to bring a quart of water from room temperature to a boil. Mental activity accounts for 15 watts of this total, while the visceral organs make 44 watts. During active exercise 1,000 to 1,500 watts is given off. Put in calories, the average-sized man sitting or lying down makes 70 to 80 calories of heat, a large man 88, a woman or a small man 56.

The more people in a room, therefore, the hotter it gets—an advantage in energy conservation in winter, but a drain on air conditioning in the summer.

Heat Waves: The Risks and Records

During World War I, great quantities of wheat were needed for the troops and the price rose accordingly. It was only natural for farmers in the prairie states to plow up land that had been covered with grasses and shrubs for grazing and to grow wheat there. The war ended and times changed. Some farmers increased their herds of cattle and set them to graze on the plowed land. The vegetation was still marginal, and the cattle quickly consumed what there was of it. Years of drought prevented regrowth and dried the earth. As the animals roamed to and fro in search of fodder, their hooves ground the topsoil into a fine powder.

By the 1930s a dust bowl had been created, a stretch of barren ground which at the end of the decade was to extend over 25,000 square miles. The dust storms reached their full fury in 1934 and continued year after year. Strong winds would raise huge clouds of topsoil and swirl it into the air to form suffocating clouds of dust that seeped into everything it touched, clogging machinery, in time clogging the lungs. These were the years of the Great Depression, and the dust storms added to the impoverishment and misery of the farmers.

These storms took place from December to May, the time of year when the soil was most bare. Then came summer, with enough plant growth to hold down the earth but bringing suffering of a different kind. Heat waves that rank among the greatest in American history took place every summer between 1930 and 1936. The temperature in Iowa reached or surpassed 100 degrees on fifty-three days of the 1936 summer. C. D. Reed, who headed the Iowa Weather and Crop Bureau, went over the state's temperature records to their beginnings in 1819. July 1936, he discovered, was the hottest July of all. That summer the maximum temperature was 121 degrees Fahrenheit in Kansas and North Dakota, and 120 was measured in South Dakota, Texas, Arkansas, and Oklahoma.

On July 10, 1913, the air temperature at Death Valley, California, reached a world's-record 134 degrees, only to lose this distinction on September 18, 1922, when 136 was recorded in Azizia, Tripolitania, in northern Africa. Ground temperature readings of 165 degrees in Death Valley and 186 degrees on the black rock surface in parts of the Sahara Desert have been achieved many times.

Hardly a city in the United States has escaped summer heat waves. The temperatures can equal those of any area close to the equator. Even Portland, Oregon, has recorded a temperature of 107. So terrible have some of our heat waves been that they have become a part of the folklore. A few aged people can still remember the heat wave that swept through the plains states in 1901. Temperatures in Lawrence, Kansas, that July were 100 degrees or higher on twenty-one days, eighteen of them consecutive.

The heat wave of 1955 affected larger areas than any of the earlier ones, covering the country from Los Angeles to Minneapolis to Boston. That summer, Yuma, on the Arizona-California border, which had lived up to its reputation as "hottest city in the United States" (gained in 1937 by 101 consecutive days of 100 degrees or higher), exceeded 110 degrees for fourteen days in a row.

The heat wave of 1980, which reached as far north as the Dakotas, was notable for its length as well as for its temperatures. Starting on June 23, Dallas suffered forty-two consecutive days of temperatures 100 degrees or higher. On one of these days a garbage collector collapsed on the street from heat exhaustion; it made the front page of the *Dallas Morning News.* Wichita Falls recorded 117 on June 28. In many states, streets buckled and automobile windows shattered in the heat. The heat wave dragged through the summer and continued in the fall. Well into September, a temperature of 112 degrees was reported in Casa Grande, Arizona, and readings above 100 were still being obtained in heat-weary Tucson and Las Vegas.

With our wide range of conditions, some states have a desert climate of dry air, which makes the heat easier to endure, even though the temperature reading may be spectacular. But in many parts of the United States the summer humidity rivals that of the jungle. The temperature-humidity index (THI), reflecting both measurements, is familiar to everyone who watches weather reports on television. It was devised in the mid-1950s by the U.S. National Weather Service for use during warm periods of the year. The higher the index number, the greater the discomfort. Most numbers are between 70 and 80. Almost everyone is comfortable at 70, half feel discomfort at 75, and almost everyone is miserable at 80. The air temperature may be much higher than the index; it is only one component of the formula— THI = 0.4 (dry-bulb temperature in degrees F plus wet-bulb temperature) plus 15. A dry-bulb thermometer is an ordinary mercury-in-glass thermometer and gives the temperature of the air. A wet-bulb thermometer is covered by a wet wick and cooled as a result of evaporation, so the reading is always lower than that of the dry bulb. (If it is very humid, not much evaporation or cooling can take place, so the wet-bulb reading will approach that of the dry bulb.)

In New York City, where humidity is high, the temperature need not reach record levels in order to be lethal. "As soon as the temperature is up over 90 degrees Fahrenheit for three days in a row, the number of deaths go up," comments a New York City Health department statistician who prepares mortality tables.

In 1980, when temperatures in St. Louis were 95 degrees or higher for eighteen of the twenty-eight days between June 21 and July 19, 886 people died, 230 more than in the same period of 1979, which was different only in being less hot. The Medical Examiner's Office reported 108 heatstroke deaths between July 2 and July 18, with 24 taking place on a single day, July 13. Those fond of black humor made much of the story that a male orangutan, native to the jungles of Malaysia, died of heat prostration in the St. Louis Zoo. In Kansas City, 148 heat-related deaths were reported during a July that saw temperatures of 102 degrees or above for more than two weeks.

Yellowing health records reveal that 3,000 people and 2,000 horses succumbed during a ten-day heat wave in 1896. The great heat wave in the plains of 1901 accounted for 9,508 deaths. The growing use of air conditioning has cut down the mortality rate. Still, even in recent heat waves, well over 1,000 heat deaths—1,265 in 1980—have been recorded, and in any current year without a major heat wave, about 175 people in the United States are listed as dying as a direct result of summer heat.

That is what the mortality records show. A search of the medical literature, however, reveals that specialists estimate that at the very least 4,000 individuals in the United States die yearly of heatstroke. How then is one to explain the low death rates given in the official tables? The statistics are "unreliable in that a brief pathologic exam may only reveal that the patient died of a myocardial infarction or of a central nervous system accident. This leads to confusion and the totality of the picture may be missed," says Dr. Lewis Goldfrank, Director of Emergency Medical Services at Montefiore/North Central Bronx Hospitals. "Most often these patients are treated as having septicemia and a high fever."

Participants at a Climate and Health Workshop held in 1976 by the National Oceanic and Atmospheric Administration analyzed the causes given on death certificates issued during a ten-day heat wave a decade earlier. So many certificates named cancer that it might have seemed that a cancer epidemic had struck. But Lawrence Truppi of the Health Effects Research Laboratory thought not. He pointed out that heat stress was a contributing factor in bringing on many of these deaths prematurely. Heat had not been included in the list of causes, he said, because the health statisticians had not recognized its importance.

Heat can become lethal when prolonged exposure causes so great a malfunction in the thermostat in the hypothalamus that body temperature soars out of control. This can quickly lead to irreversible injury to the proteins and enzymes within the cells. Normal body temperature is close to the upper limit that humans can endure. Despite our hot-region origins, we are less well able to survive high fever than temperatures that are far below normal. A Chicago woman who recovered from accidental freezing, occurring while she lay on the street in a drunken stupor on a winter's night, had a temperature in the low 60s. A patient with a brain cancer was cooled to 39.56 degrees to protect his body during hazardous surgery. In contrast, in medically induced hyperthermia, or fever treatment the temperature is allowed to rise a few degrees only. When body temperature reaches 110 to 113 degrees brain damage and death are probable. Beyond that point, even with the best medical care, death is almost certain.

The absolute outside limit of human heat endurance has been given as 115.7 degrees, a measurement obtained in 1980 from a heatstroke victim in Atlanta. Prior to that, 115.4 degrees had been the record for survival. Oddly, although suffering acutely from the heat, the stricken person usually sweats very little or not at all. In the early stages of heatstroke the skin is flushed or pink and is dry and hot to the touch. Later it can appear ashen or have a purplish cast. The metabolism rises, causing acute discomfort. As all body systems are forced to work more rapidly, waste products can accumulate to dangerous levels. Nausea and stomach cramps are common. The next step can be convulsions and, finally, lacking effective treatment, coma and death. The nervous system is so heat-sensitive that some damage may be permanent, even if the victim is rescued.

Heat-wave deaths follow a pattern. There is usually a time lag of a day or so between the onset of extreme heat and the increase in the number of deaths. Should the heat wave be prolonged, the death rate remains high and may mount appreciably. The effects of heat are cumulative. The overburdened heart and circulatory system can stand the extra stress for a while but gradually are worn out. After the heat wave breaks, there is again a time lag before the death rate declines. A period then follows when deaths are fewer than normal, because so many that were imminent were speeded by the heat stress.

On July 13, 1977, the start of the New York City heat wave that was to be made memorable by the blackout of electric power, deaths from all causes were below the normal July citywide daily average of 196. A second day of heat pushed the toll up to 237. Record temperatures continued long after the lights came back on, and deaths remained consistently above the normal summer rate. The highest temperature— 104 degrees—came late in the heat wave and was matched with the heaviest death toll, 298. Even though the temperature plummeted to 88 the following day, deaths stayed high at 291. But by the following week, after days of 78 and 82, the toll fell to 173.

Who dies of heat waves? Old people are most likely to succumb. One Sunday in July a Dallas woman went to visit her parents. The house was very quiet as she entered, and she soon came upon the body of her mother, aged seventy-six, lying in bed and her father, eighty-six, on the floor. Both had died of the heat, which had been at 100 degrees or higher for days on end. During a heat wave in St. Louis, seven people, most of them elderly, were found dead of heatstroke in their own hot apartments. Each lived alone and died so.

The typical heat-wave victim is a chronically ill woman over sixty-five. But the fact that most heat-wave deaths are of women is not due to intrinsic female weakness. If anything, it is due to greater female strength. More women than men survive into old age, when heatstroke susceptibility increases most markedly.

When exposed to heat, the body's first response is an increase in heart rate so that extra blood can be pumped to the surface to be cooled. The declining ability to deal with heat, therefore, parallels the declining function of the aging cardiovascular system. During the record-breaking July 1980 heat wave in Kansas City, the median age of those who died was seventy-three, and 72 percent of the deaths were among people age sixty-five or older. In the summer of 1966 when the temperature in St. Louis remained in the 90s for twenty-four days, death claimed 681 persons who could normally have been expected to live out a summer of more moderate heat, according to an analysis made by Dr. Stanley H. Schuman of the University of South Carolina's Department of Family Practice. More than 40 percent of the excess deaths were of individuals with arteriosclerosis, other cardiovascular disorders such as hypertension, or chronic respiratory illness. Deaths among diabetics were 81 percent above normal for the group, with blood glucose levels sharply elevated shortly before death.

The onset of sweating is slower in the old, and both body temperature and pulse rate rise more sharply than in the young. This problem can be exacerbated by drugs, which impair heat as well as cold resistance. Narcotics and the phenothiazine tranquilizers, such as chlorpromazine, slow the sweating response even more and mask the sensation of being too hot. Diuretics, the tricyclic antidepressants, and belladonna and atropine to relieve stomach distress are among the many medicines commonly taken by the old which reduce effective responses to heat. The amphetamines not only hold down sweating but make a person hotter.

A significantly higher number of deaths occur in nursing homes without air conditioning, observed Dr. Michael Marmor of New York Medical Center's Institute of Environmental Medicine, after doing an investigation of the city-run facilities for the aged. Because the reduction or cessation of sweating is a sign of impending heatstroke, the administrator of a non-air conditioned nursing home instituted "sweat rounds" during heat waves, to check the reactions of the patients.

About half of all those who develop heatstroke die, most of them for lack of proper care. (The person who runs a high fever because of an infection is in as much danger of heatstroke as the city dweller during a heat wave or the explorer in the jungle but is more likely to survive, being in most cases under the care of a doctor.) Fortunately, effective first aid by friends has rescued many. The natural reaction, lowering body temperature by any means at hand, is the right one. Lowering the victim into a cold bath, sponging with alcohol or water, wrapping in wet sheets, and running an electric fan have all proved lifesaving. During one summer heat wave the number of patients brought to the emergency room of Montefiore Hospital in New York City was so large that several victims at a time were immersed in pools of ice water. Ambulance drivers were ordered to have icy sheets ready and to use them quickly.

On the night of June 20, 1756, 146 members of the British garrison in Calcutta were forced by the soldiers of the nabob of Bengal into a guardroom. The room, the infamous "Black Hole," measured 18 feet by 14 feet 10 inches and had two small windows. By morning only 23 men were alive. It has generally been assumed that the men died of heatstroke; however, an account written at the time puts this diagnosis in doubt. Far from displaying the dry skin and extremely high temperatures of heatstroke, the victims had been producing great quantities of sweat. As a result, those who did survive had only a moderate rise in body temperature. Thus the deaths may have been due to heat exhaustion, which is usually not lethal, coupled with the lack of air.

A person need not be in a Black Hole to suffer heat exhaustion. It is common during heat waves. Where the victim of heatstroke is surprisingly dry, rather than wet, the person suffering heat exhaustion sweats heavily but is cold to the touch. The skin is clammy and pale. The oral temperature is normal or low, while the rectal temperature shows a slight rise. Weakness, giddiness, nausea, and vomiting are frequent symptoms, with the dizziness being most acute upon standing up.

Heat exhaustion is a result of dehydration caused by the heavy sweating. The normally protective mechanism dilating the blood vessels in the skin backfires, and so much blood is diverted to the skin that too little remains to supply the brain. Heat exhaustion is treated by quickly replacing the lost fluids.

Heat cramps is the other common form of injury induced by excessive sweating with too great a salt loss. Because women sweat less and lose less salt than men, they are in less danger. Heat cramps are not the mark of a weakling but occur most often in fit people who refuse to yield to heat by stopping activity. The pupils dilate with each spasm, and the skin feels cold and clammy. Abdominal cramps may be so severe as to be mistaken for acute appendicitis. When finger, arm, or leg muscles cramp during sports activity, it is natural to assume that the muscles are strained by the exercise, but trying to work heat cramps out by further exercise only makes matters worse. Since sweating is the cause, replacing the lost fluid and salt is the cure.

During the last century, ships' doctors observed that cramps were not as common among the men who stoked the furnaces of Norwegian vessels as among stokers on British ships. In the British Navy these severe muscular cramps were so frequent as to become known as "stokers' disease." Eventually the cause of the cramps was recognized and 10 grams of salt were added to each imperial gallon of water. The Norwegians had escaped the cramps because they already ate large portions of heavily salted fish and meat every day.

Not even inhabitants of the Arctic are immune to some form of heat injury. During the summer everyone from time to time suffers from heat asthenia, a state of weakness in which one feels like doing nothing at all, but only to lie with few clothes on and a long cooling drink within reach. Easily exhausted, one nonetheless finds it hard to sleep at night. Sweat rolls off the body if the humidity is at all high, the pulse is fast, and breathing shallow. This condition is easily treated by doing just what one feels like doing.

With the exception of cramps, age and state of health affect the probability of a heat injury and its severity. Chronic illness and drug use which might lead to heatstroke in the aged are more likely to produce heat exhaustion in younger individuals. On a July weekend in 1978, a crowd of 50,000 people, most of them young, packed into the Dallas Cotton Bowl for a rock concert. As the temperature soared to between 120 and 130 degrees, about a hundred concertgoers collapsed from heat exhaustion. Physicians at Parkland Hospital found that many of those stricken had heart problems, and others were taking drugs.

The pilot who makes a forced landing in the tropics will not succumb to heat as quickly as the sick, the elderly, or the infants on his plane. Infants cannot tolerate excessive heat because their thermoregulatory mechanism is not fully developed. A British physician has recently suggested heatstroke as a cause of some unexplained crib deaths. Heat injuries are uncommon only because parents usually keep infants in shady places, offer plenty to drink, and dress them lightly in hot weather. By the age of one, resistance to heat is improving, and this keeps on, year by year, to reach a plateau about the age of twenty, only to start falling off in middle age.

Regardless of age, the person who develops a heat injury—and possibly dies of it—is more likely to be poor than rich and living in the inner city than in a suburb or rural area. As the Centers for Disease Control in Atlanta commented in its report on the 1980 heat wave in Dallas, "A map pinpointing the location of the heat-related and heatstroke deaths showed few in affluent, suburban, or young singles areas." And the heat-related death rate in Kansas City, Missouri, that year was 9.6 per 10,000 among the poor in the inner city, compared to 0.09 per 10,000 among the well-to-do.

The obvious reasons for the higher incidence of death and heat prostration among the poor are that the inner city really is hotter and more crowded and its residents perhaps poorly nourished to begin with and working at heavy, menial jobs. But in addition, slum dwellers are often unable to get out of the heat even for short periods during the day to obtain relief. While it is commonly believed that going into a cooled motion-picture theater, restaurant, or store is bad for a person during a heat wave because the contrast is such a strain, quite the reverse is true; the more breaks one can get from heat exposure, the more the stress on the heart is reduced. The only disadvantage is that acclimatization is slowed.

Hundreds of thousands of inhabitants of temperate zones work in extreme heat, which subjects them to heat stresses quite comparable to those faced by laborers in the tropics or the desert. Workers in the gold mines of South Africa are transported by elevator to a shaft 5,000 feet underground. There they travel by rail dolly for another mile before getting off and scrambling along a narrowing tunnel. They work in permanent semi-darkness at a temperature of 90 degrees and a humidity of 95 percent. Less colorful to us (and less harrowing in working conditions) are the American industrial plants—steel, aluminum, glass—but the heat there may be even greater than in a gold mine. In one glass container plant, for example, temperatures surpassed 100 degrees in most locations, reaching 130 degrees in front of the furnace. Three large aluminum corporations reported 96 heat injuries among employees, and two steel plants noted 26.

Not surprisingly, National Institute of Occupational Safety and Health scientists have declared that sufficient water is the best way to protect workers under these conditions. In order to remain fit, a person should lose no more than 1.5 percent of body weight in a day, and this should be restored before starting work the next day. The water should either be lightly salted (0.1 percent) or salt tablets should be offered. A quart of water an hour is needed by those doing heavy labor in the heat.

Some people take salt tablets routinely during heat waves, no matter what their way of life. But as salt tablets can upset the stomach or cause cramps, many physicians favor merely salting the food a bit more than at other seasons, just as farmers in the old days added salt to home-brewed beer during haying season.

Proper diet can also reduce the chance of heat injury. The elderly are prone to live on tea and toast and the young on a hot day prefer soft drinks or beer and pretzels to a well-balanced meal. Yet heat drains the body of substances other than salt and water; normal potassium and calcium levels fall too, as biochemical studies made during a heat wave on more than 600 outpatients at a university hospital clinic revealed. Raw vegetables and fruits and ham, turkey, chicken, milk, and ice cream fill these potassium and calcium needs. Orange juice and prune juice are better summer drinks than cola, and salted potato chips and peanuts better snacks than pretzels.

The instinct to eat lightly is sound; protein and fat consumption are best reduced in hot weather, because they contribute so much to metabolic heat. What is more, heavy meals are harder to digest; larger quantities of blood must be diverted from the skin, where it could be cooled, to the gastrointestinal tract.

How closely food intake is related to heat intake has been calculated by the Second Commission on Calorie Requirements of the Food and Agriculture Organization of the United Nations. When the outside temperature is 50 degrees, a healthy man of average size requires a daily consumption of 3,200 calories and a woman 2,300. Caloric intake should be dropped by 5 percent for every 18-degree rise in temperature; when outdoor temperatures average 86 degrees, that same man would need 2,880 and the woman 2,070 calories in a day. Age must be figured in, too; the older one gets, the less food one needs in any climate, because of the slowing metabolic rate. Caloric requirements fall by 3 percent per decade from twenty-five to forty-five, and by 7.5 percent in the next ten years. At sixty-five, a person needs 21 percent fewer calories than at twenty-five.

Because people are usually better able to protect themselves from cold than from heat, it is not as necessary to increase food intake when temperatures are low as it is to reduce them for heat. The UN recommendation is for an increase of only 3 percent for every 18-degree drop in temperature.

Caloric intake is affected by the amount of activity; anyone performing heavy labor must have extra food no matter how hot the climate, as some 4,000 calories a day are easily burned up.

Natives of many tropical regions have traditionally consumed the kind of diet recommended by the commission: low in calories and particularly low in heat-producing fats and proteins. The Indonesian diet consists mostly of rice, potatoes, sweet potatoes, soybeans, soybean curd, and green and kidney beans, with small quantities of beef, fish, and shrimp. In other areas, the staple rice, millet, plaintains, corn, and cassava offer only small amounts of proteins.

A number of religions forbid the eating of certain meats: the cow is sacred to Hindus, who never touch beef; the meat of the pig is viewed as unclean by Muslims and Orthodox Jews. Other people refuse to eat meat altogether, considering vegetarianism akin to godliness.

The custom of eating a vegetarian diet and raising the practice to a mystic, almost cult level was probably based on the natural and sound desire for such food by people living in hot climates. Unfortunately, the economic facts of tropical life have often enforced a diet so low in calories and protein that health and the ability to work suffer, even if the ability to endure heat is enhanced.

Clothing, like food, should be scantier in the heat. In April of 1929 an expedition under the auspices of the Australian National Research Council and the University of Hawaii was sent to explore the hottest parts of Australia. In the steaming jungles, they measured temperatures of 106 degrees in the shade. Even so, members of the expedition were distressed to find tribes "who did not possess a single rag among them."

But though the explorers may have been shocked, the natives were quite properly responding to the high temperature and humidity. As Frederick J. Wulsin noted in a study done for the National Research Council of the National Academy of Sciences, "A naked savage sitting under a tree and dabbling his feet in a brook has made an almost perfect adaptation [to his environment]."

In marked contrast is the behavior of many Americans. One hot and humid September evening in 1973 the wind instrumentalists of an Alabama high school marching band put on their heavy woolen high-waisted trousers, vinyl jackets, and Busby hats of flax fur, and went to the football field. At the half, the band performed a seven-minute precision drill routine and then knelt in position while the band of the competing school took its turn. When they returned to the grandstand, a girl band member fainted, and within the next ten minutes five others had become ill. By the time the game was over, 57 students, mostly wind instrument players, and a chaperone had to be treated for headache, nausea, weakness, and dizziness. Mass hysteria over losing the game was blamed. But somehow the effect of the loss was not so upsetting to the band's percussionists, who were in shirt sleeves, and the color guard, who wore miniskirts.

While warm clothing is inappropriate in hot weather, warm drinks are best. The tea-drinking custom universal among natives of the Far East produces sweat and cools the body. Americans, on the other hand, like nothing better during a heat wave than iced drinks that provide only a temporary illusion of coolness.

Many people find liquor particularly inviting during a heat wave. As with hot tea versus iced, some natives of hot climates disagree. The Far Eastern religions forbid the use of alcohol, a taboo of particular significance in torrid regions. The iced gin and tonics favored by Americans feel cold as they go down, but they can increase the risk of heat injury, because alcohol makes the blood vessels, already dilated in the heat, expand even more. The straining heart and circulatory system are given an extra burden. At the same time, the alcohol is producing more calories of heat than either protein or carbohydrates could do.

At moderate temperatures about half the water consumed leaves the body in the urine. During a heat wave or a vacation in tropics or desert, so much water goes off in sweat that the amount of urine is reduced. This protective mechanism is nullified by the consumption of alcoholic beverages. Although beer is not so high in alcohol content as is scotch, gin, or vodka, it is a very potent diuretic. The drinker must urinate more frequently, adding to the body's water loss. The foreman of a crew drilling for oil in the desert said that he could always tell when the men had been out drinking beer—long after the glow of good fellowship and even the hangover had worn off. For two or three days they were more quickly tired by the heat, as a result of the dehydration that had taken place.

4

Athletes and
Acclimatization

"Today we die," said Czech long-distance runner Emil Zatopek before the marathon race at the Melbourne Olympic Games of 1956. The day was humid and the temperature 85 degrees.

Zatopek had won the marathon four years earlier when the games were held in cool Finland, but this time neither he nor the other northern European and American runners excelled. The marathon on that hot day was won by a French Algerian, Alain Mimoun, who was accustomed to exercising in heat and humidity. And even he was affected, taking 2 hours and 25 minutes to complete the race, compared to Zapotek's 2 hours, 23 minutes, 3.2 seconds in Finland.

The records of the summer Olympic games show that many marathon winners have been natives of warm climates: Mamo Wolde and Akebe Bikila of Ethiopia, Kitei Son of Japan, Kenneth McArthur of South Africa, Delfo Cabrero and Juan Zabala of Argentina, and, in 1896, Spyros Loues of Greece.

"I hope the marathon will be held at a sensible time in Melbourne and not in the heat of the day," Roger Bannister, the first runner to break the four-minute-mile record, had remarked earlier. The opinions of Bannister and Zatopek were ignored in Melbourne—and in subsequent races.

In 1967 the United States Pan American Marathon Trial was run in a temperature of 92 to 95 degrees. Many of the runners could not finish; a number had stopped sweating and were close to heat-stroke—and these were seasoned athletes. Today, running has become almost anyone's sport, and marathons covering the traditional 26 miles, 385 yards are entered by thousands, of all ages and in varying degrees of physical fitness.

The American College of Sports Medicine urges that no distance race of 10 miles or more be run when the wet-bulb temperature is higher than 82.4 degrees Fahrenheit. During the summer, in places where the daytime dry-bulb temperature can be expected to exceed 80 degrees, distance races should be scheduled either before 9 A.M. or after 4 P.M. Marathon runners do best at temperatures below 60 degrees. The speeds attained by runners in the New York Marathon of 1980, with Cuban-born winner Alberto Salazar coming in at 2 hours, 9 minutes, and 41 seconds, were considerably higher than in previous years; the difference was attributed to the unusual coolness of the October day on which the race was run.

Acclimatization can help. A Massachusetts high school football team competed against a Florida team on a warm humid day. The two teams were evenly matched on the basis of past performance, and the game started out with each point hotly contested. By the fourth quarter, however, the northern team had faded badly and lost. The Florida team was used to playing in hot sticky weather.

But acclimatization is not always enough to prevent heat injury. Heavy exercise puts so great a strain on the body that heatstroke deaths are regularly reported even among high school and college football players, the healthiest of individuals. Fifteen football players died from 1933 to 1963 and eleven from 1963 to 66, notes Dr. Anderson Spickard of Vanderbilt University School of Medicine. And these figures do not begin to show how many players developed heatstroke but survived.

After a break for lunch on the first day of practice at Austin Peay College in Clarksville, Tennessee, the players, in full uniform, ran up a hill, walked down, and ran up again. After getting to the top the eighth time, one collapsed with heatstroke. Everything had gone blank, he reported later, on previous climbs he completed, but he had persisted anyway.

If experienced coaches can miss symptoms and trained athletes can push themselves to the point of collapse, it is hardly surprising that

Sunday sportsmen are susceptible to heat cramps and exhaustion. Many are unaware that overheating can occur on days when the temperature is only 65 or 70 degrees and the relative humidity a fairly average 49 to 55 percent—provided that the sun is shining and the exertion beyond their capacities—and few have familiarized themselves with the symptoms of incipient heat injury. These can be quite misleading! A person may feel too hot or be chilled; sweating may be heavy or the skin may be dry; gooseflesh and hairs may rise on the upper arms and, in men, on the chest; a throbbing pressure is in the head, a feeling of being unsteady on one's feet, a headache, nausea. The runner then needs to leave the race, the player drop out of the game, and the liquid that was lost in sweat immediately replaced.

A loss of 6.6 pounds of body weight means that a quart of water has left the body in sweat. At the 1968 United States Olympic Marathon Trial, the runners lost nearly 14 pounds on the average during the race. This figure can be best understood in comparison with football; coaches comment that if a player loses more than 5 pounds during a practice, he is carefully watched for ill effects and urged to drink back all he lost as rapidly as possible. The Austin Peay football player had already lost 6 pounds in morning practice on the day he collapsed.

Experienced runners will improve their chances of getting through a race by drinking a couple of glasses of water 15 to 30 minutes in advance and as much as possible at each water station. Although sugar brings quick energy, and very small amounts are added to the fluids offered runners by coaches, overly sweetened water or orange juice can make the stomach feel uncomfortably full. As a result, the athlete is unable to drink enough at the next water station.

There is considerable argument as to whether one should have iced drinks, the American favorite, when overheated or exercising. The coach for the Ohio State University football team once remarked, "During the 1971 game in California we used hundreds of pounds of ice for the team." The more common belief is that iced drinks may cause the athlete to develop stomach cramps.

Many coaches provide tablets containing the potassium, calcium, magnesium, and phosphates lost in heavy sweating. Potassium needs are greatly increased during sports or heavy labor, as shown in a study of aluminum workers and steelworkers made by Pittsburgh University's Occupational Health Department. The aluminum workers consumed more salt than the steelworkers, yet a larger number suffered muscle cramps of the abdomen, arms, and legs. Blood tests showed that sodium levels were normal or even high; however, the serum potassium was below normal. Perhaps too high a salt intake produces the very symptoms that lesser amounts control, inducing potassium depletion which, in turn, impairs muscle function and causes cramps. This could be why men who take a great deal of salt while exercising in the heat have been found to be less rather than more tolerant of high temperatures.

A male ballet dancer who suffered severe leg cramps following a performance on a hot July night worried that his technique had been faulty. His physician, however, considered potassium loss more likely.

Jockeys and participants in other sports where slenderness is required frequently drink coffee instead of water to help them "make" the weight. They succeed in this, because coffee acts as a diuretic, but as such it is a poor substitute for water, increases the probability of dehydration, and should be avoided immediately before exercise.

The last meal before entering a marathon or other endurance contest, particularly when heat adds an extra stress, should be low in foods containing a great deal of fiber, which can produce gas and bloating. The traditional meal of a big steak is not a good choice either, because the athlete cannot now afford the extra water for protein digestion. An easily digested meal mostly made up of carbohydrates is best.

Frequent rests can save the overstrained body in the course of exercise or heavy labor in the heat. During the 1977 New York City heat wave a temperature of 145 degrees was recorded in the boiler rooms of two Staten Island steam-powered ferryboats, but stokers and water tenders had to be there to keep the boilers going. "It's really murderous," said the ferry terminal supervisor. The men endured the heat by working for stretches of thirty minutes at a time and then going up on deck for a break.

Many who collapse in the heat have failed to take any precautions, not realizing what the combination of violent exercise and high temperature can do. Sixty-five children at the Broad Channel Day Camp in Queens, New York, had to be treated for heat prostration. Although the temperature surpassed 100 degrees, they had been kept at their normal schedule of softball, basketball, and races.

Those who are unaccustomed to heat have the most trouble. The first day of football practice, for example, is the most hazardous; it was on such a day that the Austin Peay College football player developed heatstroke. Five of nine deaths among high school football players occurring between 1956 and 1963 took place on the first day of practice, and two on the second. During World War II the 125 deaths attributed to heatstroke did not occur in the South Pacific but in training camps in the United States. In the summer of 1978, two Army recruits died of heatstroke after the first day of training in a temperature of 99 degrees.

While it is easy enough to see why heat should adversely affect the elderly and chronically ill, it is hard to determine why one magnificently healthy young person should collapse where his fellows do not. This can be attributed in part to individual variations in response to heat. Excessive heat like cold, rage, and fear, calls forth the "fight or flight" reaction in which all body systems mobilize to meet a threat. Heart and endocrine responses are more efficient in some people than in others. The individual who is tall and slender and has very long arms and legs and a short torso is best endowed by nature to tolerate heat. The higher the proportion of skin to body weight, the easier it is for the hot blood to reach the surface and be cooled. This kind of build is to be found among many natives of tropical regions. Narrow hips and a small amount of subcutaneous fat on the limbs are also typical.

While the right build can help, it is not essential. Even among peoples of tropics and deserts, one will find many who do not fit this heat-releasing ideal. Acclimatization is the more significant factor. Regardless of the individual's initial capacity to withstand heat, it can be greatly increased. The Massachusetts football players and the marathon runners from northern Europe need not have "died" in the heat had they worked out in heated rooms and acclimatized themselves sufficiently before the competition. In the same way, the number of deaths among young football players could be reduced. In the British Army, it has been the practice to house soldiers awaiting transfer to duty in a hot climate in overheated barracks. The body of the native of the North can take on many of the physiological traits that characterize the native of the tropics.

The most important of these traits have to do with sweating: the ability to begin sweating more rapidly, to sweat in greater quantities, and to produce sweat that is more dilute and less salty. In one 1956 study it was found that Filipinos had more sweat glands than Russians had. Japanese investigators checked the sweating capacities of the Sasak tribe of Lombok Island in Indonesia, where the climate is more tropical than that of Japan. The Sasak had many more active sweat glands in all parts of the body tested—the forearm, the thigh, and the chest—than the Japanese.

Some peoples native to tropical areas cut or pluck off much of their body hair. The motive is quite different from that of the American woman waxing her legs, shaving under her arms, and then applying an antiperspirant. Their purpose, sensible in the heat, is to allow sweat to evaporate from their bodies unencumbered by hair and cool them more effectively.

The ability to sweat efficiently can make the difference not only between health and collapse in the heat but between winning and losing. Long-distance runners were followed by physiologists on a 12½-mile race one July. Those who began sweating the most rapidly and produced the greatest amount of sweat finished first. In a test at California's Institute of Environmental Stress, five girls and five women walked on a treadmill for two periods of fifty minutes each at a temperature of 118.4 degrees. Only one girl was able even to start the second period, and just two of the women completed it. These three females had the highest sweat rates of the group.

The fact that women sweat less is a particular disadvantage during athletic events as well as during heat waves. Performance may deteriorate to a greater extent than in the male and heatstroke be a greater danger. Acclimatization for women, therefore, is essential.

Some degree of acclimatization occurs naturally with the changing seasons and the gradual warming of the days. The young man who plays tennis in July will start sweating sooner than he did during the winter, though he played on an indoor court maintained at summer temperatures. Metal workers who are in the same hot factory all year around are better able to endure the indoor heat during the summer than the winter.

This seasonal change helps to make heat waves in Indian summer less hazardous than those earlier in the season. During the fall of 1970, for example, heat waves occurred in both New York City and Washington. The rise in the death rate in New York was smaller than during summer heat waves and there was no increase at all in Washington, where the summer lasts longer and is hotter and people are better acclimated. The process of seasonal adaptation can be circumvented to some degree, but not entirely, by remaining in air-conditioned rooms for most of the day and night.

Nearly half a century ago, physiologists worked out an experiment designed to select those people who would adapt particularly well to hot climates on the theory that employees and soldiers properly chosen for tropical or desert assignments would not be so likely to collapse or go to seed. A group of volunteers was asked to remain in a heated chamber for a number of hours, and then their sweating rate was measured. The concept, physiologically sound, was that those men who sweated best would acclimate best to heat. In practice, this did not always work. Psychological reactions to heat proved to be just as important as the sweating mechanism. Some individuals simply cannot bear to feel hot and sweaty, even though the sweat is keeping their internal temperature down. And emotionally unstable people are prone to irritability, anxiety, and inertia, no matter how well they sweat.

In most cases, however, the person who is physiologically well adapted comes to accept, if not enjoy, heat. Such adaptation requires not only speeding the sweating reaction but also slowing the heart and maintaining the body temperature within comparatively normal limits. The metabolism of sharecroppers accustomed to working in the cotton fields of the Mississippi Delta alters little with exertion, in marked contrast to the sharp rise in metabolism of men picking cotton in humid heat for the first time. A man walking at a rate of four miles per hour on a day when the temperature is 77 degrees will have a heart rate of 115 to 120 beats a minute. The first time he attempts the same exercise during a 120-degree heat wave, a pulse rate of 186 can be expected; only over time does he come closer to a normal beat.

Women, already at a sweating disadvantage, have a faster heart rate than do men to begin with, and when they exercise in the heat, the rate rises more rapidly. Scientists at the University of Nevada's Laboratory of Environmental Patho-Physiology tested endurance by taking physically fit teenage boys and girls on two-hour desert walks. Even though the girls walked in the morning before the temperature was at its maximum, and the boys in the afternoon, the girls had to quit more often because their heart rates threatened to exceed the limit set for safety.

"The sex of the individual is less important than the state of cardiovascular fitness or overall health," points out Barbara L. Drinkwater of the University of California in Santa Barbara. "Men are more likely to be fit because our society has encouraged them to follow an active life-style and discouraged women from pursuing activity. This does not add up to a basic sex difference, but to an artificial difference imposed by society." Men, therefore, are encouraged toward acclimatization.

Shortly after Pearl Harbor, physiologist H. S. Belding prepared to investigate cold- and high-altitude adaptations to aid soldiers, should they be stationed in Arctic regions or on high mountains. But the cold and altitude rooms could not be gotten ready in time, so the impatient Belding decided to use a hot room that was available. The temperature was raised to 104 degrees and relative humidity set at 23 percent before Belding started to walk uphill on a treadmill. When forced by exhaustion to stop after an hour and twenty-five minutes, his rectal temperature was 104 degrees and his pulse was racing at 170 to 200 beats per minute. The next day he tried again and did a little better, and eventually he was able to keep going up the incline for four and a half hours. At the end of that time his temperature was a little over 101 and his heartbeat 140 to 160. In the beginning the rectal temperature soared because the sweating mechanism had not gone into action quickly enough. Once acclimatized, prompt sweating prevented such overheating, though his temperature still rose somewhat.

If the Sunday tennis player were to take his temperature after the game, he might be alarmed to find he was running a fever. But in fact this fever is normal and is not accompanied by discomfort. The thermostat in the hypothalamus is "set" at a higher temperature for exercise than for rest. Warming up for a race or ball game brings it to 101.5 degrees.

Well-trained athletes can break all temperature rules. Their basal metabolism may increase thirtyfold during a competitive event, and this is reflected in a rise in body temperature to a level that would normally be dizzying and incapacitating. During the Paris Olympic summer games of 1924, Donald Lash, who ran 6.2 miles in 30.5 minutes, finished with a rectal temperature of 106. Another champion, Gregory Rice, ran three miles in 14.2 minutes on a summer's day when the air temperature was 85 degrees and the relative humidity 65 percent. His rectal temperature also was 106. Athletes often get this hot, and only occasionally are symptoms of heatstroke observed. Acclimatized workers doing heavy labor in hot factories also frequently run temperatures of 104 to 105 with no ill effects. Efficient sweating and circulatory adjustments provide the needed safeguards.

Because the blood is being carried to the skin to be cooled, subtle alterations in the walls of the blood vessels must take place to enable them to expand. In order to keep the dilated vessels in the skin filled, there is an increase in the amount of blood circulating in the body. The blood is diluted with fluid coming from other tissues. This is the basis for the expression, "The blood is thinner in the tropics." If a person becomes dehydrated as a result of heavy sweating in the heat, however, the blood volume decreases and the blood that is left is thicker and higher in hemoglobin. This is a temporary situation. Once dehydration is relieved, the blood thins again.

How long does it take to become acclimatized? The process begins the very first time a person is exposed to heat and increases day by day. The more active one forces oneself to be, the faster the acclimatization. During the colonial period, it was the practice of the British civil servant to go to the club to play tennis each day. This really did help transplanted individuals to adjust quickly to their new environment. The U.S. Army recommends daily exercise in well-heated gymnasiums for at least 100 minutes and preferably two to four hours, with frequent rests, particularly at first. Acclimatization is accomplished in four to seven days.

This exercise schedule is more rigorous than the average civilian is likely to carry out. Even without going so far, almost any healthy active person can become acclimated within ten days. The inactive individual adapts somewhat, but not as well. Just lying in a hot bath produces some acclimatization.

Workers in factories where temperatures are high also must become acclimatized. The National Institute of Occupational Safety and Health has recommended that this be achieved by having an employee begin by working only half a day in the hottest part of a plant. The time in the heat is then increased by 10 percent each day.

The length of the acclimatization period, established by physiological studies, is known empirically by people who have moved from temperate to tropical climates. Immigrants will comment that they have gotten a "second wind" and are feeling vigorous again, and this second wind comes about ten days after their arrival. By then there has been time for a 10 to 20 percent increase in the sweat rate, so the body is cooler, and changes in all body systems have taken place.

How well the pituitary, thyroid, and adrenal glands function affect one's response to heat. Thyroid-deficient individuals tolerate hot weather, while those who are hyperthyroid are uncomfortable. A number of people are somehow incapable of acclimatization. Whether because of endocrine dysfunction, obesity, cardiovascular problems, some other chronic disease, or simply too strong a dislike of feeling hot, their bodies resist making the necessary changes. The personnel manager of a large steel mill observes that if new employees do not begin to feel more comfortable after ten days on the job, they would be well-advised to seek employment in another industry.

But even those who readily adapt to heat can lose their capacity with surprising speed. Full acclimatization lasts for only about two weeks. The loss is so evident that the National Institute for Occupational Safety and Health has urged that when a worker goes away on vacation or is ill for longer than nine working days, a period of reacclimatization must be offered. After a man or woman working in tropical or desert climate has been on home leave, the return can be difficult. The longer the time away, the harder it is to get the body back into hot-climate shape. And in temperate regions the first hot day of summer reminds us each year of how much our bodies have forgotten about heat.

5

Survival: "One Does Not Play with the Desert"

On a summer's day in 1905, Pablo Valencia was traveling on horse-back through southwestern Arizona. One mile of desert looks much like another, and eventually he faced the fact that he was lost. His canteen held only one day's supply of water and he had carried no food with him. The temperature during the daytime rose to over 103 degrees Fahrenheit and even at night never fell below 81.

Valencia rode for 35 miles and, when his horse collapsed, walked and crawled for eight days and nights, covering 100, possibly 150 miles over the rocky, pitted terrain. His clothes, worn to tatters, fell off, and he was naked by the time he was finally rescued. Although he had been badly cut by the stones he was crawling over, he did not bleed. He had lost 25 percent of his body weight in water and his blood was too thick to flow. "He had done nothing right, had no survival training. But he wanted to survive and he did survive, through nothing but willpower," observed the author of the U.S. Air Force manual on survival.

Fortunately for Valencia, willpower is less quickly sapped by great heat than by great cold. When deep-body temperature falls only 7 degrees, lost mountain climbers are ready to lie down in the snow and give up; unless rescued, they will die there. Travelers lost in the desert or tropical jungle may become overheated and miserable, but usually they make active efforts to save themselves for some hours or days.

A crew of three survived a crash landing when their bomber was shot down while on a reconnaissance flight over what is now Somaliland. The plane had landed in a thorn bush, and the men had to force their way through it, scratched and bleeding, to begin their march. They searched for shelter, food, and water, but only a few scrawny acacias offered a minimum of protection against the blistering sun. When the small quantity of water they had with them was used up, they were driven to moistening their lips with alcohol from the compass.

On the sixth day after the crash they stumbled into a small hole with a trickle of water where they could barely wet their parched throats. Four days later they came upon a well-filled water hole. By then two of the men were too exhausted from exertion and sick from the heat to go on. The third filled a canteen and set out on his own. He was collapsing on the dunes when he was found by two Bedouins, who led him to another water hole and helped him onto a camel. As he rode across the desert, conspicuous on camelback, he was spotted from the air and rescued. In the strength given by his desperation, he had walked 50 miles in just twenty-four hours. Days later, when a search plane finally rescued his two companions, vultures were circling overhead.

The engine of an Air Force plane caught fire over the Arizona desert and the pilot was forced to bail out. Once safely on the ground, he folded his parachute, fastened his flying suit, and pulled his helmet firmly down over his forehead as protection against the sun. Walking across the arid ground, he found a cactus and chewed the pulp for its moisture. Before setting off again, he filled the pockets of his suit with pulp. This proved to be a wise move, for he did not find another usable cactus for two days. On the fourth day he saw a lizard, the first living thing that had come his way. He killed and skinned it with his belt buckle and ate it raw. His next meal consisted of the wings of a large fly. With this paltry amount of food and moisture, he endured five days before rescue.

Four men were lost in the southern Libyan desert. They died, one by one, until only a single man was left. He doggedly made his way over 210 miles in ten days. By the time he was picked up, he was so exhausted that he did not realize he was being saved. When he came to himself some hours later, he assured his rescuers with some bravado that their efforts had been unnecessary; he could have reached the base, another 80 miles away, by himself.

An Army study of 103 experiences of desert survival reveals that most of the men, though tormented by heat, dehydration, starvation, and exhaustion, traveled over about 50 miles of harsh terrain, and one plane crew covered 350. Most survivors independently set a schedule of walking for an hour and resting for half an hour while fresh. The walking time dropped steadily, until ten minutes at a stretch was the most that could be managed. Rest periods extended to three hours. In the beginning when a man is fresh, he can go 12 to 18 miles in a day. (Less is known of female endurance, because the bulk of the research has been done by Army physiologists on male soldiers.) And of course the will to survive has caused some exceptional individuals, including Valencia and the flier who covered 50 miles in a single day, to force their bodies to do what would be impossible in any other circumstance.

While desert annals have focused on soldiers crashing while on missions, disaster has also struck many who ventured out just for fun. Seven French soldiers on duty in the Sahara went gazelle hunting for something to do on a dull Sunday. They did not return that day or the next, so a search party went out after them. Four of the men were beyond help by the time they were found, and the other three were close to death. "One does not play with the desert," was the sage comment of the French desert experts.

While the Army study found 382 survivors, it also learned that 142 men, who had started out with others, had been lost. Many had wandered away from their fellows, "playing with the desert" with some poorly conceived idea of how to survive.

"Survival," notes the Air Force training manual in seeming seriousness, "is one thing that must be done properly the first time."

Today there are many who take a ride across a desert by car for sightseeing, making no provision for a breakdown, not troubling to study survival manuals. Some do not even carry a canteen to fill, should they reach a source of water. A surprising number have had only their shoes to use as water containers.

A tourist group died in the Egyptian desert not long ago when their cars became stuck in the sand. They had been so casual about setting off for a day's outing to an oasis less than 150 miles away that they had taken only a couple of bottles of water along.

Desert experts remark that if an American is crossing a desert alone by jeep and the vehicle breaks down, he jumps out at once and rushes here and there on foot across the burning sands, going as far as he can in search of help. In this way he uses up his energy and the water in his canteen and probably gets lost. Should the car of a Bedouin break down, however, he would promptly lie down in the shade cast by the crippled vehicle and wait patiently for rescue or for the sun to set before beginning to go to seek help.

Walking is best done by night, with the day spent resting. If no shelter is found, most of the body can be covered with sand, which not only protects against the blazing sun but also helps to prevent the evaporation of sweat. Soldiers who marched 20 miles at night were no more dehydrated when they reached their destination than others who went a mere 5½ miles in the heat of the day.

An American engineer working in the Arabian desert remarked, "I've been here seven months and I haven't seen it rain." Still, that desert is occasionally washed with rain, allowing some plant life to provide minimal shelter, food, and moisture. And American deserts do contain cacti and other vegetation. But in the Sahara it may not rain for ten or twenty years or more, and one can journey for thousands of miles without seeing any plants at all.

Many of those stranded in the desert set out in clothing too scanty to offer protection from the sun by day and from the cold at night. In the Sahara the temperature during the nighttime hours is frequently 45 degrees lower than it was that same day. Following the example of the Bedouin, one should cover the head and protect the back of the neck with a scarf or rolled-up T-shirt. Slacks are better than shorts, and a long-sleeved shirt unfastened at the cuffs so that the sleeves hang down will protect the hands from the sun. At midday in the desert, black clothing is some 30 to 40 degrees hotter than white. The practice of taking off as many clothes as possible to allow free evaporation of sweat, which is advisable in more temperate regions, is a mistake in the desert. Keeping the body covered is essential both to prevent sunburn and to conserve body water.

We think of deserts as endless golden sand plateaus, with rippled dunes, but only one tenth of the Sahara is sandy. Far more consists of gravel. The desert traveler can all too easily become mired in quicksand or sucked a few inches into soft marshy ground. The Egyptian-

Libyan desert is hard to traverse, because of chotts, swampy areas covered with a thin crust that breaks beneath a person's weight. And after the chotts come miles of alkali flats or salt lakes. Heavy shoes or high hiking boots are clearly needed, yet many tourists drive into desert areas wearing only sneakers or sandals. The realization that these will quickly be ruined in a march across the desert persuades the economical to go barefoot; after all, it is certainly hot enough. The result is usually painful burns from the sand and the salt and cuts from the gravel. What is more, one must usually live with the initial faulty decision, as feet swell so badly on the hot ground that it is virtually impossible to get shoes back on.

But of course it is not the terrain, nor the heat, nor the blazing sun, nor the cold of night that makes the desert so hazardous. It is rather the unavailability of water at a time when the body's need is high. In addition to the major losses in sweat and urine, nearly a quart of water passes out through the unbroken skin every day. This unsuspected water loss goes on at all seasons and in all climates but matters most under conditions of great heat and exertion.

Soldiers building target ranges in a region where temperatures reached 105 degrees or higher every day drank about eight quarts of water apiece a day, and railroad repairmen have downed ten to twelve. But it is perfectly possible to survive on much less.

The body can endure considerable temporary dehydration without harm. The runners who lost nearly 14 pounds in competition returned to run another day. A 110-pound woman can manage a water loss amounting to 11 pounds, and a 200-pound man 20 pounds, provided that the water is promptly replenished. This does not mean that the individual is in good condition. A 10-percent loss of body weight is so weakening that it is hard to get to a source of water that is not right at hand. Even the runner, stimulated to overcome problems that would normally be incapacitating, usually must be handed a cup of water by a trainer standing near the finish line. Nor is thirst a good guide as to how much fluid is needed. Many dehydrated individuals stop drinking after replacing only about two thirds of their loss.

The person struggling through the desert begins to be in physiological trouble well before 10 percent of body weight is lost. Maddening thirst, discomfort, loss of appetite, a fast pulse, and high body temperature, a feeling of impatience alternating with drowsiness, and sometimes nausea are tormenting symptoms. By the time a tenth of body weight is lost, the victim is dizzy, has a headache, difficulty in breathing, a tingling in the arms and legs, and a tendency to stumble when walking. The mouth is dry and the skin looks bluish in color.

Because so much water goes off in sweat, the amount of urine excreted drops sharply, falling by about one fourth very quickly. Difficulty and pain on urination have been described by almost all survivors of desert marches of more than three or four days' duration. Cramps add to the discomfort, as the lack of fluid in the system results in constipation. One soldier who returned to headquarters after a month on the desert with adequate food but limited water supplies reported having had no bowel movement for twenty-one days.

In the case of the traveler lost in the desert, when the water weight loss reaches 15 percent or more, urine ceases to flow altogether. A person so dehydrated may be delirious, hear with difficulty, and see dimly. The eyelids are stiff, body movements jerky, hands and feet numb. The tongue is swollen, sometimes feeling so large that there seems to be no room for it in the mouth. The act of swallowing becomes hard or impossible. Under conditions when great heat and great exertion combine, a 15 percent loss may be lethal, unless rescuers come in time. And, Pablo Valencia notwithstanding, when about 20 percent of the body weight is lost to dehydration, the damage is usually irreversible. The circulation slows to such an extent that blood cannot move from the internal organs to the surface of the body to be cooled and as a result the deep-body temperature rises to fatal limits.

How long can one live in the desert without water? Survival is possible for only two days when the maximum shade temperature during the daytime is 120 degrees, says the classic 1947 study by E. F. Adolph and associates—and a person could only endure that long by remaining in one place during the day, awaiting rescue. If an attempt is made to walk after dark, there is just that one night to find rescuers or a water supply.

In a slightly cooler desert, with a high for the day of 100 degrees, the individual would not be losing as much water in sweat and could survive five days of quiet waiting, three of walking at night. A canteen containing one or two quarts of water would provide some comfort, but the relief would be more psychological than physical. In the 120-degree desert, two quarts of water would not extend survival beyond two days of inactivity and would give only one extra night of walking. A gallon of water was found to be the minimum to make a difference;

it allows an inactive person two and a half days in the 120-degree desert, seven at 100 degrees.

"Money meant nothing to them. Water meant everything," said a U.S. Border Patrol agent after helping in the rescue of what was left of a group of middle-class Salvadorans who tried to enter this country illegally in the summer of 1980. Some had hidden money and jewelry but brought it out in an attempt to buy water.

How had they come to this pass? They had started out confidently after paying a "travel agency" to smuggle them into the United States by plane. But when they arrived at the border, they learned that plans had changed and they would have to walk across the Organ Pipe Cactus National Monument Desert. Some backed out, but a group set off in 115-degree heat. Never were desert travelers so ill-prepared. Several of the women were in high-heeled shoes, they were weighed down with suitcases filled with winter clothes, and they carried a most inadequate supply of water.

The following morning most of the group wisely suggested waiting until nightfall before setting out again, but others insisted on pressing on. While it would seem that those braving the sun were the ones to be doomed, they improved their chances by taking most of the water with them. So brutal was the desert heat that by noon of that first day all were in serious trouble. They drank anything liquid: aftershave lotion, deodorant, cologne, urine.

That night two border patrolmen came upon three of the men, who said not a word about the others. The story only came out the following day, when one of the women managed to struggle to the highway and flag down a border patrol vehicle. Thirteen people were found dead, dirt and sand in their mouths showing how they had tried to find water in the ground. However, fourteen survived the two days of heat and dehydration.

In this as in many other situations, some individuals have managed to do without fluid for periods that defy the calculated survival figures. In fourteen of the desert crashes studied by the Army, a number of crew members lived for three days without water, and some for as long as five.

Even those aware of the hazards often do not carry sufficient water, because it weighs so much. Each member of the crew of a large bomber had been issued a ten-gallon container. But when, after being forced down, the water was needed most, the larger amount had to be poured out onto the sand. A container with two gallons proved to be as much as they could carry on the difficult desert march.

Because thirst is accompanied by a dry mouth, some of the soldiers believed that they would be less parched if their tongues were kept moist. However, sucking pebbles or chewing gum or paraffin did not help. Chewing grass was useful, because no matter how dry it appeared, some moisture could be sucked up by the determined. One group of men returned to base recalling how they had spent hours discussing the superiority in taste of one grass over another, with advocates of each type becoming so excited that violent arguments broke out. These were counterproductive, however, because breathing through the nose, holding the lips together, and talking as little as possible keeps the hot desert winds from drying the mouth further.

Every television or movie viewer knows that those journeying on foot through the blistering desert heat must husband their precious water supply and stretch it out for as long as possible. The individual who drinks a lot of water at the start of the march is compared to the careless sparrow, which, unlike the careful squirrel, does not prepare for the future. But humans would do better to emulate the sparrow. Those who have survived desert experiences have learned that the best place to carry water is inside the body, not in the canteen. There is no physiological benefit to stretching out a limited supply of water, and the effort of carrying a heavy canteen in the heat can be an extra strain the tortured body can ill afford. The only advantage the water in the canteen has over the water in the body is psychological. And that is not enough when dehydration is weakening the marcher.

During World War II the concept that water supplies should be eked out was so generally accepted that soldiers sent out on missions over the desert were given this advice. And so men who crashed in the desert usually set off on their marches determined to hold out and not drink for as long as they possibly could. Most, in fact, did not drink at all during the first day out. Then they started spacing out the water, at first allowing themselves one mouthful an hour. Later as water became more scarce, this was reduced to a mouthful at each rest stop, next only at night and in the morning, and finally only once at midday. There was a belief, held by some athletic coaches as well, that not drinking or drinking very little before or during maximum effort was a sign of virility and toughness. Yet the soldiers did not improve their condition by this restraint or extend their period of energy in the slightest. To the contrary, they were more quickly dehydrated and hence exhausted and unable to march vigorously. They would have done better to have drunk their water at the outset and then covered as much ground as possible. One man rescued after three days in the desert declared, "Next time I go out on a mission, I'll drink all I can hold before I get into the plane."

Is it possible to learn to live with less water? The idea is a tantalizing one. With much World War II action taking place in tropics and desert, there was a concerted effort to train men to function when dehydrated. The effort failed. No matter how many times and for how long the men went without water, they did not improve their ability to be active. They became fatigued just as quickly and displayed symptoms of dehydration at just the same point of water loss.

Most of the Army studies of desert survival exploits showed that those who were lost for extended periods before rescue had found some source of water. Upon reaching the water, soldiers who prided themselves on their self-control drank sparingly and slowly, in keeping with another popular misconception: that it is dangerous to drink rapidly when terribly thirsty. But the truth is, the faster the better. The severely dehydrated person can drink a quart or more right off, only stopping for breath. Recovery then is rapid. The water should be warm or just barely cool; ice water drunk at such speed can upset the stomach.

Two American aviators taken prisoner during the war escaped their German captors and hid in an attic for six days. They had just one pint of water between them. When the town was liberated and they left the attic, they were so weak that they could hardly stumble to the water faucet. Each drank three pints as rapidly as possible and felt energy return. But even this is nothing compared to the consumption of a Swedish explorer who in 1898 was forced to go without water for some days and then found a water hole. He drank six pints on the spot.

As the desert is regularly traversed by nomads, wells and cisterns have been dug into sand or rock, but few of those not born in the area can find one. A downed airman was led by a Bedouin to a place that at first glance looked like every other. But the Arab spotted a small circle of pats of camel dung around a tiny hole; he put down a stick and struck water. The pilot had been within a few yards of the spot for two days without recognizing it for what it was.

Occasionally water is found under the most unpromising circumstances. A British paratrooper liked to tell how he had journeyed across 200 miles of the most arid desert without suffering thirst. He had found abandoned cars, trucks, and jeeps along the way, and drained the water from their radiators.

The chance of finding an oasis is better in the more desolate Sahara than in the Arabian desert. Some are so large as to have become oasis cities, while others are no more than a pond surrounded by a few date palms. Considering the number of oases, it is surprising that only one of the 382 survivors questioned by the Army had succeeded in finding such a place unaided. This man recalled later how his spirits had lifted at the sight of the palms rich with fruit.

Some of those struggling over the arid desert have been maddened with thirst to the point of drinking gasoline, blood, or urine. An engineer with an oil company was lost in the Arabian desert and at last came upon a small water hole. It was yellowish, foaming, and reeked of camel urine, but he drank it nonetheless. Another man stranded in the desert traveled by night until first the water in his canteen and then his strength were gone. As he crawled painfully forward, he fell over some small shells lying on the ground. He broke one open with his teeth and found fluid inside. But when he sucked it out, the taste and smell were so repulsive that he vomited. Still, he took the shells with him, as he doggedly dragged himself on. And by the following day his thirst had reached such proportions that the fluid no longer seemed so putrid and he cracked and consumed the contents of thirty shells, one after the other.

A tourist lost in eastern Africa came upon a land tortoise. His efforts to crush the shell and extract the meat failed, but he pulled off some of the muscles holding the shell and chewed them, and then forced himself to drink the creature's blood.

Because the terrain lacks landmarks, it is so easy to be lost that each desert has contributed to the annals of survival. A young couple traveling across the Arizona desert by car became desperate with thirst. They found a barrel cactus, forced a knife through the tough rind, pulled out the pulp, and squeezed the juice. As the juice began to flow, their spirits fell because they could see that it was milky, usually a sign of sap that is not fit to drink. However, the barrel cactus and the dandelion are exceptions to this general rule. The couple drank the sap, despite its rather unpleasant taste, and were refreshed.

Alcohol has also been the liquid of choice for some of those on hazardous duty, even after being warned that it increases the likelihood of heatstroke. A World War II pilot going out on a desert mission decided to take his weekly beer ration with him, as he knew it would be consumed by his companions on the base if he left it. The plane crashed and the pilot had to march over the hot sands for three days. "I couldn't have stood it without the beer," he declared when rescued.

In comparing notes, it turned out that seven survivors of a similar disaster had done it on wine. Two other pilots filled their canteens with whiskey before setting out on a dangerous mission. Forced down, they, too, survived.

Dr. Richard A. Howard, an Army consultant on the desert, had only this to say: "Alcohol accelerates dehydration, but the bolstering of morale might have been a compensating factor."

In each case, authorities hasten to add, rescue came comparatively soon.

Annals of survival also include the privations of those shipwrecked and in planes downed over water. The problem of dehydration on the ocean, particularly in tropical seas, is just as great as on the desert. Some marine birds have a salt gland in the nasal passages that can excrete great amounts of salt. Humans are not so endowed, and as Coleridge's ancient mariner bemoaned, seawater is unfit to drink.

Salt water can help the body to retain its fluids if, instead of being drunk, it is used to keep clothing wet. Four men who spent thirty hours on an unshaded life raft after their ship was torpedoed in the South Pacific saturated their clothing and took turns submerged in the water hanging onto the side of the raft. When rescued, they showed fewer symptoms of dehydration than did other survivors who were rescued in only three and a half hours but who had not thought to use seawater in this manner.

Dehydration is accompanied by a loss of appetite, verging on an aversion to food. This is of psychological benefit in desert regions, because finding plants and animals is hard in most of them, all but impossible in others; the physiological need for food obviously is not reduced and its lack increases the exhaustion.

Many pilots would not eat before a mission, complaining that the foods served in the mess gave them gas. Those who were rescued after a crash commented that never again would they set out without having a full meal first, regardless of the discomfort.

Food, as well as water, must be a part of any survival pack, but it has proved extremely difficult to decide what to take. Military quartermaster corps have repeatedly tried to devise a survival ration that would not increase thirst, but none of their attempts has been greeted with enthusiasm. The foods that relieve thirst best are fruits and vegetables, but they are too bulky and perishable to be used as survival rations. One crewman ordered to bail out of a disabled airplane put a handful of oranges under his shirt before jumping. Tourists leaving a car that has broken down in the desert frequently consume a dozen or more vitamin pills in the mistaken belief that this will sustain them through days of hunger and thirst.

The food carried by those on camping trips or as Army survival rations for other regions are singularly ill-suited to desert disaster. The dehydrated meals that are lightest in weight are useless in the absence of water. Canned foods provide their own liquid but are too heavy. The concentrated chocolate bar in military kits was universally disliked by those on forced desert marches. Hard candy was preferred, particularly acidic lemon or lime.

The already great difficulty of finding food, water, or a way to go in the desert is made even greater by the sameness of much of the landscape. Sand dunes and gravel flats dull or deceive the eye. Sometimes it is hard to be sure that what one sees is really there. A starving traveler lost in the Sahara was delighted to see a small rabbit directly ahead and promptly aimed his rifle. Before he could fire, the rabbit turned and jumped into what seemed to be a water hole. As the dazzled man followed, he moved on and on through endless sand.

The lone figure in the novel, tormented by sun and sand, desperate with thirst, sees a shimmering pool lying between the dunes just ahead, and there to the right is an oasis where Bedouins and their camels are refreshing themselves beneath the palm trees. But though he rushes forward, stumbling in his haste, the oasis never comes closer. At last he falls exhausted upon the sand, realizing that he has been duped by his senses. But mirages are not merely popular in fiction. However bizarre the visions described, they are equaled or surpassed by those that have lulled people lost in the desert into false hope.

While mirages are commonly believed to be unique to desert or ice-covered regions, many living in temperate climates have seen them too. On a very hot day when one looks out over an expanse of city streets, for example, a lake may seem to be gleaming on the distant pavement, but, not being desperate with thirst, the city dweller rarely pays attention.

Both in city and desert, this illusion is created by the heat distortion of the light waves. Usually the density of air decreases with altitude, and light waves pass through in a manner we have become accustomed to evaluating accurately. But air over asphalt or desert can have marked alterations in temperature. The ground becomes so hot that the layer of air close to it becomes overheated. The light waves in this haze bend and give mirror images. The "lake" is a reflected view of the distant sky. Sometimes the reflection may deceive one into thinking the sun is rising in the west. In the early morning when the contrast between the cold desert soil and the warmer upper air is great, objects can look much larger and closer than they really are. And occasionally the variations in temperature of layers of air cause the light waves to travel in such ways as to make one see two, three, or even more versions of the same image.

A tourist whose car failed while he was crossing the desert in southern Egypt walked all night and was stopped just before dawn by a huge boulder blocking his path. Too exhausted to climb over it, he prepared himself for the effort by resting an hour. Then, although he thought the boulder was just ahead, he kept walking. Eventually he came upon a small rock that he kicked aside. And yet on other occasions travelers have walked confidently along, only to be stopped by a cliff that had appeared from afar to be just a little stone.

The crew of a downed British plane kept watch for aircraft overhead, planning to set signal fires as soon as a rescue plane came into sight. But even when they were aware that one was circling overhead, they could not tell whether it was friend or enemy. "It looked as if seen through cheap and wavy window glass," said the navigator. The men also could not determine the location of the circling plane. When sightings were taken, the discrepancies between them were as great as 30 degrees.

A bomber was so badly damaged by German fighter planes that the crew had to bail out. When they met on the ground, the navigator said that he was confident he could navigate on the desert as well as in the air. While floating downward on his parachute, he had seen a flashing beacon to the northeast. This should be their goal, as surely where there was a beacon there would be people to rescue them. The pilot, however, considered the beacon to be an optical illusion, caused

by the glare of the stars and urged a different direction. Although
ordered to remain with the group, the navigator decided that air force
discipline did not apply under these conditions and set off on his own.
He disappeared into the desert vastness and was never found.

Survival training is urged upon soldiers, campers, and others who
are to visit or journey over hazardous terrain. As desert expert Douglas
H. K. Lee put it, "The desert does not yield to the timid, the vacillating,
or the ignorant. Between abhorrence and conquest of the desert lies
a middle zone fraught with tragedy."

Is it harder to survive in the desert or the jungle? The sun is not
so punishing in the jungle, where it often slips behind clouds. Even
when it is directly overhead, the heavy hanging foliage blocks its rays.
The daily temperature range in the tropics is only half that in the
deserts, and the noontime peak substantially lower. The stress placed
on the body by dry air, hot soil, and relentless sun of the desert is
two to three times as great as that of the jungle. Anyone who can
endure the desert heat should be able to manage more easily in the
jungle.

But being able to endure does not mean to endure with pleasure
or ease. The physical discomfort of being in the jungle can be great.
The traveler in the desert is maddened by the strong wind blowing
sand into mouth, nose, and eyes, but it carries away sweat and cools
the body. There is little or no wind in the tropical jungle. Wind measurements taken over long periods in the Everglades of southern Florida
have seldom produced readings of more than one mile per hour. With
so little air movement, some of the sweat drips from the body, and
another part remains on the surface, forming a film. Under these circumstances, sweating is not increased enough to cool the body. The
average sweat output of 97 men hiking through the desert has been
found to be 5 quarts per 24 hours. But when another group of men
was tested in the jungle, their sweat output averaged only 2⅓ quarts
for the same period.

Six soldiers carrying thirty-pound packs hacked their way with ma-
chetes through the thick underbrush of the tropical jungle in Florida.
They advanced for only three hours a day and rested for the balance.
Even so, they became exhausted because of the heat, the 84-percent
relative humidity, and the almost motionless air.

Less water is needed to support such labors in the tropics than in the desert, and more water is available. Not all of it is safe to drink, however. Diarrhea can begin just half to three quarters of an hour after drinking polluted water and make it impossible to continue a tortuous trip through the jungle. Since many jungle pools are contaminated, the traveler who is caught without water purification tablets watches for animals' tracks and drinks where they do. One group of anthropologists on safari in East Africa began following elephant tracks to their water hole but soon realized it was not necessary to go so far. The footprints made by the heavy beasts were themselves so deep that rainwater had collected there. The huge leaves of jungle plants catch and hold rainwater as surely as on a soup plate. Vines and tree trunks can be tapped for the liquid within, and fruits and berries with high water content found easily.

During World War II, sixty survivors of a company of Japanese soldiers were cut off from the rest of their division in the Philippines. They fled to a deserted and uncultivated area where they made camp. Among them was a Chinese botanist who had been serving in the Japanese Army. Searching for edible plants, he found twenty-five species. The men were in good health when their camp was discovered sixteen months later.

Few of those lost in the jungle have a botanist with them, to be sure, and many plants, such as the taro tuber and pokeweed berry, are toxic when raw. A party of tourists became desperate with thirst and hunger after their jeep broke down. As they staggered along, they came upon some bushes laden with berries but had no idea whether these were poisonous. Each person refused to be the one to test them, so, somewhat delirious from the heat, they decided upon an all-or-nothing approach. All would eat the berries at the same time, and all would then either live or die. This story would not be known had the berries turned out to be poisonous.

Whatever the realities of contaminated water and poisonous plants, there is an atavistic fear of the jungle. A missionary, Père Faurie, to take a typical jungle horror story, was killed by leeches, which entered his sinuses and became so fattened with blood that they could not get out, thus cutting off his breathing. Lions, tigers, crocodiles, poisonous snakes, malaria-bearing insects, biting spiders, ants, and scorpions, piranhas—the list is long of the creatures that endanger the unwitting or helpless. The horrors are exaggerated, but they are not altogether without foundation. Most people who travel in the jungles will not encounter a lion or tiger; however, poisonous snakes inhabit all tropical regions of the world, except for Chile, New Zealand, Madagascar, and the Caribbean Islands (excluding St. Lucia, Trinidad, and Martinique).

Two World Health Organization physicians recently estimated 10,000 snakebite deaths a year in the savannah region of Nigeria. Even so, for the careful and clothed traveler, the fear of poisonous snakes exceeds by the far the likelihood of being bitten and, still more, dying of the bite; most of those bitten have unwittingly angered a snake by stepping on it when wandering barefoot in the tropical heat. Only the king cobra guarding its eggs, the bushmaster, the tropical rattlesnake, and the mamba have been known to attack. Some varieties of cobra can spit venom over a distance of 10 to 12 feet. Being hit by the venom does no harm, unless it gets into the eyes, where, if not washed out immediately with whatever fluid, however unattractive, is at hand, it may cause blindness.

An American anthropologist in Africa wrote back to her friends of a snake so deadly that if it bit, "you might just as well lie down, because you would be dead before you could run for help." The advice was sound only in the avoidance of running; exercise speeds the circulation and the action of the toxin. But what is done during the first minutes after being bitten by a poisonous snake can make the difference between life and death. With treatment, fewer than 1 percent of those bitten have died, and even without, no more than 10 or 15 percent. It is mere superstition to believe it will do any good to apply kerosene, a freshly killed chicken, potassium permanganate, gunpowder, or whiskey. Instead, circulation above the bite should be stopped with a tourniquet, a small but deep cut over each fang mark made, and the poison sucked out by victim or companion.

Nightmares of being strangled in the coils of the python or boa constrictor are common, but these large snakes will not attack anyone unprovoked or, for that matter, tackle any prey too large for them to swallow.

It may be small comfort to the person bitten or embraced by a snake to consider that snakes are more often eaten than they are eaters. Like fruits and vegetables, meat is plentiful in the jungle, and one need not be a big-game hunter to capture harmless snakes, fruit bats, hedgehogs, lizards, birds, fish, and the many other creatures traveling along the ground of a tropical forest, clinging to the trees, flying overhead, or swimming in the waters.

Yet, like fruits and water, some fish are poisonous, and, like snakes, some strike with lethal effect. There are fish that will sicken or kill even the person who has not eaten them but has been unlucky enough to step on or near them. A sting by the poisonous spines of the stonefish can be as deadly as that of the krait or mamba and must be treated the same way. Cone snails possess teeth as sharp as hypodermic needles. The bite is agonizingly painful and produces swelling, paralysis, blindness, and sometimes even death within hours.

The best-known dangerous fish is the piranha of the rivers of northeastern South America. Although each individual fish is small, they travel in schools that can completely consume a person or large animal in a few minutes.

In order to exploit the mineral deposits in the jungles of the western Amazon in Brazil, construction crews hacked a road through the steaming snake- and insect-infested jungle. The men were attracted by the pay but soon found that there was no way to spend it in so remote a region. Even the prostitutes who went regularly to other mining camps could not make their way through the dense jungles. Desperate for relief from heat and boredom, the men plunged into the Trombetas River, indifferent to the risk from their fellow swimmers, the piranhas.

Other tropical fish are placid and harmless swimming companions but poisonous when eaten. A person who consumes just one ounce of the flesh of the puffer fish will be dead in twenty minutes. In most cases the severity of the illness and the likelihood of death depends on just how much and which parts of the fish are eaten, with the liver, intestines, and eggs of the fish containing the highest concentrations of poison.

The illness produced by fish poison is one of the most terrible to afflict humans. The catalog of symptoms is terrible: nausea, vomiting, dizziness, paralysis, the loss of the ability to speak, a numbness of lips, tongue, fingertips, and toes, a terrible itching, and a strange sensation in which hot objects feel cold and cold ones hot. Although induced vomiting and purging are considered worth a try, no specific antidotes exist. Fish poisoning is quite different from the food poisoning that follows eating spoiled fish, an uncomfortable bout of vomiting and diarrhea which passes relatively quickly. A poisonous fish does not need to be spoiled. It produces illness no matter how fresh it may be.

The poisons have no taste, and the fish filets usually look just like those of harmless varieties. Some travelers follow the example of the birds. If a bird can eat a fish, they reason, so can a human. But birds are not much harmed by fish poisons. Dogs and rats are very susceptible to the toxins but may not show symptoms for 24 hours.

The fact that a fish in one region is not poisonous is no guide to the safety of the same species in others. The red snapper caught in the Gulf of Mexico and the Caribbean is a delicacy. If caught in some other tropical waters and consumed, it can lead to death. It is usually safe to do as the natives do, but not always. A party of tourists went fishing off a reef and, having been warned about poisoning, threw back most of the fish they caught. They kept just one species which they saw the natives eating. But this time both tourists and native fishermen became ill. The species, which in the past had been safe to eat, had suddenly developed a poison, always a possibility with tropical fish.

Most poisonous fish live in shallow waters of lagoons or reefs, where they are particularly easy to catch and tempting to amateur fishermen. Still, as a U.S. Air Force training manual remarks, this propensity of poisonous fish for the shallows has an advantage: "Survivors on life rafts on the open ocean have less to worry about from fish poisoning." Pollyanna could not have said it better.

6

The Menace in Sun Worship

It causes premature wrinkles, dryness, scaling, mottling, loss of elasticity, and frequently skin cancer. When the health reports of nine Presidential contenders were released in 1980, they revealed that two men— President Jimmy Carter and Senator Edward Kennedy—had suffered sun-induced skin injuries. Yet the source of all these ills is courted rather than avoided.

A suntan is viewed as a sign of beauty, of health, and, in northern climates, of wealth. Certainly, a suntan does make a person look well and, for a time, youthful. And the connotation of wealth has validity in that the rich have the leisure time and the means to sunbathe beside the pool, to "follow the sun" in winter to tropical resorts, to relax on the beaches. Even those who obtain their tans from sunlamps in health clubs have the money for membership, the time to spend there, and a sense of the importance of looking tanned. The advice, "Get a suntan if you would look rich and successful," has been attributed to many a well-publicized, self-made millionaire.

Many resorts are located in hot desert country. Staying too long in such areas produces what has come to be known as an "Arizona-type" skin, leathery in texture and crisscrossed with tiny lines that cannot be removed easily even by face-lifting. (This type of skin is not, of course, unique to Arizona.) Yet the skin of those parts of the body that are seldom if ever exposed to the sun, such as the buttocks and abdomen, remains soft and appears far more youthful than the lined, dried hands, face, and neck. A woman of thirty-five who has had a yearly sunburn since she was a teenager will look older than the woman in her fifties who has avoided the sun. This obvious fact has no impact on teenagers, who know they will never grow old. The southern belle of the past who guarded her complexion jealously and never went out without her wide-brimmed hat and parasol is viewed as amusing rather than intelligent.

Sunbathing does benefit health, but not to the extent that is generally believed. The view stems in part from the fact that illness is more frequent in winter than in summer. But that is owing more to the way that people are crowded together indoors, passing viruses and bacteria back and forth, than to the lack of sunlight. It is common in winter to exercise less and get less fresh air than in summer. Tanned individuals often really are healthier because those rich enough to sunbathe regularly also follow good diets, engage in sports, have well-heated homes and air conditioning, proper protective clothing, and excellent medical advice and care.

This is not to ignore vitamin D synthesis, the acknowledged beneficial effect of sun exposure. A precursor vitamin already present in the body requires ultraviolet rays for activation and transformation into vitamin D. In the past, the sun was the best—sometimes the only—treatment for tuberculosis, skin disease, and a general feeling of being "run-down"; the opinion that sunbathing is a health necessity is, therefore, in part a survival. Rickets, the bone-deforming disease resulting from a vitamin D shortage, was once common among the poor. Children who lacked winter clothing would stay indoors for days at a time, while living on bread and potatoes. An American doctor visiting Vienna after World War I was appalled by the number of children with rickets-bowed legs. They had been kept home for safety, he was told, and had little fresh food. As soon as these children were admitted to the hospital and sent out to play on the sun porch, the progress of the disease was halted.

Until effective drugs were developed, patients with tuberculosis went to sanitariums in the mountains, where they sought health in long hours of sunbathing. Tuberculosis specialists had a saying that those patients who developed the best suntans made the best recoveries.

So fleeting is fame that few today could identify Niels Ryberg Finsen, the Dane who won the Nobel Prize in Physiology and Medicine in 1903 for treating lupus vulgaris, a tuberculous skin disease, with ultraviolet rays delivered by the Finsen lamp, his version of the sunlamp. The use of sunlamps for good health rather than good color continued for some decades thereafter. During the 1930s well-to-do parents purchased sunlamps and insisted that their children spend a certain number of minutes under the light each day. The conviction, current then and still common now, was that the ultraviolet rays could cure a cold. In truth, nothing but time produces a cure, and sunlight, as every sufferer from cold sores has learned, brings out the latent herpes virus and causes the blister to reappear. Athlete's foot is likely to have a flareup, too.

Even vitamin D synthesis does not require a suntan or day on the beach. Just a short daily walk in the noonday summer sun will provide the body with all the vitamin D needed. Even without sunshine, sufficient vitamin D can be obtained from fish-liver oils, eggs, and irradiated milk.

It is still a fact today that patients with bronchitis, rheumatism, or a "run-down" condition are urged by their physicians to go south. Those who do so feel better. The national health plans of many European countries provide for a stay at a sanitarium. While it is true that vitamin D contributes to a sense of well-being, most of the benefit is derived from the warmth, dry air, and freedom from winter storms and winds and the relaxation from work-induced tensions, rather than from the sun's rays. The sun is often recommended for skin diseases. Psoriasis is sometimes relieved and dandruff lessens. Some acne sufferers are helped by the drying and peeling produced, but others are not.

The feeling of the warm sun has a sensual quality; the skin gets a particularly pleasant odor, which is usually but not always hidden by the stronger smell of sweat, as sweating is also stimulated by the sunshine.

The standard cliché used to describe those seeking suntans is "sun worshipers," the word harking back to the times when great temples to the sun were erected in Sippar, Heliopolis, Cuzco, Teotihuacán. Thinking to feed its strength, the Aztecs gave the sun the bleeding dripping hearts of thousands upon thousands of captives.

A survival of the worship of the sun is evident in the halo, or aureole. The rays of the brilliant sun surround the heads of the trinity and the saints. The day of rest, the most important day of the week for Christians, bears the name of the sun. (The moon, for all its significance in the lunar calendar of the Jews and other peoples, gives its name to the workaday Monday.)

So valued is the golden warmth that makes the food crops grow that rulers have taken the sun to be their symbol since the days when the king of the Mesopotamians was the "sun of his land" and the pharaohs of Egypt were sons of Ra, the sun god. Closer to modern times, France's Louis XIV wished to be known as "le roi soleil," the sun king.

The brilliance and magnificence of the sun derive from its heat, which at the center is estimated at close to 20 million degrees Celsius (about 36 million degrees Fahrenheit). Even the outer surface is roughly 6,000 degrees Celsius (some 10,800 degrees Fahrenheit). Of all the rays of the sun, only the ultraviolet produce sunburn. And of the ultraviolet rays, only those at the shorter end of the electromagnetic spectrum are responsible. The wavelengths that cause sunburn also transform precursor substances in the body into Vitamin D. The B band of the spectrum, which includes those ultraviolet rays between 250 and 320 nanometers in wavelength, does the most damage to the skin, with those of less than 300 being the most significant. The A band of 320 to 400 nanometers will produce tanning without burning the skin.

The danger of severe sunburn would be greater by far were it not for the protective layer of ozone in the atmosphere. The ozone absorbs a great deal of ultraviolet radiation, particularly the most dangerous shorter wavelengths. More of these intense rays would reach the earth, should part of the ozone layer be dissipated by exhaust from supersonic transport planes, aerosols, other manmade pollutants, and dust. Clouds in the sky do not keep ultraviolet radiation from reaching the ground; many bad sunburns occur on cloudy days.

The human eye, which can only detect wavelengths from 400 to 650 nanometers, cannot see ultraviolet rays. Therefore, it is not possible to judge just how dangerous to the skin the sunlight really is on any given afternoon at the beach. Most people with severe sunburns will tell you they did not know what was happening until too late, but one dermatologist says that the first signs can be spotted by the vigilant. He learned this from a patient who was a fashion model. After being in the sun for a short time, she would glance under the fabric of her bikini. If there was the slightest difference in color, she would get out of the sun.

It takes surprisingly little time for skin to burn. Just how long depends on the skin type, whether very fair or dark. The average person will display the first hint of sunburn in just fifteen to twenty minutes during the peak hours of the day—from 10 A.M. to 3 P.M., with 11 A.M. to 1 P.M. the times of greatest risk. The closer to the equator, the shorter the time it takes for the bikini strap mark to show. Those who vacation in the tropics can start a sunburn in just twelve to fifteen minutes.

It is possible to tan without burning by spending about a minute a day less than it would take for the skin to begin to turn pink. This requires having the self-control to cover up or go inside after a mere eleven to nineteen minutes, depending on where one is sunbathing. That amount of time can be doubled on the second day, trebled on the third. It usually takes no more than three days, four to five for those with very sensitive skin, to become tan enough not to burn.

Those who spend an hour or two in the sun every day all year round in the same latitude, subject to the gradually changing intensity of the sun's rays, keep a protective tan. But most people are out in the sun in summer only, and each year they burn.

Some of the rays strike the skin directly; others are scattered and reflected back from the ground. Holding a silver-colored reflector under the chin to concentrate the sun's rays on the face—a practice abhorred by skin specialists—does exactly that, speeding the burning and tanning process. Sun is strongly reflected by sand and water, so the same amount of noontime ultraviolet radiation is more likely to produce a sunburn on a beach than in the park. Freshly fallen snow reflects back 70 to 90 percent of the radiation, and as the intensity of the rays increases by 4 percent for each 1,000 feet in altitude, skiers get burns as dark as those of sunbathers on the beach. Snow in the city seldom helps residents to lose their winter pallor, because it gets dirty so quickly and reflects back only 50 percent of these rays.

Certainly, sunburns are sometimes gotten in parks by those who work at it, and city dwellers who stay out of doors during the daytime for long periods of time will become somewhat tanned. But the association between suntans and vacations remains valid. The buildings cutting off the rays, the dull nonreflective surfaces, and the amount of clothing customarily worn reduce the probability of a city sunburn.

Writing in 1900 of her travels in Syria, Lady Gertrude Bell described a May day when the midday sun was so hot that "my foot was burned through my boot." While in more temperate regions one not likely to be severely burned through a boot, or even while wearing a beach coat or T-shirt, some of the sun's rays do get through. Even sitting in the shade under a beach umbrella or large-brimmed hat does not completely remove all risk; some radiation is reflected back from sand or sea. And swimmers have been sunburned, because the sun's rays can pass through water. Window glass and many plastics are more protective, which is why the sunporch, more popular in another era, deserves a revival.

The very best way to protect the skin is to keep it out of the sun— chemically if not physically. Not all preparations sold are protective; many of the suntan oils do not keep out any ultraviolet rays, as their purpose is merely to lubricate the skin. Considering how drying the effect of the sun can be, this is of itself helpful. As one cosmetics saleswoman advised a trainee, "The weather is your friend. If it is cold, the wind dries out the customer's skin, and if it is hot, the sun dries it out and moisturizers are needed." Contrary to popular belief, the oils do not promote tanning.

Zinc oxide, titanium dioxide, talc, and some other opaque substances keep the sun from penetrating the skin, and one will often see white-nosed or white-lipped people on the beach. But these sun blocks are too unsightly and messy to be used over much of the body. Lipsticks and makeup offer some protection against the sun; in fact, a number contain titanium dioxide or other blocking agents.

A great many sunscreens have been developed which keep out the damaging ultraviolet rays and let in those that produce a tan. Preparations vary in "Sun Protection Factor," a value scale recommended by the Food and Drug Administration and set arbitrarily from 2 for skin that requires the least protection to 15 or higher for the fair-skinned person who needs the most. The use of these products greatly increases the amount of time that can be spent in the sun with safety. The sunscreen should be reapplied every time a person goes swimming or sweats heavily. A look at the labels of a variety of sunscreens will show that the chemical used most often is para-aminobenzoic acid (PABA), followed by benzophenones, cinnamates, salicylates, and anthranilates. PABA builds up in the skin and so can be put on a couple of days before the first summer weekend, in preparation for exposure.

While all the sunscreens keep out the most harmful ultraviolet B rays, the benzophenones and anthranilates also keep out some of the longer A waves, which while they do not cause sunburn, may bring on photosensitivity reactions. The most extreme of these reactions are suffered by those with systemic lupus erythematosus, porphyria, or urticaria. Redness, swelling, rashes, and skin eruptions may appear in sensitive individuals exposed to the sun while taking drugs, such as the tetracyclines, sulfonamides, certain antifungals, oral antidiabetic agents, diuretics, and tranquilizers.

Many plants can bring on the same kind of photosynthetic response. Sometimes this occurs after a person has merely touched a plant containing a chemical affected by ultraviolet radiation. The chemical has been found in the leaves, roots, fruits, and seeds of buckwheat, parsley, dill, carrots, figs, celery, fennel, parsnips, caraway, coriander, citrus fruits, rue, and some grasses. The reaction is often mistaken for poison ivy, but unlike poison ivy, these plants do not harm so long as they are in the dark. Indoors or after sunset it is perfectly safe to get the chemical on one's skin.

Wearing perfume to the beach is seldom recognized as a possible source of trouble, but dermatologists are often consulted about mysterious dark spots appearing on the skin after a day on the beach. Bergamot, lavender, lemon, lime, and rosemary oils that go into fragrances can lead to unpleasing reactions. The germicidal deodorant soaps that are also popular in the summer among beachgoers can do the same thing.

Few people have failed to become severely sunburned at least once in their lives, and the average individual starts each summer or each vacation with a burn. The red, hot, blistered skin is acutely painful and there may also be fever or nausea. The area is exquisitely tender to touch; even a light shirt feels heavy and scratchy. The friend who thinks it hilarious to hit a sunburn in false cameraderie seldom finds the victim ready to laugh. The discomfort usually reaches a peak within the first twenty-four hours, though it may last for about three days.

Many people believe that cold water is bad for a sunburn, perhaps reflecting the masochistic view that if it feels good, it must be bad for you. Fortunately, a cold shower or cold compresses are medically sound, as they cause the blood vessels to constrict and reduce the swelling. Aspirin can help, though a truly severe sunburn may require medical attention.

While it seldom appears obvious to the sufferer, sunburn is a protective mechanism. One sunburn a season is all that most people need to prevent continued burning. Whether tanning has occurred gradually and painlessly, or rapidly and painfully, it makes the individual adapted to sunlight and able to endure longer periods of exposure.

The very first time one goes out in the summer or tropical sun, a series of reactions is set in motion by the ultraviolet rays striking the skin. Some of the living cells within the epidermis die and are added to the horny top layer of the skin, the corneum. As the corneum gets thicker, it offers more protection against sunburn. Those parts of the body where the corneum is always thick, such as the palms and soles, do not usually become sunburned in the first place.

While the reactions within the skin are going on, a substance is released that makes blood vessels dilate and produce the characteristic redness and soreness. Even so, the brilliant color is partially in the eye of the beholder. White skin reflects not only the yellow-red but also the green-blue rays of the light spectrum. However, when skin is reddened by sunburn, there is a sharp drop in its reflection of the green-blue rays. As a result, it looks even redder than it is.

The relationship between sunburn and the skin's ability to protect itself lies in the melanin pigment within the skin. The epidermis gets its color from the melanin, which consists of tiny grains of black or brown pigment. The amount of pigment available for protection varies among the races of the world. The darker-skinned peoples are less likely to become sunburned, because they are so well supplied.

Melanin pigment starts offering its protective function to white skin as soon as sunburn occurs. The amount of melanin both increases and migrates to the upper layers of skin, reaching the corneum. Once the inflammation subsides, the pigment remains, revealed in a glowing suntan. Melanin protects the vital parts of the skin cells from being damaged by the ultraviolet rays and is most heavily concentrated around the skin cell's nucleus, which contains the DNA (deoxyribonucleic acid).

In 1887 a German scientist, M. Wedding, painted sheep black with tar and found that this prevented them from developing skin lesions, a common photosensitivity reaction, when they ate buckwheat. He thought that a similar protection from sunburn should be offered to humans. Observing that blacks were relatively free from the problem, he suggested an experiment. When the next German merchant ship set off for the tropics, the skin of half the crew should be stained a dark walnut color, while the rest would serve as controls. Wedding found no ship's captain willing to go along with his idea, so the experiment was not carried out and the German scientist never learned that a stain on top of the skin is not the same thing as either a sunblock like tar, or the stain of melanin within. Similarly, the suntan produced chemically by instant tanning preparations will not protect against sunburn the way an ultraviolet-ray-induced suntan can do.

The possession of large amounts of melanin is advantageous under most but not all conditions of hot region life. The fact is that it makes a person hotter. Negro skin absorbs about 30 percent more sunlight than does white. The problem is akin to that produced by dark-colored clothing in the summer. Most people wear light colors, which makes them feel cooler by reflecting rather than absorbing the heat. However, by absorbing the sun's rays, melanin heats the skin and stimulates profuse sweating, which is the body's best way of cooling itself. It might then be considered a trade-off.

Under conditions where water loss is hazardous, this too could be a drawback, and dark-skinned inhabitants of such regions are wary. It sometimes seems odd to tourists making a first trip to Mexico or the Caribbean to observe that broad-brimmed hats are worn by natives who would not seem in much danger of sunburn. Similarly, laborers on the deck of ships in Hong Kong Harbor hold large black umbrellas over their heads. And when the peoples of Guinea, Nigeria, and Mali travel down the great Niger River by boat, each desert nomad comes on board bearing the three items considered essential to survival in the Sahara: an umbrella, a blanket, and a sword.

An anthropologist in the Australian interior where temperatures average more than 100 degrees for four or five months of the year observed that finding shade at midday was a prime concern of members of the aboriginal tribe he was studying. When none was readily available, tall branches were set in a semicircle and roofed with grass and the natives sat on the ground within.

Dark skin coloring, it seems likely, was an evolutionary advantage in the dark rain forests. The melanin provided an effective camouflage, making it easier to hide from predators and enemies. The pigment confers other benefits that are not so obvious. Melanin protects certain light-sensitive vitamins in the skin tissues and blood from being decomposed by the ultraviolet, suggest University of Minnesota scientists Richard F. Branda and John W. Eaton. If the vitamin folate is destroyed by sunlight, anemia results, which affects general health, growth, and reproductive capacity. Dark skin in this way guards against deficiency diseases.

In recent years an additional advantage of dark skin is becoming increasingly evident: While blacks are no more immune than whites to other forms of malignancy, they are seldom afflicted with skin cancer. The protection lies in the heavy concentration of melanin around the cell nucleus with its essential DNA. Damage to the DNA is an important factor in producing skin cancer.

The difference between dark and light skin in carcinogenesis is being observed in Brazil now that the forests have been cleaned out in the state of Espirito Santo. Some 300 square miles of land that had been covered with fragrant jacaranda trees and lush hanging vines and flowers is now baked and dried, holding only a few thin, dying trees, a multitude of weeds, and a few hardy shrubs. The population of this region is made up of members of two very different racial stocks, dark-skinned Brazilians and light-skinned descendants of German settlers of a century or so ago. As the forest has receded, the incidence of skin cancer has advanced. Today, many of the lighter-skinned inhabitants have cancer or the lesions that precede it; the darker-skinned Brazilians are less often stricken. Similarly, the albinos among the San Blas Indians of Central America and the albino Negroes of South America have a greater incidence and an earlier onset of skin cancer than do their fellow tribesmen who are pigmented. And the Irish, Scotch, and Welsh are very vulnerable to skin cancer, possessing both light skin and a genetic predisposition.

The most common and least serious type of skin cancer is the basal cell carcinoma, which may first appear as a small raised lesion, sometimes with a pearly border. The squamous cell type appears in response to a somewhat greater intensity of ultraviolet radiation. A red, scaling lesion which gradually grows is a frequent first sign. The least common and most dangerous, malignant melanoma, arises from a dark blue, brown, or black mole. Although this form of cancer is extremely uncommon, it is the source of an inordinate amount of concern. Everyone has moles and so has the opportunity for worry. But most changes in moles, as during pregnancy, are harmless.

There are 300,000 new cases of basal and squamous cell carcinoma annually in the United States, and 9,600 of melanoma, according to National Cancer Institute estimates. Each year 4,000 people die of melanoma, 1,600 from the other skin cancers. When diagnosed properly and treated promptly, nearly 98 percent of all skin cancers can be cured.

The anti-sunbathing movement gathered strength, once a clear relationship was found between exposure to the sun and the development of skin cancer. In the hottest, driest portion of sunny Queensland, Australia, 16 percent of all men over the age of twenty-one have had at least one skin cancer. Australia and South Africa have the highest death rates from skin cancer in the world.

"Skin cancer incidence of each cell type was found to be positively correlated with the annual ultraviolet count," states a report prepared for the National Cancer Institute. Scientists had measured ultraviolet radiation in ten widely spaced locations in the United States and compared these figures with local skin cancer incidence. The ultraviolet radiation is high in Fort Worth, Texas, with a northern latitude of 32.8 degrees; so was the number of cases of skin cancer. Basal cell cancer affected 394 per 100,000 men and 205 per 100,000 women, while the squamous cell type affected 124 of 100,000 males and 51 of the same number of women. The situation was markedly different in Des Moines, Iowa, at a more northern latitude of 41.5 degrees and with much less sunshine. The incidence of the basal cell type per 100,000 people was 123 for men and 69 for women; squamous cell was 47 for men and 13 for women. As for the malignant melanoma, an incidence of 3.24 for men and 7.30 for women in Forth Worth compared to 3.64 and 2.93 respectively in Des Moines.

In Hawaii, with its latitude of 21 degrees, the amount of carcinogenic radiation is high and, in contrast to the higher latitudes, the sunlight is brilliant all year around. This is a delight to natives and tourists, but it means that there is no time of the year when the skin can rest from the ultraviolet radiation. This does not much trouble the native, darker-skinned inhabitants of the islands. In 1955 and 1956, Honolulu's dermatologists reported 293 cases of skin cancer to the health department. Of this total, 276 were Caucasians, 9 Japanese, and 2 Hawaiians and part-Hawaiians.

Dermatologists frequently tell patients an anecdote designed to keep them out of the sun. Cabdrivers in the United States have more cancers on the left side of the face, which is exposed to the sun while they drive, than on the right. In the United Kingdom, where the driver is on the opposite side, more cancers appear on the right.

Hereford cattle, which have spotty pigmentation on their eyelids, develop cancers in the spaces between the spots. As with cattle, so with people. More cancers appear on the lower lid than on the upper, which is shielded. Between 80 and 90 percent of skin cancers are on the head and neck, with the majority on the parts of the face that protrude the farthest, such as the nose and the cheeks over the facial bones. The upper lip is shaded by the nose, the top of the neck by the chin, and fewer cancers develop in either place. The tops of the ears, the scalp, and the neck below the chin shadow are most exposed, as are the hands and arms. Those places on the body that become sunburned first are the places where the cancers most often arise.

Not all those exposed to the risks of skin cancer or sunburn are taking in the ultraviolet radiation for pleasure. According to the National Institute of Occupational Safety and Health, some 4.8 million outdoor workers are often exposed to sunlight, and another 320,000 industrial workers to artificial ultraviolet light.

Damage to the eyes is less common than to the skin but is a real hazard. In *The Four Feathers*, a 1930s movie about the British in India, Ralph Richardson portrayed a British officer who became lost while on the desert. Exhausted, he fell down on a sand dune. As he rolled over and over, his helmet came off and dropped away beyond his reach. For hours he stumbled through the desert, collapsing to the ground at last, to lie for hours unshielded from the pitiless sun. When he was finally rescued and returned to his company, he had become completely blind. The result of this misadventure was more extreme than is likely, but it cannot just be dismissed as fanciful filmmaking. A considerable degree of injury can result from the inflammation due to excessive ultraviolet exposure. Lesions may form on the cornea, leaving it scarred. The most common form of damage is known as "welder's flash" or by the unpleasantly but accurately descriptive term, "ground-glass eyeball." This form of conjunctivitis results when the mucous membrane linings of the eyes and eyelids absorb too much ultraviolet light. The injury is usually temporary, although if the exposure lasts very long, cataracts may develop. Closing the eyes against the sun when the glare is too brilliant out of doors or under a health-club sunlamp is not enough protection; the sun can burn through the lids. Sunglasses dark enough to keep out 85 to 90 percent of the light are needed. When directly under a sunlamp even for just a few minutes, it is particularly necessary to keep the eyes covered by protective goggles.

In the nineteenth and early twentieth centuries the belief was current that the sun could somehow "fry" the brain and spinal cord. Physicians attached to the British armed services advised that soldiers sent to India be provided with a topi containing a thin metal plate to keep the sun's rays from entering through the scalp. They were also to wear a pad along the spine to protect that area and, beneath it all, orange-colored underwear that was believed to stop the actinic green, blue, and violet and ultraviolet rays. The "actinic" underwear was not replaced with white until the 1920s, and it was another decade before the metal protection was removed from the helmet and the men allowed to use lighter-weight headgear.

The ancient Japanese believed that the sun should not shine upon a divine person, and the Mikado did not venture out into the light. And a tribe of South American Indians used not to allow those men chosen to be future rulers to go out of their houses for as long as seven years at a time. In this way, they were certain that there would be no ill effects from the sun.

Our current knowledge of the harm excessive exposure to the sun can bring does not detract from the joy it offers. The Mikado and the Indian rulers must have found the years of solar deprivation hard to endure with equanimity. Absence of the sun leads to depression.

"It is because of its short duration and its contrast to the rest of the year that so many activities and traditions are so closely linked to summer, the good time, the green time. The outcome is a marked sun-and-summer oriented culture," says Ole Svensson, a Danish city planner. Records dating from the first days of Arctic and Antarctic exploration tell of the brooding despondency that hung over an expedition as the days of winter dragged past, with noon indistinguishable from midnight. Some men wandered out onto the ice plateau in their despair and died there. "Cabin fever" in Alaska might as reasonably be called darkness fever. Clinics have been set up in Alaska to help those suffering from this form of depression.

Another way of utilizing the sun has come into prominence with the oil crisis. Solar heating, to be sure, is not exactly new; city builders of thousands of years ago were orienting buildings toward the sun. However, the idea still seemed so novel in 1950 that "5,000 people paid a dime to see this house—and that was when a dime was worth something," declared William Keck, architect, of his solar-heated home in Glenview, Illinois. Today, tapping the sun's power is seen as the ultimate and perfect solution to the world's energy needs. The sun is the one energy source that will last as long as the planet lasts, has no disposal problem, and, when technology has been perfected, might be cheaper than oil. In the deserts of Arizona, the Sahara, and the Kalahari, the mean annual amount of surface sunshine gives about 250 watts per square meter. Taking the contiguous United States as a whole, the annual average amount of solar energy has been calculated at roughly equal to ten or more barrels of oil per acre per day. A square yard of brilliantly sunlit ground takes in the equivalent of a cupful of gasoline a day.

The potential of solar energy is limitless. How much of it will be realized is not known. Much depends on government commitment and funding and public enthusiasm. Obviously, solar energy is most easily applied in those parts of the world where the sun is intense for much of the year. As the decade of the 1970s drew to a close, rooftop sunlight collectors could be found on countless homes; more than 2 million solar water heaters were in use in Japan, 300,000 in Israel, and 30,000 in the United States. In Australia a law was passed requiring that solar heaters be installed in all new buildings.

Solar energy can be tapped even in regions far from the tropics. By 1980 more than 200 buildings in Wisconsin were being warmed by the sun. Solar-heated houses are being built in rainy Ireland and in Denmark. A New York woman has been cooking for years on a solar oven in her back yard. Chicken takes three hours and is juicier than when done in a gas or electric oven, she insists. "I can hardly wait for winter," declared the director of the New York Botanical Garden's Cary Arboretum, as solar heating equipment was installed.

Solar-powered telephones linked Whiteface Mountain and the Olympic command post in Lake Placid. The new police headquarters in Camden, New Jersey, is heated by the sun; in Jacksonville, Florida, Anheuser-Busch has established a new solar pasteurization unit for beer; and in Nepal a solar-powered refrigerator keeps vaccines cool.

It becomes apparent that there are many ways of worshiping our sun.

7

Heat, Growth, and Reproduction

Upon retirement the businessman is honored with a gold watch and a dinner before being relegated to a less productive and influential position in society. For most, the occasion is more bitter than sweet. In western cultures, where old age is little revered, no effort to postpone its coming seems too great.

More than four centuries ago the Spaniard Juan Ponce de León set off on the voyage that was to become a symbol of the eternal search for youth. He sailed for the land of Bimini, north of Cuba, where, according to a legend told him by the Carib Indians, he would find a fountain flowing with miraculous waters. The fountain of youth eluded Ponce de León, as it has others with the same dream, but the quest goes on.

Today the fountain of youth is sought in the laboratory, where scientists wrestle with the problem of why the systems of the body run down. Why do humans grow old and must they do so? Could not youth and life itself be longer?

The moments when aging begins and death must come are genetically programmed for each species. The mayfly must carry out all the activities of its life in a single day, while the blowfly lives for thirty days, the rat two years, the beagle twelve years, the horse twenty years, and humans well beyond seventy. The time clock is set in the DNA (deoxyribonucleic acid) within the cell nucleus, with orders passed on by another molecule, the RNA (ribonucleic acid). Proteins are formed, among them the enzymes capable of triggering change and activity. However, at some point in the life of an organism, the pattern changes and error creeps in. And as it does, body systems begin to break down. Perhaps aging is nature's greatest mistake. Unlike other mistakes, however, the timing and form it will take is set from the first.

The results of tests performed at the Gerontology Research Center (National Institutes of Health) in Baltimore carry the startling suggestion that the speed of the biological time clock is to some extent governed by heat and by nutrition. More or less of these two factors can either shorten or prolong the period of proper enzyme production, of youth, of life itself.

Rotifers, aquatic creatures microscopic in size, were given the first chance at prolonged life. The Baltimore scientists kept some rotifers in heat of 95 degrees and others at a moderate 77 degrees. Those in the cooler surroundings were longer-lived than those in the hot environment. Rotifers kept hungry lived for fifty-four days, compared to thirty-four days for those provided with plentiful food. The smaller quantities of nutrients retarded growth, and so these rotifers developed more slowly and became adult at a later stage than the well-fed. When rotifers were both hot and heavy, their life span was three to four times shorter than is normal.

If environmental temperature is high and diet is plentiful, the processes within the cell whereby proteins are formed are speeded and everything that happens does so at a faster rate. It is also likely that random errors in protein synthesis creep in with greater frequency under conditions of heat. More chromosome abnormalities occur at 104 degrees than at lower temperatures. Even cells growing in a culture medium age more rapidly at very high temperatures, note researchers K.V.A. Thompson and R. Holliday at London's National Institute for Medical Research. Cells of connective tissue survived roughly half as long at 104 degrees as at 93.2 degrees.

The height of children between the ages of seven and ten increases rapidly in the spring and summer and then slows in the fall and winter. Such seasonal differences cancel one another out, according to the rules governing our biological time clock.

In 1928, long before the rotifers were being made hot and fat, a scientist, R. Pearl, presented a "Rate of Living" hypothesis: "The length of the life of a cold-blooded creature depends on the rate at which it spends its energy in growth, movement, and maintaining itself." The larvae of the fruit fly, *Drosophila*, develop more rapidly in heat, and, once hatched, the flies reach maturity sooner and age more rapidly. Growing that speedily, however, keeps them small. In general, the higher the temperature, the tinier the insect is when it attains full growth. The effect of heat on shortening life is more marked among male than female flies. Fish are also affected; eggs which develop at high temperatures hatch out smaller larvae than do those in cooler waters.

Pearl's theory could be expanded to include warm-blooded creatures. The rat, for example, has a shorter lifespan at high than at low temperatures, and reduction in food intake, particularly of protein, appears to be the only way to counteract the rapid development induced by the heat. Rats living at 82.4 degrees and eating as much as they wished reached their full growth in 300 days, compared to 470 days for those which were underfed. When kept at 93.2 degrees, those rats that voluntarily ate little survived for a longer period than rats reared at 82.4 degrees but eating heartily.

Whether the findings of the laboratory studies can be applied in some manner to higher animals or humans is intriguing, but not practical to date. Certainly, we would not be willing to inflict the retarded growth and smaller size of the underfed experimental animals on human subjects. The suggestion has been made that caloric restrictions be postponed until after full growth has been reached. The same increase in lifespan can be obtained by feeding animals half their normal diet or a liberal low-protein diet. In humans, however, this might have the unfortunate effects of reducing energy and mental powers and producing unhealthy children.

The temperature reduction that aids the cold-blooded rotifer or laboratory rat seems even harder to apply to humans. Few people can or would wish to move to cooler climates or to arrange their lives so as to be cold all the time. Certain drugs, such as the tranquilizer chlorpromazine, alter the heat-regulating mechanism of the body and achieve lower temperatures. However, tranquilizers may affect performance and have other side effects, making it inadvisable to give them to people who do not require them for psychological reasons. And so, even if temperature-reducing measures could retard aging, it seems obvious that people would not function well enough to be healthy and enjoy their extra years of youth.

In any event, in the world of nature many factors aside from temperature affect longevity. The elephant of the steaming tropics does not reach maturity until fifteen to twenty-five and lives to sixty, sometimes seventy years of age. The camel of the hot desert does not become adult until sixteen or seventeen and lives to be forty to fifty. Ironically, these animals in prehistoric times moved from what is now Europe to keep ahead of the ice-age glaciers, instead of remaining where they were and theoretically extending their lives. And while lack of food is an effective life-extending technique in the laboratory, it is more likely to kill creatures of the wild than an overabundance is to shorten their days.

Among humans the average life span tends to be longer in temperate than in hot climates, but this cannot be attributed to cooler weather and less food, but rather to better nutrition and control of disease. Because natives of the tropics and hot deserts seem old at ages when those of the northern regions look and feel young, it has been customary to believe in an earlier onset of maturity and a speeding of the whole life cycle. The English-language *Mexico City News* not long ago described the wedding in traditional white, though with a see-through nylon lace bodice, of a 26-year-old topless dancer. The bride, being married for the fourth time, had as attendants her children, ranging in age from seven to thirteen. Before the rise in teenage pregnancy in the United States, such reports were taken as proof that girls in hot climates reach puberty and are able to conceive sooner.

Little-girl mothers, however, are even more the exception in tropical than in temperate zones. Girls in cooler regions begin to menstruate at much earlier ages than in hot areas. In the United States the median age for onset of menstruation for girls of European descent is 12.8 years, and this age is roughly the same throughout Europe. In marked contrast, the Melanesians of New Guinea live in one of the hottest areas of the world and yet have the latest age of menarche, 18 to nearly 18.5. Africa is hot indeed, but in Rwanda members of the Hutu tribe reach puberty at 17 and the Tutsi tribeswomen at 16.5 years. Impoverished Bantu in the Transkei of South Africa menstruate at 15.4 years, while those who are better off do so at 15. The well-nourished natives of the Yucatán reach puberty at 12.5, while the impoverished

Maya do not until they are 15. Chinese girls from rich families in Hong Kong menstruate at 12.5 years, those from the middle class at 12.8, and the poor at 13.3. Urban populations typically achieve menarche earlier than rural, chiefly because of somewhat greater prosperity and fewer periods of hunger due to crop failure and famine. In Appalachia, where much of the population is undernourished, menarche comes at a later age than the nationwide median. The main difference is not outdoor heat but wealth or lack of it.

The classic statement, "As health goes up, age at menarche goes down," is proven repeatedly. In the nineteenth century, when nutrition on the average was poorer than today, the average age of menarche was 15 years in England and nearly 17 in Norway and Finland. This is in contrast to ancient Greece, where nutrition was good and most girls, Hippocrates reported, were menstruating by the age of 13. Over the last hundred years, the age at menarche dropped by three to four months per decade in most of Europe. Now, with the standard of living fairly constant, the age is virtually unchanged from one decade to the next.

Poor nutrition, however, remains a problem in much of the tropical world, and when the amount of body fat is too far below normal, menarche is delayed. Even if menstruation has begun it may stop. The same physiological response to emaciation can be observed in avid women joggers, professional athletes, and dancers who exercise to the point where body fat is greatly reduced.

The average amount of food available for each person in the developing, mostly tropical or desert, countries is equivalent to only 1.8 average United States meals a day, according to Environmental Fund estimates. In Zaire, the figure is 0.7, in India 0.9, Nigeria and Ecuador 1.0, Nicaragua 1.6, and Egypt, 1.9.

Such starvation results when populations are greater than can reasonably be supported by available resources. It might seem that, held down by hunger, late menarche, and disease, the birth rate would be lower than in temperate regions. Logically, then, an improvement in the economic status of natives of the tropics would reduce the age of fertility, extend the years of childbearing, and cause the population to grow even more. But that is not the way it works. However limited by poor physical condition, couples not using birth control still more than reproduce themselves. In many Muslim countries, "as many as God will send" is viewed as right. On the average, this means seven children. In fact, as Karan Singh, India's former minister of health and family planning, once remarked, "Development is the best contraceptive."

The rates of population growth in Asia, Africa, and Latin America are from two to six times as great as in Europe and North America. These regions hold better than three-fourths of the world's population. Marked drops in the birthrate in many hot-climate countries in the past decade have been hailed, however. "It is important to remember that while birthrates are declining in Asia and Latin America, the *number* of births is increasing," warns Marion O'Connor, Chief Statistical Section officer in the United Nations Development Programme. And in Africa even the birthrate has remained fairly constant at about 46 per 1,000 people, which can be compared to roughly 15 per 1,000 in North America and 14 in Europe.

Neither uncontrolled tropical passions nor an irresponsible attitude toward using up resources is behind the tradition of large families, but rather extreme poverty and the need to obtain labor and provide for old age. Bangladesh villagers seek to assure themselves of only three sons, but " 'family planning' to these people doesn't mean three children—it means ten or more," commented Dr. James R. Echols, population consultant to the government of Bangladesh. "The problem is that of ten or eleven or even twelve children, half will be girls and not count, and three or four may die before reaching puberty."

"The men regard many children as proof of their manhood," a travel writer was told by an old fisherman on the island of Mauritius in the Indian Ocean. Yet fish, the sole means of livelihood, were insufficient to support the results of such manhood. "Our solution lies in big numbers," declared South African Zulu Chief Calalakubo Kaula, seeking to advance the political future of his people and providing additional incentive for population growth.

Yet along with the emphasis on childbearing, a contrary tradition of population control exists in most cultures and has kept the situation from being even worse. Folk medicine has provided herbs to prevent pregnancy, marriage has been delayed, periodic abstention from intercourse required by taboo, coitus interruptus made a common practice, and the period of breast feeding prolonged.

While infanticide has been abandoned, a "masked" form exists in regions of terrible poverty: Infants are "allowed" to die of diarrhea or other ills, as physicians in Candelaria, Colombia, discovered. Attempting to offer their services, they were taken aback by parents refusing their help. Although contraceptives were available, abstinence was the means of birth control most commonly tried. And when they did have sexual relations, many women were determined not to reach orgasm in the mistaken belief that conception was more likely to occur during an intercourse that culminated in climax.

In many countries, taboos surround the proper timing for the intercourse meant to produce the desired son. According to old astrological calendars picked up in Taiwan, only about a hundred days each year are suitable for sexual intercourse.

In China, where early marriage is frowned on, barefoot paramedics dispense contraceptives, economic advantages are offered to those with small families, and adherence to the slogan "One is best, two is most" is urged.

Marriage in earlier times in India often predated menarche, thus providing the opportunity for impregnation at the first moment of fertility. On the other hand, suttee held down reproduction on the part of older women. And even among groups not practicing suttee, a law forbidding widows to remarry naturally had a contraceptive effect. In more recent times a striking change came when the minimum age of marriage in India was raised to eighteen for girls and twenty-one for boys. No head of government has pushed contraceptive methods, chiefly the most effective and least reversible of all, sterilization, more ruthlessly and rigorously than Indira Gandhi during her first time in power. Villagers applying for loans to buy seeds or fertilizers were ordered first to undergo a vasectomy, and teachers were refused raises until they had convinced a large enough group of parents to become sterilized.

A change in attitude toward family planning has come in the tropical world. According to a 1978 report to the United Nations, modern contraceptive methods were available in 105 developing countries checked, and only nine held to "As many as God will send" as government policy. A subsequent World Fertility Survey found that more than half the married women questioned in Colombia, Peru, and Sri Lanka wanted no more children. Although in Pakistan and Bangladesh, fewer than 10 percent of women were using birth control, 78 percent of those in Costa Rico and 65 percent in Panama were doing so.

Scheduled intercourse, whether based on taboos or menstrual periods, is still a basic method of birth control for those who object to artificial contraceptives. This method is far from foolproof, but body temperature does provide a guide to fertility. A woman's temperature fluctuates throughout her menstrual cycle, and at mid-cycle, a drop immediately followed by a rise indicates that ovulation has taken place. Then, unless pregnancy intervenes, it falls with menstruation. Physicians often advise women who are having difficulties in conceiving to keep a basal body temperature chart. They are to take their temperature each morning, marking it on a chart, so as to see clearly when ovulation is occurring, and have intercourse then. Pregnancy achieved in this way is dubbed "thermogenic conception" by infertility specialists. Those who would, instead, practice "thermogenic contraception" avoid intercourse at this time. The similar rhythm method, based on date, not temperature, is less accurate but more widely used in tropical countries.

Considering how difficult it is to reduce the growth of the huge populations of the developing nations, it may appear odd that considerable evidence has been amassed to show that conception and childbearing are adversely affected by heat. Male infertility has been linked to overheating of the testes, and may explain why athletes have this problem with surprising frequency. "The physiologic principle is that of increased intrascrotal temperature as a result of wearing a plastic cup and long periods of immersion in hot whirlpool baths," comments Dr. Stephen L. Corson, a Philadelphia specialist on infertility. Some doctors say that the best advice to give a man with this problem is to stop wearing jockey shorts, which heat the genitals, and shift to less close-fitting boxer shorts.

If the testes were not in the scrotum, which is distinctly cooler than the internal organs, the sperm could not form or develop properly, regardless of the underwear or bath temperature. Many nerve receptors for warmth are present in scrotal skin to rapidly pass along the message that it is overheating and so activate local cooling mechanisms. Should some accident cause the temperature in the scrotum to rise to merely what would be normal temperature in the rest of the body, the sperm will fail.

"Heat depresses spermatogenesis," explained Dr. Rudi Ansbacher of San Francisco, at a meeting on infertility. "Since the spermatogenic cycle is 74 days, the boxer shorts should be worn for at least three to four months before a man comes in for a sperm count test. I forbid saunas or very hot showers, and if a man with an infertility problem is a long-distance driver, always sitting near the heat of the engine, I urge him to get off that job."

The height of summer is not a peak season for conception. When scientists at the Negev Institute for Arid Zone Research in Israel traced births to the period of conception, they observed a drop of 12 percent during the hottest months of May to September. In addition, larger numbers of pregnancies started then ended in spontaneous abortion or stillbirth. Similarly, in the southern United States, the rate of conception decreased as the temperature increased, according to a study by Paul Sabol of Maryland University and Don R. Dickson of Utah. (Only the citizens of Las Vegas appeared unaffected; no guess as to the reason was hazarded by the scientists.)

An exception to the general rule occurs in countries at very northern latitudes, such as Sweden; the conception rate there reaches its height during the summer, when daylight is virtually continuous. But this is due to the joyousness with which people greet the end of the long and dismal winter, rather than to stimulation of the reproductive organs.

Most conceptions take place in the spring in Italy, Portugal, Spain, Greece, Yugoslavia, Syria, Israel, Jordan, Egypt, Korea, Japan, and Mexico, according to a comprehensive Dutch work on biometeorology edited by S. W. Tromp. These are the countries in which the spring is warm but the summer very hot. In countries where both summer and spring are exceedingly hot, autumn sees a rise in fertility. This is true of the southern United States, India, Pakistan, the West Indies, Argentina, and Australia.

Most conceptions occur in Montreal in June, observed Clarence A. Mills, Professor of Experimental Medicine at the University of Cincinnati. June in Montreal, naturally, does not present the same heat stress as May in the Negev. He pointed to temperatures between 40 and 65 degrees F as most favorable for conception in climates such as Canada's.

Does the date of conception have an effect on a person's accomplishments? In the 1920s Ellsworth Huntington looked up the birth dates of famous people living in temperate climates and figured back to the time of their conception. A significantly large proportion had been conceived in May or June, making the traditional June wedding eugenically as well as romantically sound. It was his belief that the advantage lay in the level of vitality of the parents. This was at its high when their bodies were in balance with the environment, being neither too hot nor too cold.

Dutch biometeorological studies took another tack, declaring the sex of an infant to be affected by the season of conception. Thyroid hormone production is at its height in cold weather; the metabolic rate and probability of maleness is greatest then. When pigeons were given thyroid hormone, they did indeed produce more male chicks than usual. And so these scientists believe male human infants are more likely to be born when conception takes place during the winter, and females when pregnancies begin in warm weather.

A moralistic note was added to the data by German statistician W. Otto: June was the month when most children of married couples were conceived; illegitimate babies were more often conceived in May. He neglected to comment on their sex or achievements.

8

In Heat

The male mallee incubator bird never rests; it is he rather than the mother who takes the responsibility for maintaining the eggs at a temperature of 92 degrees Fahrenheit no matter what the rigors of summer heat and autumn cool in the desert of the Australian interior. Preparation begins six months in advance of the spring laying season, when the male digs a hole three to four feet deep. Leaves are dragged in to fill it to the top, and then the mound is covered with a pile of earth. In this arid region little rain falls, but the brief winter showers are sufficient to moisten the soil cover of the mound and the leaves beneath so as to start the heat-giving fermentation process. In a season of drought, the incubator bird cannot breed.

In spring the male bird digs a small hole in the mound to receive the egg, and it is only then that the gravid female approaches. If the hole does not appear suitable to her, she retreats and waits for the male to dig another, and yet another, until one is the right size. Throughout the spring and summer an egg is laid every four to eight days. The energy cost to the female is great, too; only 3½ pounds in weight herself, she lays eggs weighing about ½ pound each.

If unchecked, fermentation would raise the temperature within the mound to a lethal 115 degrees, and so each morning before dawn the father bird pushes the earth away from the mound to let the steaming leaves release their heat to the early morning coolness, before covering them again. Summer is the most stressful time for the father and the most risky for the young, because additional layers of earth must be piled up over the mound as insulation against the brutal sun during the hottest part of the day. Then the earth must be removed to allow the heat of fermentation to escape in the cooler hours of the evening, night, and early morning.

Toward the end of the breeding season, as the weather grows cooler, the male uses reverse strategy, uncovering the eggs during the hours when the sun is highest so as to gain the heat, and then covering them again with the sun-heated sand and leaves for the night. The male bird determines when to cover, when to add leaves, and when to expose the eggs to air or sun by sticking his beak into the mound; so sensitive is this system that appropriate action is taken to keep the eggs at the optimum 92-degree temperature throughout the incubation period.

Other members of the Megapodiidae family of birds with big feet, to which the mallee belongs, survive because of a different adaptation, this time requiring extra labor for the female. The eggs of these birds, native to the forests of the tropical Celebes and Molucca islands, require a constant high temperature during their seven-week incubation period. If the eggs were laid in a cool place, they would not hatch, and if the parent birds were to provide sufficient warmth by sitting on the eggs, only a few clutches could be laid during a breeding season. And so, each day of that season the females make their way over 15 or 20 miles to the beaches to lay their eggs in a place as warm and constant in temperature as the brood patch beneath a bird's abdomen. They recognize such a place by its color. Patches of black sand, left from lava flows of long-ago volcanic activity, absorb more of the rays of the sun than the golden sand. At night the female returns to the forest to feed and mate, only to go back to the beach to lay another egg the following day, and so on throughout the breeding season.

Where some species of the Megapodiidae place the heaviest burden for incubation on the male and others on the female, the white-winged doves of the lower Sonoran Desert of Arizona enjoy perfect equality and share in the task of egg-sitting. These doves build a flimsy nest on the branches of trees and cacti which have little or no leafy cover to shield the eggs from the blistering desert sun and air temperatures of over 100 degrees F. The eggs are kept from dangerous overheating by the parent doves, who have lower body temperatures than most other birds, and of the two, the male is the cooler. As the air reaches a maximum heat around midday, the male dove rests his body more heavily on the eggs and cools them off; the females take over in the late afternoon, when it is cooler. The small difference in size cannot account for the sex difference in temperatures, says Stephen M. Russell of the University of Arizona's Department of Ecology and Evolutionary Biology, but it is possible that females become more agitated than the males: "Excitement may cause an increase in body temperature—perhaps because more muscle fibers contract."

The body of the female python also serves as an incubator when necessary, but in a manner quite different from that of the bird, with its brood patch. She coils around her eggs on cool days and warms them by rhythmically contracting her muscles. Some mothers among the skink lizards seek out a sunny spot, bask there, and, when sufficiently heated, return to cover the eggs with their warm bodies.

The female Malaysian river terrapin lays her eggs on the sandbanks of the Perak River and then pushes a protective layer of warm sand over them. She compacts the sand by falling over the eggs, rising up again on her short legs, and falling again. The sound of her 44-pound body falling makes a sound like *tun tong*, which has become the Malaysian name for the terrapin. The sound of twenty or thirty terrapins dropping up and down to cover their eggs properly makes a drumming sound that carries for miles up and down the Perak River.

The developmental stages of embryos are speeded by heat. Cleavage of the sea urchin egg, for example, takes place in twenty-four minutes in the summer, more than thirty in the winter. When oysters that normally spawn off the coast of Virginia in water temperatures of 77 degrees were moved to colder Long Island waters, they failed to deposit their eggs.

In order to protect embryos against excessive cold or heat, planarian flatworm eggs have thick shells in the winter and thin ones in the summer. The bloodsucking leech, also a worm, resembles mammals in that the embryos are incubated within its body in a special sac from which the young emerge. The sea anemone of tropical seas also protectively retains larvae within its body until they are ready to be born.

The most primitive mammals, the monotremes, have body temperatures so low that in the nineteenth century they were thought to be cold-blooded. Combining the reproductive traits of several families of animals, they lay eggs but provide their young with milk. The spiny anteater of Australia and New Guinea and the duck-billed platypus of Australia, the members of the order, produce eggs with large yolks and leathery shells. The spiny anteater lays a single egg directly into her pouch; the platypus lays hers in a burrow where they are safe until they hatch. The platypus has milk for her tiny newborn, but no nipples for it to suck. Instead it must lick milk from the many minuscule openings on the abdominal surface over the mammary glands. Despite the primitive nature of these adaptations, they enable the infants to avoid the environmental hazards of heat, drought, and lack of food.

In 1770, when Captain Cook and his men first saw a kangaroo in what is now North Queensland, they thought it was a new type of huge jumping rodent. In time this was identified as the most conspicuous living member of the marsupials, another primitive mammal, only slightly more advanced than the monotremes. Most marsupials are now found in Australia and New Guinea, with the exception of the opossum of the Americas. Their name refers to the marsupium, or pouch, which serves as a perfect incubator, keeping the young warm but not too warm, regardless of the temperature outside, and in position to obtain nourishment. Kangaroos are born after so brief a gestation period—forty days—that they are quite undeveloped. Only an inch long, they are blind and have rudimentary ears, no fur, and budlike hind legs, but the forelegs, ending in claws, are well developed. Immediately after birth the infants climb up the mother's abdomen into the pouch and fasten onto one of the nipples, remaining about six months. They are too weak to suck at first, so the mother squirts milk into their mouths by contracting her muscles.

The wombat, a marmotlike creature, has just one infant, which it carries in its pouch for six months to a year. This marsupial, only three feet long today, was as large as a hippopotamus in prehistoric times, according to fossil evidence. The fierce carnivorous thylacine, or Tasmanian wolf, looks like a wolf or, being striped, like a tiger. It is quite different in an evolutionary sense, however, also carrying its young in a pouch. The most lovable of marsupials, the koala, resembles a bear but, like the thylacine, followed a different line of descent.

The young, only three fourths of an inch long at birth, remain in the pouch protected from the weather for six to eight months and are carried by their mothers for a few months longer until they are capable of climbing trees in search of food. These fussiest eaters of the animal kingdom will eat only the leaves and shoots of a particular species of eucalyptus at a particular stage of development.

The placental mammals, which include humans, carry their young within their own bodies. Although the fetus is not altogether independent of the temperature stresses that its mother is enduring, it has the best possible form of protection. Pregnancy is long, so the infants are quite highly developed at birth.

The term "in heat" is usually applied to nonhuman mammals only, although it might be said that humans too can only reproduce when "in heat," because ovulation is followed by increased secretion of a temperature-raising hormone that helps to hold a pregnancy. Derived from *oistros*, a Greek word meaning gadfly, desire, or frenzy, estrus has come to stand for the times in a female mammal's life when she is sexually excitable and able to conceive. The word "heat" applies to a single estrus cycle. The male of many species is capable of copulating only during those times of year when the female is in heat. Some mammals, such as the bear, dog, wolf, fox, seal, and deer, are in heat but once a year; the sow, mare, cow, and ewe, and many creatures of the tropics, several times. The lemming, ready for impregnation by the age of three weeks, remains in continuous heat for most of the year, excepting only late fall and early spring. The result is periodic overpopulation, leading to frenzied behavior and sometimes ending in mass death in the sea. Some biologists maintain that certain cold-blooded creatures undergo a period comparable to estrus, or heat. Thus the female *Anolis carolinensis*, a lizard of the southeastern United States, has three complete breeding periods a year, each made up of at least ten cycles of hormonally induced sexual receptivity.

Animals signal one another when they are in heat; the hindquarters of the female baboon, for example, become bright red in invitation. Chemicals may be excreted in the urine, revealing the state of estrus to sniffing males. To further guarantee continuation of the breed, a chemical excreted in the urine of certain species of male mice may bring on estrus in the female.

External as well as internal warmth, in combination with daylight, affects fertility of the bird, deer, goat, and horse. The changing conception rate of horses over the course of the year can be related to the changing hours of daylight, because the light provides a signal for the release of hormones: Light toward the end of the day has more effect on hormone secretion than does light in the morning.

Because the very longest days of summer are the days when heat is so great as to be depressive to all but the best heat-adapted animals, the conception rate for mammals usually follows the golden rule of moderation. Pregnancy occurs most often when the days are long enough to stimulate the reproductive hormones but are not yet excessively hot.

Temperature, therefore, has a role in encouraging or discouraging conception and under certain circumstances affects the gender of the offspring. Incubation temperature in the nest can determine the sex of the hatchlings in a number of turtle and lizard species, states James J. Bull of the Genetics Laboratory of Wisconsin University. Newly laid eggs of the North American map turtle, common in Mississippi, were placed in nests warmed by the sun, while others were put in the shade. Nearly all the young that hatched from the eggs in nests warmed by the sun were female, and all those from the cooler nests were male. Lizards were affected in exactly the opposite way, with low temperatures producing females and high temperatures, males. When eggs of the snapping turtle were checked at each stage of development, it was seen that the determination of maleness occurs earlier than that of femaleness.

Some animals actually undergo sex changes under the stress of temperature. When wood frog larvae are suddenly exposed to extreme heat after sex differentiation has taken place, about half of the females will turn into males.

Temperature-dependent sex determination occurs most frequently, says Bull, in species lacking the sex-determination chromosomes common to mammals and birds. Perhaps the animals in which sex is controlled by temperature rather than heredity arose in environments where hatchlings from cold nests would make good males, but substandard females (or vice versa), while in warm nests the females would be superior.

Whatever environment they inhabit, animals breed during those times of the year when the climate is most favorable for infant survival. In many parts of the tropical world, warmth is constant, but sufficient water is not. Adaptations must therefore "cover" both these stresses.

In the dry season, the anoline lizard of Costa Rica and Panama lays her single egg only once every two or three weeks. Any sudden rainfall is accompanied by a speedup of laying. While it might seem more advantageous to the species for the female to lay many eggs in a single clutch, the hazards of life make this impractical. The tropical climate is favorable to animal life, and lizards are prey to so many larger creatures that a female heavily laden with eggs would not be able to run away easily.

It is almost always dry season in desert regions, so locusts, which need moisture for their eggs, are usually scarce. A few will be seen here and there, resting on the branches of barren trees or dry brown shrubs. These periods of drought are hard for the human inhabitants of the desert, too. They greet the rare periods of heavy rainfall with pleasure, watching the vegetation become green and luxuriant. But often, as happened in the late 1970s, a black cloud both figuratively and literally covers their joy. During this period of abundant food and water, locusts are stimulated to reproduce in large numbers. A single desert locust may lay three pods of eggs, a total of 200. In a short time, hundreds become thousands, and thousands, millions.

Locusts form huge swarms which can block out the sun or cover miles of earth with the dense mass of their bodies. Wherever they go, they munch, each voraciously consuming its own weight in vegetation a day. They eat most heavily in the evening, when they roost, but at any hour while on the march they stop for "snack bar" meals. As they clear one area of plants, they move on to the next, until they have left nothing but drooping dry stalks in an area of hundreds of miles. Locusts can fly at a speed of 10 to 12 miles per hour and, so long as it is warm, stay aloft for seventeen or more hours at a stretch. They may journey from Ethiopia, Somalia, and Kenya to Saudi Arabia, Yemen, Egypt, and Iran.

While they carry terror and famine to humans, locusts as a species display a remarkable ability to survive in inhospitable terrain. They are able to seize the brief opportunity of plentiful food resulting from the unexpected rainstorms to multiply in great numbers. A plague of locusts represents an evolutionary triumph.

Coolness or heat alone can slow the locust. When the temperature is below the mid-70s, the insect's flight muscles do not function well. Extreme heat produces the same reaction, and at midday the swarm may settle on low-growing shrubs so as to be off the hot ground. If the locust were better heat- or cold-adapted, it might take over the world, say scientists at London's Anti-Locust Research Centre. Unchecked by weather, predators, lack of food, or human effort, swarms of locusts occupying only two square miles could breed in numbers sufficient to blanket the globe within only four of their generations.

Although a magnificently heat-adapted creature such as the termite of the Sonoran Desert can forage for food at 122 degrees, most animals cannot be active at temperatures higher than 104. If the weather is consistently hotter than that, even in the early morning or at night, or too cold, too dry, or too wet for several months of a year in the region which is native to a species, the animal will make its way to another where weather is more clement and food supplies more readily available, and there it will bear its young. The gray whale leaves the icy waters of the Bering Sea and journeys 8,000 miles to reach the warm water off Baja California and Sonora, Mexico; within a sheltered lagoon, the female gives birth. The American golden plover escapes the winter cold and scarcity of food in northern Canada by a journey of some 20,000 miles to southern Brazil and Argentina.

Look up at the skies in early fall and watch the birds setting off for the south; look up in the spring and see them return. So well adapted are these species that they depart while the weather is still warm and it might seem tempting to tarry. Change in day length is enough of a clue to make them start the journey.

During migration, flight speed can reach 18.5 miles an hour, and the bird's body temperature rises as a result. In the course of a vast journey, a bird may not drink, eat, or rest for long periods of time, but lives off its body fat.

In order to get over the Himalayas, barhead geese fly 5.5 miles up—more than 29,000 feet. And a Ruppells griffon vulture ran into a commercial airplane flying at an altitude of almost 40,000 feet over the Ivory Coast. Most often, birds seek a height where the air temperature will be low enough for the heat produced by their straining bodies to be balanced by the amount of heat lost to the air. They fly higher by day and lower by night. If they must fly through a high-temperature zone, they open their bills and extend their feet into the airstream. When it gets cooler, they fold their legs close to their bodies.

"The bird can adjust to the enormously larger heat production during flight, primarily because of large changes in the thermal resistance of the skin and feathers," wrote José Torre-Bueno in a Rockefeller University doctoral thesis.

He found the feather depth of starlings during flight to be 2 millimeters when the air was hot or moderately warm, increasing to 5 millimeters, sufficient to change the shape of the bird's body, at very cold temperatures.

By the time the yellow warblers of the northern United States and Canada have arrived in their wintering grounds in Panama, much of the area has already been occupied by species from more southerly regions that did not have so far to fly. Oddly, the young yellow warblers that come from the distant North have plumage that is not yellow at all but dull in hue. This protects the frail young birds from the older ones that reached the territory first and would otherwise be stimulated to aggression by the sight of bright yellow feathers. The young warblers are so unobtrusive that they can slip into the flocks of more experienced birds and follow along to sources of food. When the same northern warblers return the following year, they have matured enough to hold their own in the mating game and are a proud and brilliant yellow.

With food so plentiful for much of the year, and the weather so warm, tropical birds live longer than do birds of temperate zones. An ornithologist who banded birds in Trinidad in the early 1960s found that many were still alive when he returned in 1971. Surprisingly, those tropical birds which migrate to temperate zones each summer and breed there live longer than those which spend their entire lives in the tropics. Migration appears to be so hazardous an undertaking that one would expect it to shorten life. But, in fact, migration helps these birds by relieving them of environmental stresses they would otherwise have to endure.

"The most biologically appropriate way to view these birds is as basically tropical species that make a short run up here to take advantage of short-lived insect population peaks for breeding," says Eugene S. Morton of the Smithsonian's National Zoological Park. Under such favorable conditions, these birds lay four to six eggs at a time, in comparison to the two- or three-egg clutches of birds of the same or closely related species which remain in the tropics all year round. The migrants breed once a year during their brief stay each summer. Offhand, it would seem that they are not doing as well in perpetuating the species as are nonmigrant birds, such as robins, which breed three times a year. But adding up all the figures shows that this is not necessarily the case. The migrants not only lay bigger clutches each time but also breed more often, simply because they have a greater life span.

"The migrants seem to have the strategy of returning to the South as soon as they can," comments Morton, "because they live longer as individuals by doing so."

Some creatures do not migrate when food supplies become too scarce to support activity and reproduction, water sources dry up, or temperatures rise beyond endurance. They avoid trouble by sleeping the bad times away—aestivating—and tolerate the intolerable world by withdrawing from it and refusing to function until things get better. Crocodiles, alligators, snakes, tortoises, frogs, lizards, snails, newts, salamanders, and many fishes are aestivators. They bury themselves in the mud of a drying pond or slip into the crevices of rocks or curl up in burrows. In parts of Iran the earth becomes scorched and the vegetation desiccated within the first few weeks of summer. The ground squirrel is nowhere to be seen; it has already gone into aestivation. The spadefoot toad of the deserts of the southwestern United States digs a hole two feet or so deep. The surface of the soil is heated by the sun to 158 degrees, but it is much cooler than that in the hole. As added protection, a skin forms over the toad's body.

Aestivation, sometimes called "summer sleep," is a hot-climate or summertime variant of hibernation, and there are many similarities between the two. Both cold-blooded (poikilothermic) and warm-blooded (homeothermic) animals can aestivate, but only the warm-blooded hibernate. The temperature of the poikilotherm during aestivation is usually considerably lower than that of the world outside. The temperature of the homeothermic aestivator drops too, but not to quite so low a level as that of the hibernator sleeping out the bitter winter. No food is needed in either state, the fat reserves being sufficient to support the sleeping body's needs. Oxygen consumption is decreased to the point where it is almost impossible to tell, just by looking, whether the animal is alive. The low rate of respiration and complete lack of physical activity hold down water loss. Even so, the aestivator must build up its store of body water in preparation for drought much as the hibernator increases its store of body fat in preparation for cold; in advance of aestivation, the bladders of frogs and toads become grossly distended to hold the additional fluid. The state of repose may last for however long the drought and heat continue. When rain finally begins to fall on the desert, it seeps through the sand little by little until it reaches the hole where the toad is lying; when touched by the moisture, the creature awakens.

By interrupting the reproductive cycle, both hibernation and aestivation protect a species from becoming weak or extinct. Even if the adult animal did tolerate the temperature and could obtain enough food and water to survive, infants born of gestations in periods of such scarcity would be puny, possibly deficient or deformed. Most would die of heat or cold, or hunger and thirst.

The lizard of the southeastern United States goes into a winter dormancy. The coming of spring arouses the male and, needing a safe place to breed, he fights with other males to establish territory. Slower to respond to the stimulation of the changing seasons and her own hormonal signals, the female remains dormant during the combat. She does not venture out from under the bark of dead trees or logs until the stronger males are in control, the inferior losers weeded out. Courtship ensues, culminating with the male mounting the female and inserting his hemipenis. If the female lizard were to awaken earlier in the season, she might be caught between the battling males, injured, and rendered unable to reproduce, or she might be impregnated by weaker stock. The difference in the duration of female dormancy over male thus gives the species a selective evolutionary advantage, suggested scientists at a National Institute of Mental Health colloquium on lizards.

Viewed logically, dormancy is a round-about type of adaptation, depending as it does on avoidance. Appearing to be a survival from an earlier era, aestivation is characteristic of the most primitive vertebrate known on earth today, the African lungfish. Often described as a living fossil, the lungfish has survived more than 300 million years with virtually no change in anatomy. Had it lacked the adaptation of aestivation, the lungfish would have died out millions of years ago when the swamps or bodies of water where it lived dried up.

Unlike the indirection of aestivation, the state of cold-bloodedness is a direct approach to dealing with the temperature extremes of the outside world. The poikilotherm does not need a heavy layer of fat, fur, or feathers to keep off the heat of the sun in desert or tropics or the cold of the ice in the polar regions, but instead can take its warmth from air, earth or water. The process of obtaining heat from external sources, ectothermy, contrasts with heat obtained from within, or endothermy, as is characteristic of humans and other mammals. Ectotherms do not require a large amount of food to maintain their body temperature; endotherms do.

Where warm-blooded animals can survive within a narrow range of body temperature only, poikilotherms endure wide swings from excessively low to excessively high. (Aestivation is more often a response to the drought resulting from great heat than to the high temperature itself.)

The internal temperature of the cold-blooded creature fluctuates to match that of the external world. Although called cold-blooded, these animals often have a body temperature that can go as high or higher than that of the warm-blooded mammal or bird. And they seek to achieve such a temperature—for at least part of the time. Therefore the poikilotherm practices heliothermy, positioning itself so as to obtain heat from the sun, and thigmothermy, obtaining heat from the rocks, sand, or soil. Because the sun is the major heat source, color plays a particularly big role in temperature regulation. The dark brown desert grasshopper is several degrees hotter than the pale tan species occupying the very same sand dune. The desert iguana turns a darker color when it first ventures out into the sun. After it gets warmer, it becomes lighter—receiving a sun bleach rather than a sunburn. A tropical amphibious fish will change color during its time on shore, thus regulating the absorption of heat from the sun.

Many poikilotherms keep their body temperatures higher or lower than that of the surrounding air or water. In the mountains of Peru, where temperatures are often below freezing, the lizards native to the area are so heated by the sun that their body temperature can rise up to 45 degrees above that of the air and stay at that level for long periods.

In the Namib Desert of southern Africa, tenebrionid beetles inhabit the sand dune to the south and west of the Kuiseb River, a region where easterly winds blow strongly at certain times of the day. Some of the beetles have very long legs which keep their bodies so high off the ground that they can scurry about gathering food and mating when the sand is hottest; they must go into hiding, however, when the winds are strong and would carry them off. Other beetles in the same sand dune have very short legs and bodies close to the ground.

They burrow into the sand, finding comfortable temperatures of 90 degrees about eight inches down, and come out only when the surface has cooled. On the other hand, the winds are not likely to lift them away, so they stay out and make a meal of the detritus being blown about. The sand surface can be heated by the sun to 150 degrees while at the very same time it is only 100.4 degrees in the shade. When beetles skitter in short dashes from sun to shade, it takes them only four minutes to achieve a rise or fall of 21.6 to 27 degrees in body temperature.

The patch-nosed snake of the open shrub deserts of the southwestern United States and Mexico tolerates body temperatures between 44.6 and 110 degrees, its heart rate rising from a slow-paced 6.6 beats a minute when cold to 131 beats per minute when very hot. The tiny insect *Thermobia domestica*, the firebrat, which makes its home in boiler rooms, does not succumb to heat injury until its temperature has reached 124.34 degrees or freeze until it falls to 1.8 degrees.

But the mere fact that body temperatures change with changing conditions and that the animals can survive extremes of heating and cooling does not mean that they can be active and feed and mate throughout this range. The sea snake stops swimming at 64.4 degrees; the firebrat slows down at 112. Millipedes on the Chihuahuan desert will take in their customary diet of dead plant tissues, outer parts of shrubs, and animal feces only when their body temperatures are between 68 and 86 degrees.

The spiny lizards of the deserts of southern Texas, Death Valley, California, and Mexico come out of their burrows in the early morning, cautious in their movements, because their low body temperature at this time of day makes them too sluggish to escape predators, says lizard expert Neil Greenberg of the University of Tennessee. They prop themselves up on their forelegs to keep their bodies off the cold soil until the sun is high. Then they bask, spreading out their ribs and sprawling their legs, and, when stimulated sufficiently by heat, set out to forage for food and seek a mate.

In order to travel rapidly across hot sand or rocks, the lizards raise their bodies high off the ground and run on their hind legs, a practice known to lizard watchers as "stilting." This has the added advantage of lifting them high enough to survey the scene before setting off. As the desert soil becomes too hot even for this contact, they scurry for shade or to a burrow. But if at that moment they sense a nearby predator and fear any movement would betray their presence, they just raise up their sensitive toes, or sometimes their entire feet and tail, and rest lightly on the abdomen. These reactions are not too different from those of the warm-blooded albatross, which sits on its heels so as to keep the rest of its big webbed feet off the desert earth.

Some animals do not stilt but push their bodies beneath the top layer of sand to reach the cooler layers below. The side-winding adder of the Namib Desert digs its body into the sand, rolls to the side, and so forces itself forward. The sand skink of the Sahara, dubbed *poisson de sable* (fish of the sand) by the French, seems to swim across the dunes. The fringe-toed lizard uses its strangely shaped feet to help it wriggle through the sand without sinking in too far.

The scorpion escapes the worst of the summer heat in Kentucky, Tennessee, and Missouri by rushing indoors, where its bite becomes a major hazard. From the viewpoint of the survival of the species, it is an excellent behavioral adaptation.

Crocodiles, turtles, and the marine iguana are inactive during the hottest parts of the day, coming out to forage and copulate at night. For the most part, however, poikilotherms try to keep their body temperatures closer to the warmer than the colder limit of their range.

The longer an animal can maintain its optimal temperature, the more hours of the day can be spent in feeding and mating, and the greater the number of generations that are produced in a single season. The temperature that becomes optimal for a species may be the one at which it can be active for more of the day than its prey or than animals that would consume it.

Spiders spin their webs so that changes in the position of their bodies will give them just the amount of direct sunlight they need to be warm and active. First the spider will turn its back to the sun, then offer just the apex of the abdomen, then the entire ventral surface.

The amphibious rockskipper of the eastern tropical Pacific Ocean makes brief daytime excursions onto the rocks, moving from one tide pool to another in search of food or to escape predators. In the water, this fish can survive a body temperature of 104 degrees, but on land when exposed to sunshine it dies at only 89.6. Cause of death is the drying of the respiratory surfaces, reducing the amount of oxygen the rockskipper can take in.

The upper limit for life of the poikilotherms is set by their oxygen needs. Like the warm-blooded, these creatures increase their oxygen consumption as they get warmer. However, the more used to heat animals are, the higher the temperature that stimulates this reaction. Frogs living in the tropics do not begin to take in more oxygen until the temperature is 18 degrees higher than that activating frogs in temperate climates. Salamander larvae breathe through their gills 9 times a minute when the water temperature is 50 degrees. When it reaches 68, they take 48 breaths and must rise to the surface to gulp air as well. Lizards open their mouths when very hot, although biologists argue as to whether the movements they make constitute panting.

The division between warm- and cold-blooded is not altogether distinct. The Australian vespertilionid bat has a body temperature of 104.4 degrees when awake and resting quietly, 105.8 degrees in flight, and becomes virtually cold-blooded when asleep. Many warm-blooded animals are cold-blooded during infancy, until the nerve fibers of the hypothalamus develop sufficiently. The two-day-old chipping sparrow is only 5½ degrees warmer than the air, but by seven days it has become warm-blooded—homeothermic. It is then subject to all the difficulties so familiar to the warm-blooded of dealing with extremes of temperature in a world where such extremes are the rule rather than the exception.

On the face of it, warm-bloodedness would seem to be as much of an evolutionary disadvantage as advantage. Yet it characterizes only the higher vertebrates, the mammals and birds. The cold-blooded reptiles and fish seem to be more in tune with their environment than we. But in fact, cold-blooded creatures are in tune at the cost of considerable activity. The increased biochemical reaction rate in a perpetually warm body means more activity, including that of the brain. Those mammals which evolved to become warm-blooded developed a four-chambered heart, which prevents the mixing of oxygenated and non-oxygenated blood and causes the whole animal to be more efficiently supplied with oxygen. The brain was able to reach a higher stage of development in those creatures with a four-chambered heart, and this compensated for all the obvious problems of warm-bloodedness, chiefly the difficulty of surviving in cold and in heat.

The energy requirements of being warm-blooded are very great. The needs even of the cold-blooded locust, which eats its own weight in food a day, are surpassed by many warm-blooded animals; the shrew and the hummingbird eat two or three times their weight in a day and the lion consumes its own great weight in food every week to ten days. A mouse has a metabolic rate five times that of an amphibian the same size; a mammal or bird three to four times that of the reptile. But in the long run, the extra effort to maintain a high metabolism is worth it. Warm-bloodedness gives an animal a competitive advantage in a world where the rule is eat or be eaten. Cold-blooded creatures become somnolent at extremes of temperature; the animal that is awake when others are not can attack at will.

In order to gather the great amounts of food needed for endothermy, an animal needs a good memory and the ability to obtain and process information as to sources. In the process of evolution, those with such capacities were the ones to survive.

The dinosaur did not survive. Because of its similarity to living reptiles, the dinosaur has traditionally been considered to have been cold-blooded, and this view is still favored by many paleontologists. Considering its record of 140 million years of world domination, however, and its development into close to a thousand species, some scientists suggest it may have been warm-blooded.

Today one can find only two warm-blooded reptiles, neither of them typical, the large Indian rock python during incubation and the leatherback turtle. Nonetheless, the very fact that dinosaur poikilothermy, so long accepted as unquestionable, is being challenged commands attention. Instead of viewing the dinosaur as a huge sluggish ponderous beast slowly making its way through the mud, Robert T. Bakker of Johns Hopkins sees a lively, fast-moving creature, running through the prehistoric swamp, pouncing on its prey, and jumping about in frisky fashion, despite its bulk.

What is there in the fossil evidence of these long-extinct creatures that would indicate warm-bloodedness? Posture provides a clue, says John H. Ostrom of Yale University. Among the vertebrates of today, only the warm-blooded have an erect posture and gait. The tracks left by dinosaurs are narrow, and the shapes of hip and shoulder sockets indicate that the great beasts walked with torso erect, rather than with legs sprawled and torso horizontal to the ground; some even walked on two legs, using their forelegs to hold their prey. The head of the dinosaur is located far above the level of the heart—eighteen feet up in the case of Brachiosaurus. How did the dinosaur get sufficient blood and oxygen up its long neck to feed the brain if it did not have a high systemic blood pressure? No living cold-blooded creature has a high blood pressure; that requires a fully divided four-chambered heart. Also, the fossils of bone seem to indicate a rich supply of blood vessels, which among living creatures is true only for mammals and birds. The dinosaurs laid eggs, as do both warm- and cold-blooded creatures. Some scientists read the fossil remains as indicating that they brought food and cared for their young as warm-blooded parents do, but others say a dinosaur mother would have crushed any infant she attempted to feed.

Nearly all the dinosaurs were huge—but size is used as proof of both theories. The temperature of a large cold-blooded animal changes more slowly than that of a small one, so a huge cold-blooded beast heated during the day in the subtropical or tropical climate of the Mesozoic would retain most of this warmth throughout the night.

Even if dinosaurs did have a body temperature as high as that of modern mammals, the question remains as to whether they achieved this as poikilotherms do, by ectothermy, or heat absorption, or whether they possessed an internal temperature-regulating mechanism. As Smithsonian paleobiologist Nicholas Hotten sees it, "The fact that they were very large put them in a functionally warm-blooded condition without a physiological system. And the effects of being warm-blooded would have been to make them active and able to engage in gregarious social behavior."

The strange configurations and monstrous features of the dinosaurs may have made ectothermy possible by dissipating or increasing body heat. Hot blood might have been forced to the surface of the bony plates along the back and tail of Stegosaurus and been cooled by the outside air. The elaborate bony frill, or horn, on the head of many large dinosaurs might have served to keep the head warm during the cool part of the day and dissipated the heat at high noon.

The sail lizards, *Dimetrodon grandis*, are the last stage in the evolution of the Pelycosauria, which lived in semi-arid Texas during the Permian period of the Paleozoic era. Elongated vertebrae, presumably connected by membranes, formed the sail. The weight of the pelycosaur, the daily fluctuations in temperature, and the heat of the sun of 260 million years ago have been estimated by British scientists C. D. Bramwell and P. B. Fellget of Reading University. By their figuring, it would take 205 minutes of basking in the sun to raise the body temperature of a sailless carnivorous lizard to the point where active hunting was possible. In contrast, by putting itself in a position where the sail took in the sun's rays and added to the amount of exposed body surface, the pelycosaur could achieve this rise in temperature in only 80 minutes. But the sun in the prehistoric sky would remain high for some hours thereafter, placing the lizard at risk of heat stupor, which would render it helpless against its enemies. The beast was too large to find shade behind the rocks in this terrain and the sail may have been necessary to help radiate away excess heat. If so, its sail enabled this lizard to be alert for more of the day and to produce more generations of young than the creatures it preyed on.

The lack of dinosaur insulation, except for the scales of the duckbill, has been taken as evidence of poikilothermy; warm-blooded animals, with internal temperature-regulating mechanisms, need fur, fat, or feathers. But the fossils of a crow-sized creature that may have been able to glide or fly indicate that insulation in the form of feathers might have existed. Only a handful of specimens of Archaeopteryx have been found. This creature, which has been dated to the middle of the dinosaur era, has a skeleton which, aside from a wishbone, is virtually identical to that of a small carnivorous dinosaur, the Theropod. But for the clear fossil impressions of a feather covering, paleontologists would have classed it as an ordinary dinosaur. The finding of feather fossils raises the question, says Yale's Ostrom, of whether other theropod dinosaurs were feathered as well, even though no remains have been recovered. And if they had feathers, were they endotherms too?

Does the attempt to prove that dinosaurs were warm-blooded enhance their status? Does the enduring theory that they were ectotherms like modern reptiles serve to degrade them? Should warm-bloodedness seem better to us? Lizard expert Greenberg challenges this desire to impute humanity where it is not natural or needed as "endothermocentricity" and a kind of chauvinism.

9

How Animals Keep Cool

On a hot day in June, three girl scouts were raped and murdered at a scout camp in northeastern Oklahoma. Two specially trained tracking dogs were flown from Pennsylvania to the murder site to find the killer's spoor and lead the police to him. Within a week, however, one of these sleek powerful dogs dropped dead from heat prostration, and the other, possibly careless because of heat exhaustion, was killed by a speeding car.

Could humans have endured the heat any better? If one removes extraneous factors such as cars from one's calculations and considers highest lethal temperatures only, a human can survive greater heat than the dog, somewhat less than the shrew, and much less than the hen. Like all birds, however, the hen starts out with a body temperature at least 3.6 degrees Fahrenheit higher.

Among the mammals, whether living in tropics, desert, temperate zone, or polar icecap, the rectal, or deep-body, temperature is much the same. The human's 99.6 degrees compares to the elephant's 97.16, the penguin's 99.6 to 102.2, and the dog, cat, and cow's 101.48. But the adaptations that maintain this body temperature vary widely in type and in effectiveness.

Panting is not as efficient a way to get rid of body heat as is sweating.

And a dog's temperature rises more rapidly in heat than does that of humans. The few sweat glands the dog does have are not particularly well-developed. Where, in panting, water is lost from the mouth, tongue, and respiratory tract, in sweating it is lost over great areas and so cools more of the body. No salt is lost in panting, but this advantage is countered by the fact that so much carbon dioxide is exhaled during panting that the dog's acid balance is disturbed, making the muscles work harder. In addition, panting is an exercise of a sort and so produces some heat. The cat also pants when overheating, increasing its speed of respiration from about 60 breaths a minute to 240 or even 250. Birds, which cannot pant like dogs or cats or sweat like humans, evaporate water by breathing more rapidly and flapping the loose skin beneath their throats.

Small cattle are better able to tolerate humid tropical conditions than are large ones. American dairy farmers, however, favor large beasts. As a result, during a summer heat wave in the Chino Valley of San Bernardino County, California, 700 to 1,000 cows died from the heat and humidity, additional members of the herd collapsed from heat exhaustion, and production of milk in the region fell by 15 percent.

A dairy farmer from South Dakota accompanied his former college's basketball team to Cuba to watch them play exhibition matches. While there, he was invited to visit a large dairy farm outside of Havana. The Cubans were trying to maintain purebred Holsteins by keeping them shaded from the sun and bathing them frequently. The farmer also was shown one of Cuba's sources of pride, the F-1 cow, a cross between the Holstein, which produces a great deal of milk but cannot endure great heat unprotected, and the Indian Zebu, which yields little milk but can tolerate the torrid climate with ease.

Some well-adapted animals can sweat. The zebu, for example, has more sweat glands than do Dutch Fresian cattle. The massive baboon, like the human it resembles in a number of ways, sweats rather than pants.

In animals that do not sweat, other body fluids are released for cooling. The wood stork keeps comfortable by urinating on its own unfeathered legs. Turtles and lizards may discharge a cooling liquid from their body cavities. A number of turtles salivate, as does the cat, which cools off by licking its fur.

Kangaroos, primitive in their reproductive practices, are highly sophisticated in their ability to get rid of body heat. They not only sweat and increase their rate of breathing to an extent that works almost as well as panting, but also salivate and cover their fur. The quokka, a small kangaroo living on Rottnest Island off the coast of southwestern Australia, salivates so copiously that even after it has covered its entire body, there is still some liquid left to drip off onto the ground. The wallaby also licks itself effectively. But this type of heat adaptation has a great disadvantage. The animal cannot lick itself while running to escape a predator, and overheating slows it down. The carnivorous Tasmanian devil, although also a marsupial, is better adapted to escape both predators and overheating. It does not need to stop to lick its coat; sweating keeps this otherwise primitive animal cool. Not even panting, it shows no signs of discomfort at 104-degree temperatures.

Animals of the hot deserts must be able to endure not only great heat but also lack of water. Many desert rodents drink no liquid at all, in any season, and fill their needs from plant tissues. The quokka produces its vast amounts of saliva and meets all its other fluid needs from the water contained in the plants on Rottnest, and possibly from seawater, too.

During periods of drought, Gambel's quail can rear their young with no liquids, taking moisture from the fruit of the cactus. The parakeet native to the dry interior of Australia needs a little water when the outdoor temperature is in or above the mid-80s, but during cooler seasons it can go without water indefinitely.

The carnivore is at an advantage in the desert, because meat has a high liquid content. The mulgara, a crest-tailed marsupial mouse of arid central Australia, never drinks but satisfies its needs from the body fluids of the animals it preys upon. The sparrow hawk has in captivity survived comfortably on meat alone, and so has the domestic cat when given only fish and chopped meat. A rattlesnake, caught in the Negev Desert and kept in an enclosure, was given no water to drink and a diet exclusively of mouse, yet the snake survived for the five years of its captivity. And the desert hedgehog can exist with even less water than some of the other carnivores, selecting prey with a lower water content.

The kangaroo rat of the North American deserts not only drinks no water but also eats no food with liquid content. This small creature consumes dry seeds and obtains sufficient moisture from the oxidation of carbohydrates by its digestive system. It reduces water needs by staying all day at a comfortable 68 degrees in its burrow, sealing the entrance and exits so that the little water it gives off in breathing is retained to keep the air moist. To ensure survival of the species through the long hot summer, the kangaroo rat may aestivate, lowering its body temperature from a normal 102 degrees to between 59 and 68, and in a cold winter it may hibernate, reaching a body temperature of 43 degrees. A number of other desert rodents go into brief periods of hibernation whenever there is a sudden drop in temperature or a food shortage.

Most important to the success of the desert nondrinker is powerful kidneys. This was first observed in 1822 when Louis N. Vauquelin reported on his examination of the excretions of snakes: The urine was almost completely uric acid. The ability to concentrate urine is an evolutionary advantage. Animals that need only a small amount of water to deal with their body wastes can survive long periods of drought, even a lifetime, without thirst or dehydration. The urine of many desert creatures is semi-solid. Feces are also dry and hard. Some rodents consume their feces, so as to reabsorb whatever water it does contain.

Desert animals are likely to be modest in their food demands, as large meals raise metabolism, increase body heat, and require additional water for digestion.

Of all creatures of arid regions, none typifies the desert better than the camel, which remains a major beast of burden to this day. When the Rajasthan Canal was built recently in northwest India, 50,000 people were helped by 8,000 camels. And of all creatures of the desert, none is so magnificently adapted to its environment. This fact does not improve its disposition. Camel drivers in ancient times devised the first intrauterine devices to prevent conception—stones, inserted before setting off with a female camel on a desert journey. There is no creature on earth, it is said, as evil-tempered as a pregnant camel. When not pregnant, the camel is very reliable. The Persian waterwheel, used since ancient times, depends on camel power, because once started these beasts will keep going around all day without being prodded, struck, or shouted at.

Large stores of water are kept in the camel's alimentary tract—not in the hump, as legend would have it; the hump is made up of unromantic fat. The camel and another well-adapted desert animal, the addax antelope, have several stomachs, the first being the rumen, where the food is mixed with great amounts of liquid. Again, contrary to legend, this is actually digestive fluid, not pure water, but it can be drunk, and there are countless anecdotes about thirsty travelers in the desert who have killed camels in order to get at that fluid. (Most of these are undocumented and are denied by camel lovers as hotly as any tales of human cannibalism.) When in need of water, the camel can make use of the water from its alimentary tract. The kidneys are extremely powerful and the urine is concentrated and scant in quantity for so large a creature, while the feces are hard and dry.

Camels can continue their desert march when dehydrated by 27 percent of their body weight. This compares to death at a dehydration of 12 percent for the dog and 18 to 20 percent for many other mammals. The donkey, which is also a much-used and excellent beast of burden in desert areas, is unique in enduring a loss of 30 percent of its body weight in water. While this might seem to make it superior to the camel, that is not quite true. The donkey loses much *more* water in the heat and so does not end up ahead.

The camel's ability to go without drinking for so long is due in large part to wide swings in its body temperature. As the sun gets higher in the desert sky, the body temperature rises. In contrast to the human, who sweats heavily so as to retain a constant temperature, the camel saves the water. As evening falls and the air temperature drops, so does the temperature of the camel, and at that time of day this can be achieved without sweating.

Once the camel does get to a source of water, it can take in more than 30 percent of its body weight at a time. A young female was led to a full watering trough. By the time she decided she had had enough and turned away sated, she had drunk 70.5 quarts. The record, declared Théodore Monod, who made a study of nearly 600 miles of the "empty" portion of the Sahara in the 1950s, was achieved by a lactating female. She returned to camp after six days in the desert, drank 113 quarts on the spot, and a few hours later was thirsty once more and downed another 74.

The camel clumps along on thick cloven hooves, which do not sink into the soft desert sand. Its nostrils are lined with hair to keep out the blowing dust and sand. Its thick fur provides insulation against water loss and heat in the daytime and against the cold at night. The heavy wool coat is shed in the spring, but the summer coat beneath is thick too. The color, which may be off-white, what is known as camel color, or dark brown, serves as camouflage. The coat is dull and neither reflects radiation nor absorbs the sun's rays.

Many birds of the desert are similarly dull in color, and therefore are protected from the sun and from predators. They blend so completely into the landscape that an experienced birdwatcher spotted ten to fifteen species of birds in a desolate scene where a less-practiced companion saw none at all. The desert lark, common in the Sahara, obtains equal protection by covering its plumage completely with dust.

Those who have seen the oryx, silhouetted at sunset against the desert sky, have thought they had at last found the fabled unicorn. In profile, this slender antelope appears to have but a single horn, finely carved with circular ridges running around it. Because of its rare beauty, it may indeed have been the basis for the ubiquitous myth of the unicorn. Once the oryx ranged over most of the Arabian peninsula, Israel, Syria, Jordan, and Iraq. But rather than being subdued by a virgin of purity, it was hunted almost into extinction for its meat and its hide. And somehow to this day, say hunters, great prestige is attained by the person who captures an oryx.

This animal is a marvel, not only because of its beauty and resemblance to the unicorn but for its ability to survive body temperatures as high as 113 degrees without brain damage. The oryx and another antelope, the eland, are among the creatures endowed with one of the most notable temperature-regulating adaptations to be found in the animal kingdom: the *rete mirabile*, Latin for "wonderful net." This is a network of thin-walled arteries and veins arranged in such a way as to act as a heat exchanger. The air that enters the nasal passages of the oryx and eland cools the venous blood, which in turn lowers the temperature of the hot blood in the adjacent cerebral arteries before this blood reaches the brain. Because the net helps prevent both overheating and freezing, it exists in animals such as the seal as well, and protects some less exotic beasts too, being present in the donkey, sheep, goat, ox, and pig, which thrive in a wide range of climates.

Keeping one part of the body much warmer than others by means of shunts in the circulatory system has also conferred an evolutionary advantage on a number of animals that must endure wide swings of temperature. When the desert air turns cold, the Australian lizard, *Varanus varius*, shunts the blood from its legs and tail to the internal organs. They can remain warmer than the environment for some seven hours, and by then the sun is high enough to provide external warmth. In the cool of the early morning, the head of the horned lizard may be 9 degrees warmer than the rest of the body. On the other hand, when the heat reaches levels that would be dangerous, cool blood is sent to the brain.

Aggressive and well-adapted tropical animals wrest food from weaker species. The walking catfish of Southeast Asia have rudimentary lungs to sustain them for long periods between immersions. They are able to "walk" on land, virtually upright on their dorsal fins. Though only a foot long, the fish eat so voraciously that they can strip small lakes and ponds of all other living things. Long viewed as a rarity by tropical fish farmers, these catfish are "farmed" in Florida. A year or two ago some of the fish ventured out of their pond and walked some 100 miles to Lake Okeechobee, entering and decimating life in ponds in ten counties on the way. Fortunately, they cannot thrive in cooler waters, so their boundaries are limited by heat.

Those creatures that have survived the rigors of life in the tropics are more varied in hue and in shape than those of any other region. Among them are the most beautiful animals in the world, and also the ugliest. The magnificence of the striped tiger, the long-necked giraffe, the spotted leopard, and the maned lion are in sharp contrast to the crudeness of the obese hippopotamus or the grotesque rhinoceros.

The colors and patterns have provided a species advantage by enabling the animals to blend in with an environment in which plants, too, are brilliant in hue, and patches of brilliant sunshine contrast with the darkness of heavy foliage or torrential rain. The strange configurations also serve as camouflage, weapons and food-gathering appendages. The giraffe can reach its long elastic tongue around the leaves on the topmost branches of the acacia and mimosa trees, because a seven-foot-long neck brings the total height to eighteen feet; a plant diet enables it to go without drinking water for long periods. And although an air of fragility makes the giraffe seem a creature to be pampered, its graceful spindly legs can kick a lion to death and its speed is such as to outdistance most enemies.

The mere fact of living in tropical climates does not mean that an animal is physiologically adapted to heat. It may get by on life-style. The tiger does not hunt during the heat of the day but sets out in the late afternoon and keeps going all through the night. By day it may lie in the tall grass, close to other tigers but not really associating with them. (Even when it mates, the bond lasts for only about two days.) The water buffalo, essential to agriculture in many torrid regions, is very poorly adapted to heat. It keeps cool by wallowing in water.

The hippopotamus maintains its comfort by remaining in water most of the time, coming on shore only to eat. The eyes are located near the top of the head, so that it can observe what is going on while all the rest of the body is submerged. The hippopotamus comes out of the water every five minutes or so to breathe, looking much like a heavy dinosaur rising from a primeval swamp. Despite the coolness of the water, the great beast is able to maintain a normal temperature because of its massive size and weight—three to five tons—and a hide that is two inches thick in some places. The gray or brownish color of the hide serves as camouflage, giving the hippopotamus the guise of a huge rock or floating log, and the dullness of its surface does not reflect or absorb the sun during food-gathering trips on land.

The rhinoceros, even more than the hippopotamus, looks to be a prehistoric creature that somehow escaped the mass extinctions that ended the era when dinosaurs reigned. On its vicious-appearing snout are one or two horns, consisting not of bone but of congealed hair; although the technique of the rhinoceros's sexual performance strains the imagination, powdered rhinoceros horn has long been valued as an aphrodisiac. The rhinoceros avoids overheating by remaining quietly in the shade near water for most of the day. It becomes active at night or in the early morning when seeking food. The skin is thick and tough and usually black or gray, although a few rare species, just to add to the rhinoceros mystique, are white.

Few animals are more appealing to humans than the huge elephant, as the crowds in front of its pen in the zoo attest. The largest of all land mammals in the world today, the record for size is held by an African bull weighing 12 tons and measuring 13 feet 2 inches high at shoulder level. The size presents a problem in the tropics. Huge beasts more easily retain than get rid of body heat, and the animal seems much better suited to the frigid climate that was its home in prehistoric times. Subsequent adaptations to enable the creature to endure heat are surprisingly few, the most conspicuous being a loss of the furry coating that protected its ancestor, the mammoth, from the cold and a change in the size of the ears. The mammoth possessed very small ears, which provided little surface for heat loss. The modern elephant has huge floppy ones, which serve as fans; the higher the air temperature, the more vigorously the ears flap back and forth.

The elephant is no better able than the human to withstand fever, dying when its temperature rises about 9 degrees above normal. This beast does not sweat, but it does lose some water through the skin. The elephant overcomes its size disadvantage and remains cool by staying under the shade of trees, wallowing in streams or in mud, and sucking up water in the trunk to squirt over its hot body. With every passing year, as the populations of the countries of Africa expand, however, the elephants are left with fewer stands of trees, mudholes, and rivers to wallow in. When their food sources are wiped out, the great beasts become marauders and are shot down by angry farmers.

The characteristics that make it possible for animals to survive in the wild are the very ones that make them particularly desirable to hunters. With elephants, it is the tusks, at once their basic weapon and the most valuable part of their body. As well as facing death from starvation and heat prostration and at the hands of farmers and big-game hunters, elephants are mercilessly tracked down by poachers for their ivory. In 1973 more than 2,500 elephants were counted in Uganda's Rwenzori National Park; an aerial survey in 1980 found only 150. During a three-month period in 1976, said a warden of the Tsavo game preserve in Kenya, 1,400 poachers were in the park. Many carcasses, perfect except for the missing ivory, were abandoned on the ground. One exporter, traveling by Mercedes-Benz, was caught with thirty elephant tusks.

The zebra has been hunted for its hide, the lion and tiger for their pelts, the rhinoceros for the horn. Exotic tropical animals, fascinating to natives of temperate zones, are captured for zoos or as pets. The term "laundering," which at one time seemed surprising when applied to money, is even more surprisingly—but just as aptly—being applied to wildlife. Illegally captured exotic animals are moved into free ports such as Singapore and provided with documents alleging that they were caught there and so can be legally exported. In truth, the wildlife of Singapore was killed off many years ago. The population of the island, which was inhabited by about 150 fishermen in the eighteenth century, now numbers well over two million people, and hardly any of the indigenous animal or even plant life remains.

Gradually, one species after another—many from tropical and desert habitats—joins the Tahiti parakeet, not seen since 1844, in extinction.

The smallest tiger, the Bali, became extinct in 1975; also gone forever are the Persian lion, Arabian ostrich, centralian hare wallaby, and southern Burchell's zebra. Occasionally a species revives, only to be threatened again. The yellow-tailed woolly monkey of Peru was believed to have disappeared from the earth until construction workers deep in the jungle came upon some survivors. Their reaction was to kill the appealing little monkeys, "without compassion, and to eat them," declared a Peruvian schoolteacher who came upon such a scene. The monkeys were pathetically easy to hunt down, because of their sense of fellowship; when one was hurt, the others gathered around it.

Yet hunting cannot be blamed for driving so many creatures to the brink of extinction. Many animals with far lower food needs than the elephant's are unable to fill them in the changing world of tropic and desert. What advocates call compassion and opponents call cruelty is responsible for the practice of shooting some wild animals on the theory that all would starve if the total population is not reduced.

It has been suggested that smaller wild animals serve as livestock, thus keeping their population in balance while providing the human population with a source of food. The gazelle, addax, zebra, impala, wildebeest, eland, buffalo, and wart hog would offer steaks and chops just as cattle, pigs, and lambs do in temperate regions. Taking advantage of the natural adaptations of these animals to heat and drought would relieve farmers of the difficulties encountered in keeping animals imported from cooler regions alive. The gazelle, for example, produces 14.6 pounds of meat on the same amount of grazing that enables beef cattle to supply only 7.9 pounds. And the gazelle needs little water, the addax almost none.

In many desert regions of the earth with no consistent policy of farming or containment, the animals, unchecked, are grazing virtually every shrub, compounding the problems caused by human overpopulation. The Rajasthan Desert in India, brown parched earth with a rare thin scrubby plant or tree, must support 150 people to the square mile, compared to an average of 9 or 10 for other deserts. The black and brown goats there have been described by government agronomist H. S. Mann as "desert-makers par excellence, eating every bit of green or dry vegetation." Their ability to tolerate high temperatures with little water has enabled the goats to double in number over the last twenty years, despite the loss of most of their best grazing land. "Now every patch of good land is struggled over," says an aged shepherd, "and the earth never gets to rest." Traveling over a patch of sun-

scorched earth with a party of nomads, a botanist was stunned to
see a goat slithering up a tree trunk to snap off the leaves higher up,
since the lower branches had already been stripped. The nomads were
not interested; they were used to such sights.

The acacia tree used to grow freely in and around Khartoum. Over
the last thirty years, some of these trees have been stripped by animals
and the others cut down for firewood. Today the city dweller must
journey 56 miles to the south to see any acacias. Yet at the same
time a United Nations program is under way to plant these trees,
numbered among the world's best at resisting drought and anchoring
sand dunes.

The deserts of the world are expanding—in India, Ghana, Kenya,
Indonesia, Brazil, Madagascar, Italy, Greece, west Texas, Arizona, and
New Mexico. Despite long periods of drought, American ranchers have
continued to overgraze their cattle on dry rangeland, gradually denuding
the soil. Vegetation has become so sparse in some areas of the Southwest
that 160 acres feed only one or two cattle.

Smaller animals and insects contribute to desertification; a single
jackrabbit may consume 38 grams of larrea shoots in a single day and
nibble off and leave another 10 to 14 grams. Only 26 grams of what
is eaten comes back as feces to fertilize the soil. (On the other hand,
small animals stimulate plant growth by stirring up and aerating the
soil as they dig their burrows.) Insects do more to create a desert
than the actual amount of food they eat would indicate. The sagebrush
defoliator of the Great Basin Desert fulfills its need for moisture by
consuming just the fresh shoots at the tips of the branches. Similarly,
the woodborer takes only tiny quantities of mesquite, but what it takes
is from the phloem and cambium parts of the stem; in a sense, it is
eating the heart out of the plant.

As the deserts spread, drought comes more frequently, and with it
comes death for humans and animals. As a drought is prolonged, wells
are dug in the desert soil to get at whatever groundwater is present;
these, paradoxically, speed desertification. Animals so trample the area
in their desperate search for food and water that a desert within a
desert is created around the water hole.

Animal populations are so greatly reduced by a drought that when
rain finally comes and plants begin to grow in the moist soil, there is
a brief period when enough food is available for the sheep, goats,
and other survivors. However, the animals rapidly reproduce in response
to the improved conditions, and soon all the vegetation is eaten up

and the land is left bare. At the same time, those creatures that avoided the drought by making their way to another area return and further denude the soil.

Herding practices contribute as well, because many nomads maintain scrawny, frail cattle or goats, which produce little meat or milk in return for the amount of forage they consume during a period of drought. However, among some tribes animals are used as a substitute for currency, to pay a bride price. A goat or cow still counts as a goat or cow, no matter how thin. And many nomads believe that to sacrifice the frail members of the herd to leave more food for the others removes all possibility of ever becoming wealthy. This practice would give them a few sturdy, sleek beasts instead of many emaciated ones. "A dead animal is gone forever," says a herdsman. "But once a drought is over, scrawny animals can be fattened up. And in the end, I will have many sleek cattle."

Thousands among the Karamojong nomads of northeast Uganda starved during a 1980 drought. One morning a nurse arrived at the infirmary run by the Save the Children Fund and found the bodies of three children lying outside the walls. She knew they were boys without turning them over. Girls can be traded for cattle and so during times of famine are given some food; boys are left to starve. It is, after all, the cattle which offer the hope of future prosperity.

In order to protect themselves against the losses of drought, a tribal custom of the Pokot of Kenya is to lend some animals to herdsmen in other areas. If a drought wipes out the original owner's herd, he goes to the borrower and asks back the animals lent in better times.

Nomads have traditionally moved their camels, goats, cattle, and sheep from one area to another to obtain the best possible forage. For centuries this method was useful, in that land was given time to recover. But as the populations of the countries around the deserts have expanded, grazing land has been given over to housing and crops, and the nomads must keep their animals on each acre of ground until all plants are wiped out.

"Years ago the nomadic way of life was reasonable," said Egyptian biologist Mohammed Kassas, adviser to a 1977 United Nations Conference on Desertification. "But now the rest of the world is closing in on them. Now the Bedouins ride their camels with transistor radios at their ears."

But transistors cannot help them to find fertile grazing land.

10

From Cactus to Cannabis

"Jojoba is almost like a cult. People are growing it who don't know anything about growing plants. They want to save the whale, or they've been sold some get-rich scheme," said Jack D. Johnson, director of the University of Arizona's Office of Arid Lands. Jojoba, an evergreen of the southwestern United States and the desert wastelands of Mexico, is today being praised for its oil, remarkably similar to that of the sperm whale, up to now the only natural source of a liquid wax highly valued for its ability to withstand extreme pressures. What is more, because it is said to cure baldness and improve acne and dry skin, jojoba oil is being added to shampoos and cosmetics.

The sperm whale is among the most aggressive of all whales, attacking any creature that gets in its way, yet it has been hunted so remorselessly for its oil as to need protection as an endangered species. Formidable in quite another way and in no danger of extinction is the jojoba, which can live for one, sometimes two centuries, enduring a full year without rain, indeed regenerating lost branches, and flourishing at 113 degrees Fahrenheit in the shade.

For plants of the hot deserts, the stress of drought and the stress of heat are inextricably linked, and a variety of adaptations enables them to deal with both. The rose of Jericho, a desert plant that is not a rose but a member of the mustard family, blooms briefly and then dries into a skeleton which holds the seeds. In this form it can stand years of drought, the seeds within lying dormant. But whenever rain comes and the drops touch the skeleton, it expands and opens to release its seeds. After the rain the seeds germinate within eight hours, the length of time desert soil remains damp enough for roots to get through. The way the rose of Jericho lets fall its seeds is viewed by desert natives as analogous to the birth process in humans. Folk medicine prescribes that a woman in labor drink water in which the plant has been dipped, so that she may bring forth her offspring as successfully.

The acacia of the central Australian desert does not bloom in any given season. Rather, it flowers whenever there is a rainfall. So many desert plants are opportunistic that after a rain a profusion of yellow, orange, red, purple, and white flowers springs up on soil that only a few hours before seemed totally devoid of life.

When the Roman soldiers arrived in ancient Mauretania in 32 B.C., so goes the legend, they were thirsty but were assured by the native ruler that water was always plentiful: Each night the trees gathered enough from the clouds to fill the needs of the kingdom. It was an exaggeration, certainly, yet, like many legends, not completely lacking a scientific basis. The hairnet plant of Death Valley does indeed meet all its moisture needs from virtually imperceptible amounts of water vapor in the air. Many other desert plants need no liquid besides the morning dew; some cling to rocks and make do with whatever moisture seeps down and becomes trapped in liquid or vapor form within the porous material.

A botanist found a cactus uprooted on the Sonoran Desert, took it back to the laboratory, and put it in a pot kept in a dimly lit room. The plant was not watered for six years, but lost a mere 0.05 percent of weight a day during the first weeks and months, and then only a minimal 0.015 percent. The botanist took another cactus and peeled off its cuticle, the semi-permeable membrane that covers the leaves of all plants. Without the protection, the cactus lost 85 percent of its weight in a mere two days.

So superbly adapted to its desert habitat is the cactus that it can store water for at least a year. The largest, the saguaro, is capable of retaining from six to eight gallons of water in its expandable trunk, a supply that lasts for two years of drought. The thicker the skin, the better, and the skin of many cacti is so heavy and tough that only the sharpest knife or machete will cut into it. Not only does it keep in the water, it also protects the delicate inner cells from the blistering heat of the desert sun by day and the chill at night and from specks of sand or dust blown with force by the desert wind. The stem possesses chlorophyll for the photosynthetic functions performed in other types of plants by the leaves. Instead of leaves, the cactus has thin thorns that keep away predators and reduce the surface for water loss.

When desert plants have recognizable leaves, these are hard and have little permeability. Typical are the leaves of the yucca (the state flower of New Mexico), which are stiff and spearlike. No lofty stem lifts this plant above the desert soil to make it vulnerable to winds and shifting sands. It hugs the ground, close to what little nourishment and moisture is to be found there.

The adaptations that improve the chances for fruitful life in the desert are shared by a number of crop plants, favored for this reason by farmers in arid regions. Under normal weather conditions, an acre of grain sorghum, a major crop on the hot dry plains from Texas to South Dakota, produces only two thirds of the yield of an acre of corn, but when there is a drought, sorghum can outproduce corn. The waxy substance on the leaves and stems of the sorghum that gives the plants a sticky, frosty look helps protect against water loss. Indeed, so important is this wax that when plants are being bred for drought resistance, one of the goals is to increase the thickness of the waxy coating.

A good number of plants become acclimated during the course of a dry season and manage to do with lessening amounts of water from week to week. Older, tougher plants are less susceptible to drought than are those that are young and sensitive. Heat tolerance also increases over the course of a summer.

Botanists have identified 320 types of plants in the deserts around Las Delicias, a small, desperately poor community some 400 miles north of Mexico City. Even so, the inhabitants consume little besides corn and beans. Their harsh existence is typical of many of the peoples living in regions contiguous to the deserts. Dust storms frequently rage through Las Delicias. The water in the wells is salty, so fresh water is brought in by tanker once a week and kept in oil barrels, where it becomes brackish and polluted. Dehydration and dysenteries are common. Despite all this, few even think of migrating to a more prosperous area. "Why should we leave?" asks José Morales Vázquez, community leader. "This is our home. We were all born here. We even have water, but it's underground and we need the government to get it out."

Many of the plants of the deserts can get to the groundwater themselves easily, because of an enormous and complex root system. The mesquite sends its roots 100 feet beneath the surface. The drier the region, the more of a plant is underground: some succulents are four fifths roots. The massive 66-pound root of the buffalo gourd taps enough water to enable the plant to endure in the deserts of the southwestern United States and Mexico. With just this amount of water, the buffalo gourd makes as much protein and edible vegetable oil as peanuts and sunflowers do with a great deal of water. This would be a valuable crop for such communities as Las Delicias. The starch within the root has also been suggested as a source of gasohol.

The cactus develops rain-catching roots whenever there is a shower. Roots of many desert plants expand sideways rather than downward. These roots are lifesaving when rain is scant and the ground so hot that it evaporates too rapidly to sink deeply.

Many people lost in the desert have perished because they could find neither shelter nor liquid. Bad for people, good for plants, which benefit from being widely spaced. Then each plant can obtain whatever water is present in a given area, whether deep within the ground or in rainfall. A North African olive exporter has commented that the number of olive trees is smaller in areas with limited rainfall, but each tree produces just as many olives as do trees planted in regions with more rain.

Essential to water gain or loss are the movements of the stomata, the tiny pores in the cuticle. These stomata open to let air, water, and sunlight in, and to allow gases and water vapor to get out. Plants adapted to regions where water is scarce open the stomata just for brief intervals during the daytime or do so only at dawn or at night. Once the stomata are closed, transpiration falls by 80 percent or more; only a small amount leaks out through the skin. During the dry season, plants open their pores for shorter periods than when it is rainy. By keeping its stomata closed during the day, the tropical pineapple thrives in dry as well as in rainy seasons.

Cacti do most of their transpiration at night, opening their pores to cold rather than to hot air. There are cacti that have only a brief spell of beauty, seen by few, because they bloom at night, saving water and avoiding ultraviolet light.

The speed with which plants close their stomata is directly related to their drought resistance. Even plants with sluggish reactions may, however, have compensatory adaptations. While sorghum plants close their stomata more slowly than do corn, they leak less water through the cuticle. And when sorghum have lived through a drought and are then watered, their stomata do not open quite so widely as before.

Temperatures of various parts of a plant differ from one another. Any or all of a plant may be hotter or colder than the surrounding air; the leaves in particular are often hotter, because they take in so much of the heat of the sun, comments botanist J. Levitt of the Carnegie Institute of Washington. The brighter the color of the leaf, the more solar radiation it absorbs, and the hotter it becomes. Some plants are truly heat-loving and heat-resistant, but others are equally well able to survive in tropical temperatures because the positioning, shape, and thickness of the leaves are such as to reduce the amount of radiation absorbed. Thin or wilted leaves get hotter than thick ones; hanging leaves take in less sunlight than those that stick straight out. When stomata are on the undersurfaces of the leaves, a smaller amount of solar radiation gets in and the leaves are cooler than when stomata are on both sides.

Because transpiration cools plants as sweat does humans, forest plants that tend to lose a great deal of water are often lower in temperature than the air. Plant temperatures as much as 27 degrees cooler than the air have been recorded.

The different parts of a plant endure heat more or less well. The temperature within the rice flower is warmer than the outside air by up to 1.8 degrees until the air temperature exceeds 86 degrees. At that point the relationship changes, and the flower remains cooler than the air. This adaptation supports survival, because high temperature within the rice flower would render it sterile.

High temperatures sometimes induce changes in chromosomes and produce mutants, most often freaks that do poorly. Occasionally the mutant is healthier than the parent, and plant breeders force more of such changes by exposing parent stock to heat.

Except for the best adapted, heat injury does occur, more often minor than lethal. Even protein damage is reversible if the excessive heat does not continue for too long. Injury to one part does not necessarily kill a plant. A high air temperature in bright sunlight is more harmful than the same degree of heat in shade. When walking through a forest, one will often observe burns and cankers on the side of trees facing the afternoon sun. Who has not started to eat a piece of fruit only to find a dry tasteless patch of burned flesh? Heat can cause tip burn of lettuce and potatoes and produce discolored and malformed dahlias and crysanthemums.

Yet plants favor heat; more species can be found in the torrid than in the frigid deserts of the earth. In western Australia, plants grow at 136.4 degrees in dry soil. Even the more fragile iris shoots of less rigorous climates have lived through 131 degrees for stretches of ten minutes or so. Succulents of the desert actually flourish in 130 degrees.

In Poona, India, tropical agricultural experts recorded soil temperature of 167 degrees in the shade, soaring to 186 in the sun. The surface layers of the soil are too hot for any plants, even for most algae, fungi, or bacteria. In regions where the ground, though less baked than Poona, seems too hot for life, it is cooler within the earth. At the equator, the average temperature all year around at a depth of just 4½ feet is 76.16 degrees. When the soil surface is bare and baked, plants with large thick roots are the most likely to survive. The riskiest time, even for them, occurs when a rise in soil temperature occurs just as young seedlings are beginning to push up above the ground.

The world's record for heat endurance of higher plants in a state of nature is generally considered to be 149 degrees. This has been observed in midafternoon, and the peak temperature was maintained for a short time only. Survival in such heat is possible only when the plants are not in a growing phase but are resting, as living things are less susceptible to stresses when they are not actively developing and reproducing.

Seeds in their dormant state can endure any temperature ever achieved in nature. When barley and oat grains were dried and kept at 212 degrees for an hour, they put forth shoots as soon as they were planted and watered.

If the temperature is too high when the plant is growing, it may be dwarfed. Instead of reproducing, it can become sterile. Efforts to grow crops from cooler regions in the oases of the Sahara have more frequently failed than succeeded.

A number of plants avoid problems by means of an adaptation akin to aestivation or hibernation; they completely stop growing when the heat or cold is too great and begin again only when the temperature moderates. In temperate climates, plants are awakened from a winter sleep by the coming of warmth and the increasing hours of daylight, which signal the most favorable time of the year for growth. Conversely, in desert regions where the days of longest sunlight are those when heat and drought are most stressful, the increasing daylight signals the plant that it is time to become dormant.

Excessive heat, high solar radiation, and lack of water would seem enough stresses to bear, but in most deserts plants must also be able to grow in salty soil. Some have adapted so well as not only to be able to endure salt but even be stimulated by it. Saltbushes, common to many deserts, easily get rid of excess salt. Small vesicles to hold the salt form on the leaf surfaces and burst when filled up.

A botanist making his way through the formidable Atacamá Desert of northern Chile found a clump of tamarugo trees growing in a salt crust several feet thick. Rain may not fall for seven years at a time, but the tamarugo, like the Mauritanian trees of the legend, can obtain sufficient water for its needs from occasional foggy drizzle and from small amounts of groundwater. Because tamarugo pods provide high-protein sheep fodder, plantations of them have been established. But Chilean tamarugo farmers have a special problem: Before each seedling can be planted, a hole must be forced through the salt crust.

Salt is also a problem in the humid tropics, though, oddly, some plants like it. Many species of algae flourish in salt and brackish water the world over. Lake Chad in north-central Africa is "fished" by native women for the blue-green alga, spirulina. Filtered through sand and dried in the sun, it provides a good quantity of protein. The use of spirulina as food has a long history. Before the Spanish conquest of Mexico, the Aztecs in the capital city of Tenochtitlán gathered the slime that floated on the surface of Lake Texcoco. Its Indian name, *tecuitlatl*, meaning "excrement of the stones," indicates what they thought it looked like, but the product that resulted was described in histories by the Spanish conquistadors as having the taste of a salty cheese.

While the ability of algae to survive the worst of conditions anywhere is well known, and the tamarugo looks hardy, it is surprising to discover that the delicate pomelo, a citrus fruit native to Southeast Asia, favors the saline lowlands around the river deltas and brackish marshes in

Thailand. In fact, Thai women insist that the salt it grows in actually enhances the acidic yet sugary flavor of the fruit. And mangroves grow in salt water in Florida, but most of the salt is filtered out through the roots, so that the water getting to the leaves is nearly pure.

Still, large amounts of salt in the soil throughout much of the deserts and tropics is a major handicap to agricultural productivity. As M. El Gabaly of the Food and Agriculture Organization Regional Office for the Near East in Cairo declared, "The percentage of salt-affected and waterlogged soil amounts to 50 percent of the irrigable area in Iraq, 23 percent of Pakistan, 50 percent in the Euphrates Valley in Syria, and 30 percent in Egypt."

While plants of the desert have adapted to high salt environments, few crops have succeeded in doing so. A landholder commented that he had been forced to limit himself to alfalfa as his major crop, because it is fairly salt-tolerant. Meanwhile, efforts are regularly made to breed plants that can grow in seawater, the theory being that if seaweeds flourish there, why not higher plants? Strains of barley and other grains are nourished with salt water, and those that survive used as breeding stock.

Even soil that is not salty presents problems to tropical farmers. Oddly, and for quite different reasons, the earth in parts of the tropics is not much different from that in the desert. Much of it looks red, being high in iron and aluminum hydroxide, low in organic matter.

"Unhappily, the evident fertility of the jungle is deceptive," is the consensus of Rockefeller Foundation scientists. The tropical forests do not enrich the soil as one would expect. Instead, when one plant dies another takes its place and absorbs all its nutrients so quickly that very little goes into the soil. This has become apparent over the past few decades as one rain forest after the other has been cut down for "development." Moreover, soil that has been heated too much, whether in desert or tropics, is likely to be particularly deficient in nitrogen, which is basic for plant protein development and growth. When a soil scientist measured nitrogen in the Congo recently, he found a 24-pounds-per-acre loss for every degree of temperature over 97 degrees. In addition, plants do not absorb nutrients as well when they are very hot.

A number of tropical plants have adapted by living in a symbiotic relationship with nitrogen-fixing microorganisms, much as legume crops do in temperate climates. The winged bean of Papua, New Guinea, possesses an exceptional ability to grow in nitrogen-deficient soil and yet produce large amounts of protein. It achieves such concentrations by means of the activity of bacteria living in nodules on the roots. Winged bean roots have more and larger nodules than other better-known legumes—more than 600 have been counted on the roots of a single plant. In Burma, where winged bean pods are popular, they are dipped quickly in boiling water and eaten as an afternoon snack. The entire plant is edible—tuber, seeds, leaves, flowers, and shoots. In Papua the flowers are fried in oil, and travelers who have tasted them say the flavor resembles that of mushrooms.

When the tropical rains first start, there is a brief period when the soil nitrogen increases. Farmers rush to get their seeds into the ground, hoping to get a harvest before the violence of the storms causes the widespread flooding that will leach the soil of nutrients and make it very acid.

As some plants adapt to whatever environment they are in, the oil palm, tea, and rice can grow in acid soil, but many others fail. A businessman bought forest land in Fiji and had it cleared for a banana plantation. He was sure that this would be successful, because the forest was lush, the weather always warm, and the rainfall heavy. The bananas, however, were few and unhealthy. The soil, he soon learned, was too acid to support the fruit trees. Fertilizers had to be added to bring to the tropical soil the nutrients it was lacking.

Because the nitrogen is leached from the upper layers, the crops that do well have roots going very far down beneath the soil. Coffee plant roots send out tiny tendrils ten feet down, and sugarcane roots may go down twelve feet. The same adaptation thus applies to plants of the tropics as of the desert, but for a different reason. In the desert the nutrients are in the top layers of the soil, but the root must go down deep to find water. In the tropics water is plentiful at every layer, but the root must go down deep to find nourishment.

The heavy and continuous downpour of the rainy season makes the soil waterlogged as well as acid. Weather scientists measured 128 inches of rainfall during the rainy season in Brazil, and 85 inches is common in humid Africa. Any tropical rain forest receives 60 to 80 inches of rain a year. Many indigenous plants are water loving, but except for a few, such as rice, most have somehow missed out in becoming part of our diet. Hardly anyone except the natives of the western Amazon regions of Brazil, Colombia, or Peru has bitten into the sweet white flesh of the uvilla, which grows during the wettest season in the rain forests. Pineapple is one of the few other tropical fruits able to do as well in such an environment, and that was the one favored by the colonials and exploited for export, which is why we know it.

While a great deal of effort has gone into introducing potatoes into tropical areas to which they are not really suited, little has been done to expand plantations of the potato alternatives, the cocoyam and the taro, which are native to regions of heavy rainfall. The taro, which has a pleasing nutty flavor, is cultivated commercially only in Egypt, the Philippines, Hawaii, and a few other tropical areas. It is so well-adapted to water that it can be grown in marshes or in paddies like rice.

The fruit of the durian tree enjoyed by natives of tropical countries has displeased many Americans and Europeans because of its odor, scornfully described as a "mixture of old cheese and onions flavored with turpentine" or as "custard passed through a sewer." Yet the natives of Malaya, Indonesia, southern Thailand, and the Philippines consider durian superb, and a nineteenth-century British naturalist, Alfred Russell Wallace, declared that "it was worth a journey to the East, if only to taste of its fruit. . . . It is neither acid, nor sweet, nor juicy, yet one feels the want of none of these qualities, for it is perfect as it is." Elephants, tigers, and monkeys must be driven away, as they find it irresistible. This tree does best in regions so humid as to lack a dry season altogether.

Among the plants best adapted to the weather conditions and soils of the tropics and deserts are those that produce dreams, hallucinations, and oblivion. While people who live in temperate or cold places of the earth tend to think of life in hotter zones as easier, alcoholic beverages and most of our drugs paradoxically originated in those regions, and their first widespread use was there.

The dream produced by opium begins in the beautiful opium poppy that needs but three months in its warm environment to reach maturity and flower. The farmer then pulls off the petals and, ten days later, cuts into the unripe seed pods. The milky juice he collects contains the drug that has produced visions and escape from reality for millions of people over the last 6,000 years. While the poppy grows in many climates, it gives the most opium in the tropics.

While addiction has given opium and its alkaloid derivatives, chiefly morphine and heroin, its bad name, the drug is second to none as a painkiller, and to this day all new analgesics are measured against it for effectiveness. During the American Civil War morphine was given to wounded soldiers to relieve their pain, and a large number became addicted, and more recently the Vietnam war helped create an army of addicts.

Jungle experts returning from the Peruvian wilds have described the visionary state sought by natives in ayahuasca or yajé made from the liana vine. The effects are comparable to those induced by psilocybin, the active substance in the fabled hallucinogenic mushrooms of Mexico.

The particular importance of drugs to the religious practices of many tropical and desert regions derives from the emphasis placed on visions and dreams. It is said that Montezuma, last ruler of the Aztecs, ordered anyone dreaming about the future of the empire to tell him what was to be. Many dreamers appeared and presented terrible tales of disaster. Montezuma was so disturbed that he refused to accept these as true dreams and had the dreamers killed. Hernando Cortez and the Spanish conquistadors came nonetheless. Their coming resulted in hardship and poverty for the native populations. And poverty, a by-product of colonialism and too high a birthrate in many hot regions, contributed to the widespread adoption of the drugs and liquors available in the plants so close at hand.

The San Pedro cactus can wrest all the nutrients it needs for growth in the Valley of the Moon in Bolivia. The Indians cut off pieces and boil them to produce a sugary juice. Fermented into a liquor, it has effects on the mind similar to those produced by mescaline.

In many desert regions the peyote button caps the crown of a light blue cactus plant with a lovely small pink flower. The peyote is chewed until soft—a common native practice for obtaining derivatives—and then brewed into a drink or formed into a tablet. The active ingredient, mescaline, produces alterations in consciousness, in mood, in perceptions. Brilliantly colored hallucinations flash across the mind. The cult of religious peyotism has been practiced since pre-Columbian times by many Indian peoples of Mexico and the southwestern United States. The Huichol Indians of Mexico, for example, have traditionally gone out onto the desert each year in a peyote-hunting rite. The shaman of the tribe shoots an arrow into the first cactus seen, and then the peyote button is cut off and consumed in a ritual act.

Peyote was adopted by American hippies and flower children of the 1960s, as well as by such noted intellectuals as British author Aldous Huxley, who wrote that, after taking mescaline, a bunch of flowers in a vase took on mystic proportions, revealing to him what the world must have looked like to Adam as he opened his eyes on the day of his creation. Acceptance by Huxley was viewed by some as putting the stamp of approval on the drug experience. But as a number of users developed emotional problems and "bad trips" became frequent, mescaline, along with such other mind-altering drugs as psilocybin and LSD-25, fell into disfavor in this country.

Although similar in name and to some degree in effect, mescal, the powerful alcoholic drink of the Mexicans, comes from a different desert plant, the agave, or maguey, as do the more refined tequila and the cruder syrupy beer, pulque. A number of agave species are used as sources of liquor, the best known being the century plant, the name an exaggerated description of the growth pattern. It takes many years—though by no means a hundred—for the plant to mature in the hot, arid environment. After it flowers, the agave appears to wither away and die, but around the base remain tiny shoots that will slowly begin to make their way upward to find sunshine and moisture. During the brief period of flowering, the agave yields up its sweet sap, collected in a hollow scooped into the heart. This sap is then fermented into pulque and drunk as is or distilled into mescal, which may also be consumed in that form, or redistilled into tequila. To remind the drinker of the source, an agave worm may be placed at the bottom of the mescal bottle. Some tequila producers will take the heart of the plant, a huge mass weighing a hundred or more pounds, and have it hacked to pieces, crushed, and baked to release its sugar-filled juice for fermentation and distillation.

Corn, sugarcane, and manioc or cassava, which flourish in many tropical regions, are also common sources of the starch or sugar needed for fermentation. Among many poor families in Bolivia, the corn liquor, chicha, replaces food, observes Gregorio Aramayo, a psychiatrist with Bolivia's National Institute of Drug Dependence.

The Yagua Indians of lowland Peru clear the land communally. Typically, twenty or more families start out, interrupting their labor every now and again to drink rum and aquadente (water with teeth) made from the sugarcane. It is only in the evening, when the work has been done, that they allow themselves masato, the drink made from the manioc root, which has been peeled, boiled, and mashed. The Yagua women chew the mash and spit it back into the pot, where it is covered with palm leaves and left to ferment.

In the highlands of Peru, chewing the leaves of the coca plant is a universal custom to reduce hunger pangs, because the leaves contain cocaine. The amount of cocaine in each leaf is small, but so much is chewed—two pounds a day is a frequently given guess—that many of the natives appear glassy-eyed and filled with lassitude, even while declaring that coca leaves give them energy.

From 10,000 to 12,000 pounds of the narcotic weed kat was imported from Ethiopia into Djibouti daily in the late 1970s, reported the *New York Times*, linking use of the drug to the widespread unemployment.

Betel nuts, providing a milder stimulant effect, are chewed by natives of India, Sri Lanka, and southeast Asia. Despite the name, these are the seeds of the areca palm. While betel may be chewed fresh, it is more palatable when cured. Users like to cut up the betel nut, mix it with spices, and spread it on a leaf of the betel pepper. (This is quite a different plant, a creeping-vine relative of pepper, but the two flavors mix well.) The betel chewer is easy to recognize; betel makes the saliva brick red and eventually stains the teeth.

The most widely used of the consciousness-altering drugs, marijuana, taken from the hemp plant, *Cannabis sativa*, was first described in Chinese writings of 2737 B.C. and has since been grown in India, North Africa, Europe, the United States, Mexico, and many other regions of the world. The most powerful of the cannabis substances, hashish, is obtained from the resin on the flower clusters and top leaves of the female plant. In many tropical countries this is collected on cloth, taken off by hand, and then dried. The cannabis plant grows in many climates, but it is rightly described as tropical: While the lower-grade marijuana can be taken from plants raised in many merely warm places, including window boxes outside of North American apartments, hashish is obtained from plants adapted to and cultivated in the humid tropics.

11

Plant Hunters, Exploiters, and Breeders

A feast of fruits, vegetables, saps, and nectars is waiting in the tropics. Lush green plants offer their flowers, leaves, stems, roots, and seeds. While more than 3,000 plant species have served as food over the millennia, only 150 or so have been cultivated on farms. Today, a mere 20 crops feed most of the world's population, a National Academy of Sciences committee reports. The top 16 of that list are grown in the tropics and subtropics, some indigenous, others introduced from temperate zones but flourishing in the warmth: rice, maize, millet, sorghum, wheat, potatoes, sweet potatoes, cassavas, peas, beans, peanuts, soybeans, sugarcane, sugar beets, coconuts, and bananas. Tea, coffee, and cocoa, beverages basic to our diets, are also tropical in origin. Add to all these the fragrant clove, nutmeg, and cinnamon, the vanilla bean, slightly acid mango, the pungent pepper, fleshy papaya, the passion fruit and pomegranate, the sweetly sticky date, the blandly sweet melon, the berry, cherry, orange, and olive—such is our debt to the tropics.

Plants, like animals, have an optimal temperature for growth, and this is most often attained with the greatest ease in perpetually warm climates. A number of plants prefer tropical heat but will, nonetheless, do well in temperate regions where the longer hours of daylight during the summer make up for the lesser heat. Some, such as corn, have a wide range and will flourish from the tropics to Canada. Oats, wheat, and barley have a temperature optimum of 77 to 88 degrees, can continue growing well into the 90s, and yet can endure almost freezing temperatures. Sorghum, melons, and other crops that are better adapted to hot climates or seasons do best at 88 to 98 degrees, can survive heat of 122 degrees, but will stop growing at 59 to 64 degrees.

The temperature optimum may vary with the stage of development, and, as has been found true of some animals, plants may grow too rapidly and be weak if the most favorable amount of heat is present too soon, when they are young.

In Ghana, cocoa flourishes so long as daytime temperatures are above 83 degrees—above 85 is preferable. A planter observed that during a cool spell flowers emerged two months late and were fewer in number than usual.

But cool spells are rare in the tropics; for the most part, continuous warmth encourages plant growth. Botanists have said that there are as many plant species in Panama alone as in all Europe. In the rain forests of Indonesia, 5,000 species of orchid have been identified; 3,000 species of trees grow in the Philippines; 2,700 palm trees, ranging from six inches to more than three hundred feet in height, are found throughout the tropics and subtropics, as well as in desert oases. And so it is not surprising that governments have sent explorers to scour the tropical regions for useful plants and then sought to adapt them to plantation growth.

Efforts to control access to these plants have affected the world's history, with the tropics serving as outposts or colonies of the major European powers. Although most of the produce was shipped out of the colonies, the labor was native and in many cases involuntary. In 1833, with the passage of the Emancipation Act in Britain, the slaves in British colonies became apprenticed laborers. The results were disastrous for plantation owners, wrote Alleyne Ireland in 1899, looking back on his four-year stint as overseer of sugar estates in the West Indies; many plantations were ruined. As Ireland complained, "What possible means are there of inducing the inhabitants of the tropics to undertake steady and continuous work if the local conditions are such that from the mere bounty of nature all the ambitions of the people can be gratified without any considerable amount of labor?"

The next step was importing indentured laborers from the East

Indies at a cost of $12 a year for five years, paid by the plantation owner. Eventually, laws were passed protecting these indentured laborers in the British colonies, despite the view expressed by a writer in the *Madras Weekly Mail* in 1874: "There is not a poor man in England with a tithe of the advantages open to him that are placed at these coolies' feet."

The labor problem that so troubled the colonials during the nineteenth century did not abate. The harvesting of crops in the tropics requires the handling of great amounts of foodstuffs in terrain that often defeats all attempts at mechanization. Even in the 1960s an agricultural expert commented that hand labor was unavoidable in many regions. Few advantages were placed at the feet of those who performed it; rewards were minimal.

Cloves, nutmeg, vanilla, and coconut flourish in the Moluccas, once known as the Spice Islands. But though the soil and the climate are just right for the growth of these prized and delicate plants, native laborers often still fail to benefit. In South Molucca, a farmer admitted that in all of 1976 his hired laborers had earned less than $400. And in February 1977, it was estimated that 300,000 landless peasants in the coffee-growing region around Huehuetla, Mexico, were earning the equivalent of $1 a day for the arduous task of picking coffee beans, one third the official minimum wage. The workers, therefore, could only purchase enough food for half their needs and filled up as best they could on the roots and flowers they had the time and energy to gather.

How does this picture of misery square with the "bounty of nature" providing all that natives of the tropics could want without their having to labor for it? Exploitation in the colonial era, and to some extent to this day, accounts for some of it. Tenant farming, with landlords, whether local or absentee, taking much of the crops, leaves farmers with no stores for times of famine. But the physical facts of life in the tropics contribute greatly. "The popular vision of the tropics as a perpetual garden of green growing things . . . forms a grim contrast with present-day actuality," declares the International Institute of Tropical Agriculture in Ibadan, Nigeria.

"As many as one billion inhabitants of the developing countries live in abject poverty, their most fundamental needs—food, shelter, health, clothing—unmet," reports the United States Office of Technology Assessment.

The paradox in the tropical paradise is that though the sun shines for much of the year, the air is warm, and plants grow in lush splendor, hunger is common. The glory of the season of growth and flowering is followed by the violence of monsoons, floods, wind and dust storms, or locust invasions. Fertile soil quickly becomes desiccated; the red earth already deficient in nutrients becomes dark and waterlogged or baked and cracking in the sun. The sheer numbers of the expanding population strain all resources. Frequent battles between tribes or nations waste crops, destroy fields, and denude more of the soil. Malaria, dysentery, cholera, and other diseases kill or weaken people and animals. The traditional poor farming methods in many areas cause millions to lead a life of unending toil.

In addition, as the Inter-American Development Bank reported after studying the land from Panama to Guatemala, "There exist formidable obstacles to agricultural production, including oppressive heat, mosquito breeding grounds, extensive swamps and mangroves, and steep mountainous terrain."

A second paradox is that the pleasing climate of warmth, sunshine, and moisture that encourages so rich a growth of trees, vines, flowers, fruits, and grains at the same time enhances the growth of weeds, microbes, and animal pests that damage them. In all too many regions the temperature year round is hot, ideal for reproduction by unwanted as well as wanted species. In Djakarta, Indonesia, for example, there is less than 1.8 degrees of difference between the hottest and coolest months; in Belém, Brazil, 2.3 degrees. The temperature in the jungles and rain forests is not as stressful as in the deserts, seldom going higher than 100 degrees.

Tropical waters are friendly to life; needs of aquatic weeds are met so fully that the yield per acre is often greater than that of nearby plants on land. Two water hyacinths checked by botanists, for example, produced 30 offspring in twenty-three days and 1,200 in four months; in Guyana, these hyacinths clog the river that is the chief means of communication between the coast and the interior. Sugarcane, the major crop, must be carried from the fields to the mills in small boats, but these often become mired in the heavy mats of hyacinths so during the harvest season, farmers must interrupt their work repeatedly to stop and clear the waters of the weeds.

Enchanted by its beauty, tourists used to uproot a hyacinth or two and take it home to their own waterways, with the result that the hyacinth has spread all over the tropics and subtropics including the southern United States.

Harmful insects and animals live on aquatic plants, including hyacinths, and when these weeds invade a rice paddy, the pests go with them and attack the crop. It is no coincidence that the malaria-bearing Anopheles mosquito begins to breed just two weeks after the water lotus puts forth its leaves. And the snail that serves as intermediate host for the parasite causing the tropical disease of schistosomiasis in humans finds ample nourishment in the water lettuce.

Biological control achieved by stocking the waters with fish that would consume the weeds and then be consumed themselves by people and animals is more attractive in concept than chemical control, but it has proven surprisingly hard to achieve. The white amur, or Chinese grass carp, which was ranked second by Americans in taste tests of seven fish, was introduced into the waters of Guyana, but the amur were too docile to compete with the more voracious native fish and were eaten before they had a chance to destroy many weeds. In January of 1979 thousands of amur were dumped into Gatun Lake of the Panama Canal to consume some of the weeds that were getting into ship propellers and clogging the gates of the locks. Even though the amur did not here have to contend with killer fish, the results, said the deputy director of engineering construction, were "inconclusive."

A number of biologists see an answer to the weed problem in the manatee, or sea cow, a huge slow-moving creature of the tropical seas. Believed to be a mermaid by fishermen of old, prized as high-quality meat by seventeenth- and eighteenth-century explorers, the manatee has been all but ignored ever since. Several manatees were released in the weed-choked waters of central and southern Florida, some to be killed by motorboats, others by a cold wave, before they could make any inroads on the weeds. In tropical Guyana, the manatee faces neither threat. When two of them were loosed in a canal 22 feet wide and almost a mile long, they ate up all the weeds in seventeen weeks, each day consuming one fourth of their body weight of 500 to 2,000 pounds. But manatees are not far from extinction, with a world population estimated at but a few thousand. And, unfortunately, they are passive creatures which breed very slowly in the wild and have not reproduced at all in captivity.

Weeds take over land as well as water, and farmers, like home gardeners, complain that weeds often do better than food crops or flowers, particularly when fertilizers are added to the soil and weedkillers are not. The more aggressive weeds deprive the more desirable plants of nutrients and, during the dry season, of water.

The tropical environment is also perfect for microbes, and many plants, adapted to all other hot region stresses, succumb to pathogenic organisms. The taro, for example, is highly susceptible to viral infection and plants that survive to the harvest, says a Solomon Islander, often decay in less than a week.

In addition, plants in the tropics are subject to the predations of insects, worms, birds, and rodents. Vast numbers of pest species multiply wildly in the tropics. "A big deterrent to high yields in the tropics is the pest problem [insects and disease]," declares John H. Lonnquist, former Director of the International Maize Program.

A 1974 study found that pests and diseases wiped out more than two fifths of the world's rice and a fifth of other crops. In India, adds an agricultural technical consultant, it would take a train 3,000 miles long to carry the grain eaten by rats in a year.

The African armyworm gets its name because it marches in phalanx eating everything in sight: rice, maize, millet, wheat, barley, oats, and grasses. Armyworms and cutworms may not be spotted by the farmer at first, because they feed after dark. When they reach full size, they can destroy an entire field in a night. About half the rice fields in central and northern Ghana were wiped out in one worm invasion of the mid-1960s.

The red-billed, sparrow-like quelea bird is little known in the United States, but in arid regions of Africa it is a predator on the scale of the locust, devouring grasses, millet, rice, and wheat. Both young birds and adults are voracious. Abandoned by their parents at the age of three weeks, hundreds of thousands of young birds use up their fat reserves and then go searching for food. They are called the "deaf ones" in the Sudan, because they ignore the loudest shouts by farmers. Control efforts have been massive, with flamethrowers, explosives, and poison sprays directed at the birds. In one year in the 1960s, 177 million birds were killed—to no avail, noted the Centre for Overseas Pest Research: there were still countless others to take their place.

"Practically every plant used by man has been recorded as being attacked by at least one termite species at some stage of its growth in some part of the tropics," states W. A. Sands of the Centre. Termites are particularly vicious, mounting their attack just when their plant victim's resistance is lowest—right after transplantation or in the dry season.

More than 800 species of insects have been identified in the rice paddies, with the most damage being done by 18 to 20 of them. When the stem borer struck Pakistan in 1970, the rice was so badly damaged that what was left had to be used for animal fodder. Leafhoppers and plant hoppers suck out plant juices, inject toxins, and transmit diseases. A single outbreak of these insects in Bangladesh in 1956 is still spoken of, as 20 to 50 percent of crops close to the harvest stage were destroyed, and up to 80 percent of younger plants. If crops are alternated in a field, the pests that attack the first die out when the second appears. But when farmers grow only one crop, and that one continuously, pests increase to new levels of population density.

As human population density forces such continuous cropping, another approach has been emphasized, that of concentrating on crops which are pest-resistant naturally or by breeding. Many plants that have evolved in the tropics have survived by adaptations that make them less attractive to pests. The winged bean, for example, is so free of serious pests and diseases that when a virulent nematode attack occurred in Papua, New Guinea, one year, it was talked of for decades thereafter. The hornworm may eat the spinach-like leaves of the Mexican chaya, but they are rapidly regenerated. And the tough skin and chalky wax coating of the wax gourd of Asia keeps out both insects and microbes so successfully that even after harvesting the fruit can be kept unrefrigerated for a year.

Some of the major crop plant species indigenous to the tropics are also pest-resistant but give a poor yield. And others are susceptible to pathogens and insects and peculiarly ill-suited in other ways to the stresses of the environment.

In efforts to correct the lacks, many crosses of parent plants with different qualities have been made. In 1920, agricultural experts selected 44,000 tea bushes in Buitenzorg, Java, studied them all, and took the best 2,100 for breeding. Botanists have searched the tropical world for perfect parent stock. Collectors exhausted by a particularly difficult journey in Sri Lanka stopped for lunch one day in a jungle clearing, relaxed after having obtained a treasure of pest-resistant samples. Just as they began their meal, a band of apes appeared on the scene, grabbed the bags of seedlings, and refused to relinquish them even when offered the combined lunches of the plant explorers.

A group of agronomists traveled by jeep and then by motorboat to find species that could grow in infertile ground. Finally they reached a remote swamp where the soil, particularly high in acid content, yielded more than fifty varieties of plants to use in crossbreeding with stock that gave better yields but required better nutrients.

No possible combination of plant crosses is overlooked. Advances in genetic engineering make possible the mating of widely different plants, even of species that once were viewed as incompatible. The botanist who suggests crossing an indestructable Death Valley plant with a fragile crop plant is not ignored. Because tropical varieties of corn are tall and do not yield well relative to their size, some of the more efficient United States cornbelt varieties are being incorporated.

The greatest of all efforts to improve tropical crops has been concentrated on rice. "No thinking person can fail to have an interest in rice," declared Nyle C. Brady, Director General of the International Rice Research Institute (IRRI), located in the Philippines and supported by the Ford and Rockefeller Foundations and many international and government agencies. "It provides at least one fourth of the food consumed by 1.7 million people. In parts of Asia more than two thirds of the calories and more than half the protein comes from rice."

So seriously has the work of IRRI been taken that during the war between Pakistan and Bangladesh, leaders of both sides spoke on the radio, exhorting their followers not to do any damage. The word was passed and not a truck was taken or a window smashed.

When IRRI was first formed, agriculturalists set themselves this problem: "If there were an ideal rice plant, what would it look like?" Explains Lowell Hardin of the Ford Foundation, "They drew a picture of the perfect plant and then observed that the rice in the paddies did not look like it." The pictured rice was short and sturdy with upright leaves, whereas in the paddies the plants were tall and fell over when heavy with grain or lashed by the monsoon. The leaves were droopy and so did not make best use of sunlight. And as the long record of crop losses reveals, the rice plants were susceptible to insects and disease.

In the mid-1960s after thousands of crosses, a new variety, IR-8, soon to be named "miracle" rice, was developed. At last a plant had been created that looked like the picture of the ideal. This rice is short, about 3 feet high, compared to more than five feet for the older types, and its leaves are upright. Growth is not affected by day length, and it matures rapidly. Within two years, yields in southern Pakistan had risen by 60 percent and the Philippines, long a rice importer, was declaring itself ready to export.

Use of IR-8 and newer hybrids made the harvest in India so large that farmers coming into town with loaded buffalo carts could not find any place to store their grain to protect it from the next season's monsoon. Palaces were rapidly turned into warehouses, and wheat and rice piled to the chandeliers of the ballrooms, drawing rooms, and great reception chambers. The grain that did not fit was stacked out of doors, covered with polyethylene sheets.

Even so, ten years after IR-8 had burst upon the agricultural scene, it had become evident that only one fourth of the world's rice farmers were using miracle grains. This was in part due to the fact that many native farmers were accustomed to making the most of the poorest plant stock by their planting customs. "Some years ago an American scientist went to the Philippines to show farmers how to improve their yield of rice," recalls Hardin. "He discovered to his chagrin that they were getting a higher yield with their indigenous varieties than he was. His methods were not suited to the vagaries of the climate and theirs were."

Scientists used to consider the Philippine tradition of planting rice to the accompaniment of guitar music rather amusing. But there is more logic than the sophisticates recognized; the work was done in time to the music, and the plants were spaced properly to give the best possible yield.

During a recent drought in Uttar Pradesh when even hybrid plants died, the rumor spread that farmers' wives in a desperation move were following the ancient custom of going naked into the fields at night to till the earth. The belief was that this would bring the much-desired rain and save the crop.

Many farmers have been reluctant to take a risk with something new. All could recall periods of famine. A technical aid in Colombia observed, "When we experiment with a new variety of rice, I don't know what to say to a poor farmer who tells me that if it does not work, he will have to sell or abandon his farm."

The main problem, however, has been that the perfect hybrid rice was not so perfect for everyone. It really did best when irrigated and supplied with nitrogen fertilizers, which were often unavailable or beyond the means of the farmers. And while resistance to some pests had been bred into the new lines, they proved even more susceptible than the old to a number of others. Epidemics of rice gall midges, which had occurred at three-year intervals on native rice, were happening every year with the new rice.

And so breeding efforts continued, with 4,000 crosses attempted in a single year. One hybrid was created to be so hostile to the stem borer that the insect laid fewer eggs. Many of those that hatched died, and even those that survived were slower to grow, small in size, and more often male than female.

Much of the world's rice is grown near the Ganges, Brahmaputra, Godavari, Irrawaddy, Chao Phraya, Mekong, Niger, and other rivers and has adapted to the special conditions of this environment. These rice varieties are of normal height when the river delta is low, but during seasons of flood the stems elongate and the leaves float on top of the water. In other, normally drier regions, rice lacks this characteristic, and so a huge loss ensued when rice fields in Luzon, the Philippines, were flooded for four weeks. Crossbreeding floating rice with short-stemmed rice was promptly suggested to create a hybrid able to survive occasional flooding.

Many farmers in tropical regions do welcome the new "miracle" varieties. "When a hybrid is planted experimentally, it is hard to keep the farmers away," remarks Hardin. "Word gets out even in the most isolated areas, and as soon as the experts turn aside, the farmers will steal the seed. At some places men have been stationed around the seeded plots to protect them. In India we learned that kernels of wheat that had not yet been fully tested were selling to farmers on the black market for several dollars for a small handful."

Seeds of a Mexican hybrid wheat were smuggled into Turkey by way of Pakistan in the mid-1960s, and given to a farmer for a trial. The yield was so outstanding that his neighbors sought to obtain some of the seed. The scientists in charge of government programs, however, objected to letting seed of a still-untested hybrid into Turkey. They agreed to allow just enough for 100 farmers to use. Excellent results were obtained, and the Minister of Agriculture agreed to allow 50,000 tons of seed to be imported. Again, the outcry from the scientists arose and the Ministry backed down and imported only 22,000 tons.

One hopes the hybrid passed the test and was distributed to larger numbers of farmers.

Unfortunately, many of the food crops that are dietary staples for millions in the developing countries are low in protein and what they have is of poor quality. Because the protein content of most milled rice grains is only 7 to 8 percent, 20,000 rice samples are tested every year, and those that rate highest are used as parent stock. There are already some hybrids with 9 to 10 percent protein.

While considerable effort goes into breeding rice, wheat, and corn, little attention is paid to other plants considered basic in many cultures but not selected for export in colonial times. The cassava, a staple in Africa, Asia, and South America, offers less than 2 percent protein. A physician in a rural hospital in Africa says sadly that he sees many cases of kwashiorkor, a protein-deficiency disease, in children who are not starving but whose diet is made up almost entirely of cassava. In the past the approach to such problems has been to try to induce the native population to develop different tastes and change to European or American foods, disregarding the fact that cassava, for example, is practical in regions with few storage facilities, because it can be kept in the ground, and ignoring its ritual uses in religious ceremonies and as the source of a popular beverage.

With the growing recognition that the huge populations of the developing countries need expanded food sources of all kinds, attempts to improve cassava, chick peas, pearl millet, and other indigenous crops have at last been instituted, and a number of international research centers in addition to the IRRI have been established. At the same time, agronomists have begun to urge greater use of less familiar plants.

"The apparent advantages of staple plants over minor tropical plants often result only from the disproportionate research attention they have been given," declares the National Academy of Sciences. Why not consider the sweetly sour naranjilla, known as the "golden fruit of the Andes"; the crisp carrot-shaped arracacha; the musky acidic soursop; the fragrant pear-shaped rose apple of the rain forest; the olive-oil "double" from the purple fruit of the jessenia palm; the milky liquid from the brosimum, or "cow tree"; and the fruit of the pejibaye, or peach palm, with its pleasing coconut flavor and surprisingly high protein content?

The closest most Americans have come to a breadfruit tree is in the story of Captain Bligh and the mutiny on the *Bounty*, which had been on a mission to bring breadfruit trees from the Society Islands of the South Pacific to Jamaica in the West Indies. A food staple of natives of the South Pacific, the fruit can be cooked or squeezed raw into a tasty mash. Despite the *Bounty* misadventure, breadfruit is found in the Americas. Fourth-year medical students from the University of Wisconsin went to tiny Isla del Maíz off the Caribbean coast of Nicaragua to see at first hand malaria, intestinal parasites, and other tropical diseases. They observed evidence of all these. Yet the most dangerous tropical medical problem they encountered turned out to be skulls cracked by breadfruit dropping heavily on unsuspecting walkers.

Not only food but industrial products as well can be obtained from little-known tropical plants. When the Spanish conquistadors arrived in what is now Mexico, they watched the Aztecs playing a game with a heavy, bouncing black ball. They learned that the ball was made of the latex obtained from plants, the species varying with the locality. In the arid highlands of Mexico the Aztecs gathered the freely growing guayule shrub and chewed the roots, stems, and branches to separate the latex.

Guayule has at times been commercially exploited to some degree, and at more times been all but forgotten. It gives a rubber similar in properties to that obtained from *Hevea brasiliensis,* which gained acceptance as the only source of natural rubber. Unlike *Hevea,* which is limited to humid tropical areas within 10 degrees of the equator, guayule's extensive root system can wrest water and nutrients from a harsh desert soil, easily endure temperatures of 120 degrees, and do well in regions where no other plants with commercial uses can flourish. The shrub does not merely tolerate aridity, but prefers it.

In 1910 guayule filled 10 percent of the world's rubber needs, and in 1930 the U.S. War Department set up a research project under then Major Dwight D. Eisenhower. In 1953 a federal research program found heavy-duty guayule truck tires to be equal in performance to hevea rubber ones. Nonetheless, that same year the program was terminated in the United States and guayule development continued in Mexico only. Today the desert shrub is again receiving attention as a possible source of rubber, reducing the reliance on synthetic rubber, a byproduct of costly petroleum. The National Academy of Sciences is suggesting that guayule could be an economically viable crop on Indian reservations with infertile soil.

Although the hevea rubber tree is as well adapted to life under conditions of high temperatures and high humidity as the guayule is to the desert, it is not indigenous to many of the areas where the greatest rubber plantations are now found. The hevea tree grew in its native state in the Amazon basin. In the late nineteenth century, Sir Henry Wickham brought a consignment of 70,000 seeds to the botanical gardens at Kew in London. As earlier efforts to raise rubber seedlings in England had failed, these were given such high priority that customarily prized plants were summarily removed from the hothouses to make room for the rubber. The seedlings succeeded, and the plants were sent to Ceylon, Malaya, and other parts of the Far East.

Sir Henry was as excited by the possibility of finding a new source of edible oil in the caryocar trees of the Amazon basin as he was by the idea of expanding the range of natural rubber. Not only does this tree produce two edible oils, both excellent for cooking, but its kernels, similar to Brazil nuts in taste, had been described by early explorers of the Amazon as "the most delicious nuts in the world." And the wood from some species of caryocar is so hard that it is suitable for shipbuilding, a matter of some importance to the British at that time.

With the same vigor he had applied to the rubber venture, Sir Henry sent seedlings from caryocar trees to the Far East. But where the hevea trees became virtually the only source of natural rubber, the stands of caryocar were neglected for decades, only to gain attention today, in our search for alternative sources of scarce and costly raw materials.

12

Life at the
Boiling Point

"The upper temperature for life as we know it has not yet been defined," stated Thomas D. Brock of Indiana University, after finding bacteria carrying out all their life processes in the alkaline hot springs of Yellowstone National Park in water at the boiling point (197.6 to 199.4 degrees Fahrenheit at that elevation). And these microbes evolved in a world where the average temperature is 53.6 degrees.

The beauty of the springs stems in part from the living things within. "The water was of a deep indigo blue boiling like an immense cauldron," Osborne Russell, a trapper in Yellowstone from 1834 to 1843, wrote in his journal. In the boiling lake, streams of water were white to the west, red in the middle, and light blue on the east. Russell could not quite believe that these colors represented living cells and left the explanation of the phenomenon to "some scientific tourist" of the future. The "scientific tourist" in time proved that the colors were alive. Mixtures and layering of bacteria and algae produce the red, white, and pale blue Russell described and, in other springs, form mats of flesh pink, pale yellow, emerald green, and cedar brown.

The simpler the organism, the greater the amount of heat it can bear. Bacteria can tolerate higher temperatures than algae; in waters just below the boiling point they multiply so vigorously as to double in number every two to seven hours. Temperatures at or even above the boiling point do not inhibit the growth of some species. In the superheated pools in Yellowstone, so named because the water temperature is above the normal boiling point but has properties that keep it liquid, there is constant bubbling and rippling and life is not so clearly evident. But it is present. When Brock pulled up glass slides left in the water for a week to ten days, a film of bacteria was evident.

Some bacteria, very similar to those found in the hot springs, have been identified in hot-water heaters in homes and commercial laundries. Water temperatures here range from 149 to 177 degrees, no hindrance at all to the microbes. These bacteria are not known to do any harm, and their presence is more of intellectual than other interest.

Blue-green algae, the simplest of all plants, are able to grow at 163.4 to 167 degrees, and this can be taken as the uppermost limit for any form of plant life. The more complex eucaryotic algae, which unlike the blue-green, contain a true nucleus, are limited to 131 to 140 degrees, as are fungi.

Great heat plus a complete absence of water would appear to be a combination of stresses intolerable for any form of life. However, a bacterium, *Sulfolobus acidocaldarius*, was recently found growing in hot sulfuric acid, fulfilling all its metabolic needs by oxidizing the elemental sulfur present in the spring.

Even so, bacteria and all other organisms do better in pools where the water is alkaline. Acid does set a temperature limit for life. When water in the hot springs is acidic, the amount of heat tolerated by the greatest thermophiles, or heat lovers, is reduced. Algae stop growing at 131 to 132.8 degrees, and bacteria cease their activity at between 158 and 167 degrees.

The hot springs have been dated to the Precambrian Era, and ancient rock formations contain fossils very much like certain thermophilic Flexibacteria existing today. Fossils resembling blue-green algae are evident in rock three billion or more years old. The history of this planet, born in heat, is such that it is logical for life at high temperatures to have preceded life at medium or low temperatures. Perhaps during the millennia when the earth as a whole was hotter than it is today, these thermophilic microorganisms had a much wider range. If that is so, then organisms flourishing at lower temperatures could have evolved over the ages from higher-temperature ancestral forms.

As their long history indicates, algae are exceedingly resilient and can snap back repeatedly after catastrophes. The hooves of elk and buffalo tear the algal mats when they cross the hot springs, and tourists rip off bits or drop in heavy cans and bottles. On August 30, 1967, a sudden storm hurled six inches of hail upon the lower Geyser Basin of Yellowstone. The lush mat of algae was badly damaged, even totally destroyed in some areas; not a trace of the characteristic greenish color was evident. On the eighth day after the storm, a visitor to the park noticed a faint tinge of color along the hot spring's bottom. In another two weeks the mat was forming again, and in less than five months it was just as before.

The preference of algae for warm water, and their ability to survive disaster, becomes a problem in streams where effluents from power plants and other factories are discharged, creating conditions comparable to those of the waters in Yellowstone.

While higher plants are found in hot-spring regions, they have a lower heat tolerance than do the primitive algae and grow around rather than in the boiling water. The visitor to the springs is most likely to see the monkey flower, a member of the snapdragon family, which puts out its roots in soil temperatures of 104 to 113 degrees.

Animal life exists in the cooler hot springs only, because even invertebrates are far more frail in regard to great heat than are microbes or simple plants. The upper temperature limit for animal growth is 122 degrees. One will hear an occasional report of a primitive creature such as an ostracod being kept alive in a laboratory for an hour at 123.8 degrees or for a minute at 132.35 degrees, and every so often an ostracod will be found in the wild in a stream with waters of nearly 125 degrees, but for the most part, at temperatures above the 122-degree limit the invertebrate is merely surviving, not growing or reproducing.

Because fish often swim in hot springs, it seems as though they endure high temperatures as well as the algae. But this is an illusion. Fish can stand water no hotter than 104 degrees. In 1875 the German scientist Felix Hoppe-Seyler looked for fish in a canal with a known surface temperature close to 113 degrees. Many small fish were swimming back and forth, but when he bent down to the water, he saw that the fish were not really that close to the surface. They remained in the deeper layers of the water, where the temperature was a very moderate 77. When a fish did by accident get into warmer water, it either swam back down rapidly or died. The ability to survive life at the boiling point is thus limited to microorganisms.

The high humidity and heat of tropical jungles encourages microbes to an excess of activity. The great stone monuments of the Maya, buried after the collapse of this classic civilization around A.D. 900 and rediscovered in the twentieth century, are being defaced by the vigorous growth of lichen and blue-green algae. Archaeologists are hard-pressed to read the hieroglyphics on the surfaces, blurred and sometimes obliterated as they are by heat-loving organisms.

When missiles that had been in the U.S. Army Tropic Test Center in the Canal Zone from one to five years were returned to the White Sands Missile Range, representatives of 79 fungal species and 6 bacterial genera were growing in wild profusion on them. Cork gaskets of missiles that had been in the tropics for just one year had 310,000 bacteria growing on them and no fungi. Those returned after five years were colonized by bacteria too numerous to count, and 37 million fungi had appeared. Materials containing organic matter were most heavily invaded.

The clothes of travelers to the tropics rot or become discolored with mildew, shoes are covered with mold, paper disintegrates, and the glass lenses of cameras and telescopes are damaged. Food is rapidly taken over by hordes of microbes. But the fondness of microbes for heat has consequences far more devastating than these. While most common microorganisms are destroyed by boiling, life at or above this point is not limited to hot springs—unfortunately. Some heat-resistant microbes produce terrible illnesses that are extremely hard to control.

In 1956 Dr. D. Carleton Gadjusek journeyed to the eastern highlands of Papua to study a strange disease afflicting the Fore, a people living in a Stone Age culture. The natives called the illness kuru, and victims died within a year. It took Gadjusek two years to make his way through the 169 mountain villages inhabited by these people and during that time he found 3,000 cases of kuru. Observing that the disease was known nowhere else in the world, he learned that it was a mourning custom among the Fore for the bodies of the dead to be cut up, cooked, and eaten. The disease was passed from the dead to the living by means of this religious cannibalism. Cooking did not kill the virus that caused kuru, said Gadjusek, who was later to win the Nobel Prize for his work on unconventional viruses. Only when the ritual requiring the eating of human flesh was ended among the Fore did kuru begin to disappear.

It might seem that a rare soon-to-be eliminated disease found only among primitive peoples of the New Guinea highlands has nothing to do with anyone living in the cities of Europe and the United States. Yet a tragedy remarkably similar to what happened to the Fore had its beginning in 1974 when a sixty-nine-year-old woman entered a neurological clinic in Zurich, Switzerland, for depression, anxiety, failures in muscular coordination, and memory lapses. Soon she began to make jerky epileptic motions. To help in the diagnosis, silver electrodes were implanted in her brain. Eventually the patient lapsed into a coma and died.

A few months later a woman of twenty-three with intractable epilepsy entered the hospital for neurosurgery, and nine silver electrodes were implanted. She recovered from the surgery, returned home, and subsequently became pregnant. In the course of her pregnancy, memory lapses, blurred speech, and difficulty in walking became evident. The infant was delivered by cesarean section and did well, but the mother continued to deteriorate and lapsed into a semi-stupor.

Not long after this baby was delivered, a young man of nineteen died in a state of dementia. Two years earlier, he also had undergone neurosurgery at the Zurich clinic for epilepsy, and seven electrodes had been implanted in his brain.

The electrodes were the link between the three. Those used on the young woman and the man had previously been implanted in the sixty-nine-year-old patient, whose illness on autopsy was diagnosed as Creutzfeldt-Jakob disease (CJD), caused by a virus similar in type to the one responsible for kuru. This disease possesses the dread faculty of causing a senile dementia, even in the young, coma, and death. Considering the seriousness of the disease, one might ask why the electrodes were used more than once. But as the physicians explained, the electrodes had been cleaned with benzine and disinfected with 70 percent ethanol before being sterilized in formaldehyde vapor for 48 hours or more, a technique that had never before failed to destroy all pathogens.

Although many people have never heard of it, Creutzfeldt-Jakob disease causes the deaths of at least 200 people in the United States annually. In Israel the incidence among Jews of Libyan origin is thirty times higher than among those who come from Europe. It is the custom for members of this ethnic group to eat the eyeballs and brains of sheep, which may be infected with scrapie, another neurological disease that is caused by the same kind of virus as the ones for both kuru and CJD.

These viruses are among the most heat resistant on earth, surviving not only boiling and treatment with disinfectants but also ultraviolet radiation, ionizing radiation, and ultrasonic energy. To kill these viruses requires an hour of steam sterilization in an autoclave at 250 degrees Fahrenheit and 15 pounds of pressure per square inch. (Just about all other organisms die if autoclaved for even fifteen minutes.)

While the diseases caused by these extraordinary viruses are rare, more familiar human illnesses can be traced to many other pathogens that survive most cooking methods, including, in some cases, boiling. Microbes such as clostridia, and other bacilli which reproduce by means of spores are the hardest to kill by ordinary cooking. The bacterial cells may be destroyed, but the spores live on to produce more damaging bacteria.

The heat endurance of the spores of one common soil bacterium is behind a great many human tragedies, such as one that occurred on a southern farm not long ago. It started with what seemed to be just an ordinary stomach upset for the farmer's wife. But the familiar symptoms of nausea, vomiting, and weakness were soon followed by some that were bizarre. The woman began to see double and then to have difficulty in swallowing, followed by an inability to get words out at all, and then a paralysis of other muscles set in. The doctor was called and, after puzzling for a while, asked if she did her own canning. Yes, her daughter reported; her mother had cooked and eaten some of her canned string beans for lunch the day before. No one else in the family liked string beans, which was lucky for them.

Botulism, the most dangerous of all forms of food poisoning, can cause paralysis of the respiratory muscles. If that happens, the victim may die of suffocation.

The peculiar nature of the symptoms, which involve the nervous system more dramatically than the gastrointestinal, often confounds diagnosis, particularly in areas where home canning is not the custom. The seemingly unrelated symptoms are brought about by the nerve toxin released in the food by the bacillus *Clostridium botulinum*. The enzymes in the digestive tract do not inactivate this toxin. Some patients are far more sick than others, either because they ate more of the food or because it was more grossly contaminated. Still, toxin sufficient to kill a human is infinitesimal in quantity.

In addition, the victims may not be fortunate enough to know they have eaten poisoned food. It does not invariably taste bad, and they may feel perfectly well all day and possibly much of the next day, too. Yet the failure to diagnose and treat promptly can be catastrophic. Well over half of untreated cases end in death. An antiserum can be given, but it works best when taken early, ideally when the contamination of the food is recognized and before the illness is apparent.

The toxin-producing organism can grow only in the absence of air, which is why the illness is not more frequent. A 1972 upsurge of interest in home canning was noted by food technologists; it was accompanied by an upsurge in cases of botulism. Commercial canning procedures utilize temperatures sufficient to kill the spores. Some seventy cases of botulism were reported in the United States in 1980. In a study made of twelve recent episodes, eleven were traced to home-canned foods. The largest single epidemic in the United States struck 45 persons who had consumed home-canned peppers. Foods low in acidity, such as fish, meat, poultry, milk products, soups, corn, pumpkins, figs, asparagus, and spinach, are most often responsible. In France and Spain, where home-cured meats are commonly eaten, botulism has often been traced to sausages and hams.

Tests by a Council for Agricultural Science and Technology Task Force headed by Richard V. Lechowich of Virginia Polytechnic Institute and State University found one botulinum spore to every one to seven pounds of meat products. Aside from sufficient heat, a nitrite (implicated in some animal tests as producing a possible carcinogen but not banned by the Food and Drug Administration) is the only single substance that controls the botulinum spores and prevents toxin formation.

A related organism, *Clostridium perfringens*, sickens far more people than the *botulinum* but much less severely. It is a frequent cause of the twenty-four-hour intestinal "bug" of cramps, diarrhea, and nausea.

Food spoiled by staphylococci may neither smell nor taste bad. These organisms also produce toxins, but not lethal ones. Onset of illness is rapid, and so is recovery. Shortly after getting home from a Fourth of July picnic catered by a local restaurant, a young woman was troubled with gastrointestinal symptoms. By the next day thirty of the once happy picnickers had become ill. Many others, however, were completely unaffected. In time it became evident that those who were sick had eaten liberally of a tasty chicken salad. Although the picnic was held in the cool of the evening, the tables had been set up a few hours in advance, and the dishes taken out of the refrigerator. The mayonnaise used in the chicken salad provided the staphylococci with the nutrients they like best for growth, and the hours of warmth were sufficient to encourage them to activity. Where did they come from in the first place? The local health department examined everyone who had been handling the food on the day of the picnic and discovered a skin infection on the arms of one of the cooks.

Staphylococcal food poisoning is preventable, as the organisms themselves are destroyed by sufficient boiling. However, if the food is then handled by an infected person, the staphylococci will get into the food, flourish if it is warm, and secrete their toxin. And once this has been produced, no amount of cooking will kill it.

Because most forms of food poisoning originate due to improper handling, detective work to uncover the source of epidemics has priority in health departments. In late June of 1978, food poisoning broke out in Erie County in upstate New York. The illness, diagnosed on the basis of specimens taken from the victims, was salmonellosis, caused by another very common bacterium. By comparing notes with other local health departments, officials learned that a similar outbreak was taking place in Cortland County, and before long it appeared in parts of Connecticut, Pennsylvania, and New Jersey. Estimates of how many people were sickened ranged from the thousands to the tens of thousands. But as few people with diarrhea are likely to inform a health department of their plight, it is clear that no estimate could be accurate.

Centers for Disease Control (CDC) epidemiologists were called in from Atlanta, and they traced the outbreaks to roast beef purchased precooked by delicatessens and restaurants. The Department of Agriculture responded to the threat of widespread food poisoning by issuing a directive that represented bad news for the millions who like their roast beef rare: Processors of precooked roast beef were henceforth to heat it to an inner temperature of 145 degrees or higher. Beef cooked to that temperature is medium or medium rare at best. While the order applied to commercial processors, it obviously contains good advice for home cooks, too. Heat sufficient to make meat "very well done" is not necessary: Unlike staphylococci and clostridia, which must produce toxins in order to sicken, salmonella organisms themselves are harmful. As they are destroyed at lower temperatures than are toxins, it is easier to prevent salmonella food poisoning.

It has often been suggested that orthodox Jewish and Muslim prohibitions on eating pork were originally to a large extent a hygienic measure, based on the empiric observation that illness (trichinosis) could follow such a meal. The roundworm *Trichinella spiralis* cannot survive prolonged and thorough cooking, so the danger lies in pork taken from infested swine and eaten raw or undercooked. Once in the comfortable warmth of the intestines, the worms mate and release large numbers of larvae, which mature and travel through the body. Their presence may induce diarrhea and other gastrointestinal symptoms, or swelling, fever, sweating, muscle soreness, and exhaustion, or no symptoms at all.

Pork sausages are the most frequent cause of trichinosis. One November day two Rhode Island families took a day's outing to a farm to buy a pig. Each family took half and prepared Portuguese sausages, which were smoked at low temperatures. Six people became ill. In another case on record, ten of seventeen members of a family became ill after eating home-prepared sausages. The two who had the worst cases were the cooks, who kept tasting the pork sausages while seasoning them.

A well-known stage and screen actor ate pork spare ribs at a fashionable restaurant in New York City. When he developed the most unfashionable disease of trichinosis, he blamed the restaurant for improper cooking of the ribs and brought suit. Eventually the case was settled out of court, but by then the newspapers had picked up the story.

Well over a hundred cases of trichinosis are reported to the CDC each year, states Dr. Myron G. Schultz, who heads the Parasitic Diseases Branch. The largest number occur around Christmas, possibly because home cooking, often including the making of pork sausages, is at a peak. More than 70 percent of the meat implicated was purchased in supermarkets and butcher shops, indicating the importance of thoroughly cooking all pork to an internal temperature of 170 degrees, no matter how much one trusts the butcher. Raw pork stamped "U.S. Inspected and Passed" does not mean that it has been examined for the parasite. Bear meat is responsible for another 5 percent of cases. Struck by this finding, the CDC investigated the bears of New England and learned that 1.3 percent harbored the parasite. This is thirteen times the incidence among grain-fed swine and points up the need for hunters to cook bear meat through and through. In 1979, 26 cases of trichinosis were traced to walrus meat, proof that one can never be too careful.

Meat or poultry cooked very slowly and at very low temperatures may never get hot enough to cause any parasites or bacteria that may be present true discomfort. The meat may spend too many hours above the 122-degree temperature, where growth of most bacteria is vigorous, and yet remain below the 145-degree mark, where growth is likely to stop. To be sure, many people cook in this way without getting food poisoning, because in the great majority of cases the meat is not contaminated to start with and does not pick up contamination along the way.

Contrary to common belief, freezing destroys some parasites but not microbes; it merely causes them to suspend their life processes and become dormant. Most will not grow in an ordinary refrigerator either, but they will not die. As soon as they warm up, they start growing again. This is not to contradict the truly tremendous effect refrigeration has had on reducing the incidence of food poisoning. Food that is free of harmful organisms when it goes into the refrigerator will usually be free of them when it is taken out. Molds may grow, but not bacteria and toxins.

For many years, therefore, efforts have focused on freeing food of organisms before it is sold. In the early 1900s the U.S. Public Health Service published a bulletin that was to have a major effect on national health by revealing that more than 500 outbreaks of milk-borne diseases had occurred between 1880 and 1907. The first reactions came from Chicago and New York City, which passed laws requiring milk to be pasteurized. In 1890 the death rate from tuberculosis stood at 240 per 100,000 of population. Eighty-four years later it was down to 1.8 per 100,000, a decline attributed in large measure to pasteurization.

In this process, the milk is heated for thirty minutes at 145 degrees (or less time at greater heat). This is more than enough to destroy the tubercle bacillus, the focus of pasteurization efforts, which dies in just twenty minutes of 140-degree heat. Pasteurization also prevents other diseases produced by organisms most likely to be present in milk—brucellosis, Q fever, shigellosis, a number of streptococcal infections, and salmonellosis. Because staphyloccal toxins are not destroyed, staphylococci must be kept out of the milk at every stage along the way from cow to container. The cow represents the greatest risk, as these organisms can infect the udders. Even if the cow is infected, the toxins will not be produced if the milk is refrigerated from the moment of milking to pasteurization. It is a mistake to equate pasteurization with sterilization. If milk were cooked to a temperature high enough to kill all toxins as well as all microbes, it would have an unpleasant boiled taste. Many organisms are not killed outright but are rendered inactive. The lactic-acid-producing bacilli survive pasteurization and, if milk is unrefrigerated, will reproduce wildly and cause it to sour. A few other harmless types also persist and can give milk a faint metallic or acid taste.

While microorganisms can survive both great heat and great cold, they are most active within a rather narrow range. And it is unfortunate that the favorite temperature for the growth and reproduction of myriad bacteria, viruses, and fungi happens to be the temperature of the human body. This fact is basic to all infection. The tubercle bacillus, cause of tuberculosis, grows from 86 to 107.6 degrees, finding 98.6 degrees the optimum. The gonococcus, cause of gonorrhea, can grow in a temperature range of 86 to 105.8 degrees but does best at 98.6. The meningococcus, cause of meningitis, can perform all life processes from 77 to 107.6 degrees but, again, finds 98.6 to be the very best.

Vibrio cholerae, which has the wider range of 60.8 to 107.6 degrees, still is most active at 98.6. Every year Muslims by the thousands make their pilgrimage to Mecca and cholera goes with them. In India, too, the religious journey on foot to shrines or to sit at the feet of holy men, and cholera goes with them. Although patients with severe cases are immobilized by the diarrhea, others are well themselves but harbor the pathogen and pass it along in their body wastes to contaminate water or food. The disease has been endemic in eastern India and Bangladesh throughout recorded history, with pandemics periodically spreading the disease over the world. During a 1977 outbreak, 900 new cases were reported in Syria in a single day. That month, health officials in Syria and Jordan urged Muslims to avoid the visits customary during Ramadan, the sacred ninth month of the Islamic calendar. Street vendors in Lebanon were forbidden to sell cookies and tarts to the children.

Americans are convinced that cholera could never run unchecked through the country. When cholera did strike here in the last century, many believed it was divine retribution, rather than inadequate hygiene—a retribution limited to the poor, to be sure. Cholera is endemic to countries where "Don't drink the water" is the classic traveler's advisory. If sanitation is poor, diarrhea can put trillions of bacteria into the water; after all, a patient can lose literally gallons of microbe-laden fluid a day.

So ghastly are the symptoms—and so lethal, before the treatment by full fluid replacement became standard—that in 1780 when an epidemic of cholera swept through the crew of the British warship *Seahorse*, lying off Madras, the surgeon looked at the men and said, "This is the *'mort de chien'* " (dog's death).

The custom of drinking hot tea instead of cold water, universal among inhabitants of tropical and desert areas, contains the spread of cholera somewhat. The boiling process kills or inactivates pathogens, provided it is continued for long enough.

When a case does occur in a country with good hygiene, as in Europe or the United States, it is usually quickly established that the patient has recently returned from Syria, Turkey, Jordan, Pakistan, India, Saudi Arabia, or Africa. An Englishwoman who developed the disease had returned from vacation in Turkey, and a West German truck driver became ill after going to Baghdad. In the United States even cases of such origin are so rare as to be memorable. One case was reported in Staten Island in 1911. "Since then there have been a few laboratory-acquired cases, but until 1978, there was only one other naturally acquired case, which occurred in Texas in 1973," noted Paul A. Blake of CDC's Enteric Diseases Branch.

At that time a fifty-one-year-old carpenter working in the public schools was admitted to a local hospital in shock and diagnosed by an alert physician as suffering from cholera. Proper therapy was instituted and the patient recovered, and then efforts to find the source of infection got under way. The CDC took stool samples from members of the patient's family, from all individuals who had traveled abroad and returned to the school, from local families who had recently immigrated to the United States, from fifty-two families who had stayed at a motel next to the mobile home of the carpenter, from crew members of a ship that had called at the port, from a local resident recently returned from Singapore who frequently dined at the restaurant where the patient had eaten the day before he became ill, and staff members of three university-based research laboratories in Texas.

The results of this massive search were negative. But there was one strange finding: A strain most closely matching the one that had made the Texan ill had been isolated from water in Makassar, in what is now Sulawesi, in 1959, and was the biotype involved in the seventh world pandemic of cholera beginning in Sulawesi in 1961. Perhaps the patient was infected by a long-term carrier who had originally acquired the infection during the pandemic. In any event, in the United States, with its good sanitation and water chlorination, a single case does not lead to an epidemic. The episode was considered closed.

Five years later two laboratory technicians noted an organism which they could not identify in a specimen taken from a patient with diarrhea in Abbeville, Louisiana. They sent the culture plate to the health department, and there the organism was identified as one far more familiar in Bangladesh or Saudi Arabia than here. Soon afterward, cholera was diagnosed in ten more Louisiana residents.

This time the outbreak was traced to crabs caught in the Louisiana bayous. These crabs, which harbored the bacterium, had been cooked at home for too short a time or at too low a temperature to kill the pathogens. The recommendation went out that crabs be boiled for 15 minutes. Further tests of the organisms isolated from the Louisiana patients revealed an odd connection: They were the same type as the one found both in the patient in Texas and Sulawesi. No more than that is known.

Even more mysterious is a case of cholera that occurred in Florida in late November 1980, in a patient who had not traveled recently. The apparent source of contamination was raw oysters, but this leaves the question of why the many other oyster-eaters in the area were spared. In any event, the timing of the disease was fortuitous in that the winter cooling of the Gulf waters discouraged the microbes from proliferating.

While most pathogens favor a comfortably warm environment, leprosy mycobacteria like to be cool. The first skin lesions appear on the extremities, because they have the lowest temperature of any part of the body. The skin is often 10 degrees cooler than the interior of the body, and the fingers, toes, and nose may be colder than that. After finding leprosy bacilli around the teeth of a Pakistani patient, British doctors took the mouth temperatures of 100 individuals selected at random and found that some teeth and surrounding gums were cooler than others. These are indeed the areas where lesions tend to appear in victims of leprosy.

This ancient "scourge" of humanity is still far more common than is generally believed, affecting 11 to 12 million people, according to Hubert Sansarricq, chief of the World Health Organization Leprosy Unit. Most of them are natives of the tropics and subtropics of Asia, Africa, and the Americas, but an estimated 2,000 to 3,000 people in the United States have the disease, and about 225 new cases were reported in 1980. The majority are in Texas and Louisiana and a few in California. They are a sad consequence of illegal immigration from Mexico, where there are from 25,000 to 50,000 cases, and from the Far East and Samoa.

The fear of leprosy has led to great cruelties, such as the enforced isolation of lepers on the island of Molokai in Hawaii. A middle-aged Hawaiian recalled that in 1937 at the age of six he was imprisoned for five years in a hospital ward with other leper children in Honolulu and then ordered to Molokai. No one is imprisoned in a leper colony today. The treatment and fate of lepers was revolutionized by dapsone, a sulfa drug discovered in the 1940s, and since then other effective medications have been added. Still, dapsone must be taken for two to three years to control the milder tuberculoid form of leprosy and from five to fifteen years or sometimes for life for the more devastating lepromatous form.

Hope for the conquest of leprosy lies in the development of a vaccine. Efforts to achieve this have long been thwarted because it has not been possible to culture the pathogen in the laboratory. However, two Louisiana scientists, Eleanor Storrs and Waldemar F. Kirchheimer, have discovered that the leprosy bacillus can be grown in great quantities in the nine-banded armadillo, *Dasypus novemcinctus*, known in many countries of Latin America as a particularly delectable food. This armadillo, which is about a foot long, has sharp claws, a brownish shell with characteristic bands, and no teeth.

Why the armadillo? This animal is particularly vulnerable to leprosy because of a body temperature of only 87.8 degrees. Not only its exterior but also its comparatively cool internal organs are as hospitable to the bacilli as are the extremities of humans and standard laboratory test animals. An armadillo with leprosy has far greater concentrations of the pathogen than a human victim of the disease; 150 billion bacilli have been obtained from just one liver.

"The armadillo which we consider to be the experimental armadillo of the future is *Dasypus sabanicola*, the pygmy armadillo which is native to a restricted area of Venezuela and Colombia," declares Storrs, pointing out that this animal combines the advantages of small size, ease of adaptation to captivity, and ease of handling.

Unfortunately, perhaps because their low temperature makes them sluggish, armadillos do not reproduce in large numbers. Even so, a few at a time, armadillos are proving valuable to the development of a vaccine.

13

Diseases of Tropics and Travelers

A conference of gastroenterologists was held in Mexico. Despite considerable experience in treating the intestinal ills of others, nearly half the attending physicians and their wives were struck by "turista," the name most commonly given to the relentless attacks of diarrhea often suffered by tourists in tropical regions (also known as the Aztec two-step, Montezuma's revenge, Delhi belly, and other similarly unappealing terms).

Although aware that drugs slowing the activity of the gastrointestinal tract may prolong illness by preventing the body from ridding itself of the infectious organisms, the physicians took them anyway. The treatment doctors advise when not seeking to stop the symptoms in time for a trip to the pyramids is to replace the fluids and salts lost in the diarrhea and be patient; most cases clear up in a few days. But if even the gastroenterologists could not resist anti-diarrheal medications, it is hard to expect it of less well-informed travelers.

Prevention being better than illness, treated or untreated, most tourists expend considerable effort to avoid polluted water and contaminated food. They consume only bottled water, soft drinks, beer, wine, liquor, and hot beverages made with boiled water. Some will purify water with a few drops of chlorine laundry bleach or iodine. However tempting, raw fruits and vegetables that cannot be peeled are refused, as are unpasteurized milk and milk products and food that was cooked a long time before and is no longer very hot.

It would be nice if following these golden rules guaranteed freedom from diarrhea, but many of the most careful travelers are, nonetheless, stricken. But the effort is not in vain, for these measures protect against the more serious of the diseases of poor sanitation: hepatitis, typhoid, and cholera.

Hepatitis is extremely common in the developing countries, and the longer a traveler stays, the greater is the likelihood of infection. Among soldiers and missionaries stationed abroad, cases of hepatitis begin to show up after about three months, more often after six. There is no specific vaccine against hepatitis, but inoculation with gamma globulin, which stimulates an immune reaction, is often recommended.

There are vaccines against typhoid and cholera, neither of them foolproof enough to allow the traveler to relax vigilance about water and food. The typhoid vaccine is effective for about 70 to 90 percent of those who take it and must be repeated every three years. The cholera vaccine, required for entry into a large number of countries, is only about 50 percent effective and lasts for six months or less. By contrast, a perfect record has been achieved by the oldest of vaccines, smallpox.

In October 1977, two patients with smallpox were being cared for at the district hospital in Merca, Somalia. The cook at the hospital, Ali Maow Maalin, came into their room from time to time. He began to feel ill, and on October 26 he too was diagnosed as having smallpox. The case was not a severe one and he recovered. This hospital cook has the dubious distinction of having been the last person ever to acquire smallpox from an infected individual. Every person who had been in contact with him was painstakingly traced and vaccinated, and the dread scourge of smallpox was eradicated from the earth. However, when an American planning a trip to Egypt that winter called the health department office advising on vaccinations for foreign travel to ask why smallpox vaccination was required when, according to the newspapers, smallpox was no more, the half-joking reply was, "Maybe they know something we don't know."

The World Health Organization was slow to declare the world to be smallpox-free. Public health officials had seen smallpox "eradicated" before, only to have it crop up again. "The last case of smallpox in the world will occur this month," declared a leading figure in tropical medicine in January of 1977. Two months later, cases began to show up among desert nomads in Somalia. The contacts of each patient were traced and vaccinated, and again the spread of the disease was halted.

It had long been believed that the only way to wipe out smallpox was to inoculate every person on earth. Because refrigeration of the vaccine was not feasible in much of the tropics, a freeze-dried product was devised. Because there were few physicians to cover areas of thousands of square miles, a special needle that paramedics could handle was designed. But still the gap between the vaccinated and the total population continued to be large. Transporting vaccines over vast impenetrable jungles and savannahs, often flooded or torn by civil war, sometimes proved impossible.

In December of 1966 a missionary in Ogoja province of Nigeria reported a case of smallpox to the public health officials. The missionary kept watch on the developing epidemic—six cases almost immediately, four more within the first week, twelve in the second week, and nine in the third. Health workers immediately vaccinated every member of each victim's family and others in the village who might have been in contact. By the end of the fourth week, the outbreak was over.

A new method had been found: Instead of vaccinating everybody, only the close contacts of each recognized case would be selected. The primary task of public health workers thus became detection. In Bangladesh, where smallpox had been common, fifty surveillance teams made up of four men each journeyed through the rice fields, forests, and towns, stopping each person they saw and entering each house. They carried with them photographs of victims of smallpox. "Have you seen anyone with these marks?" they would ask.

In tropical regions, smallpox remained endemic for decades after it had disappeared from the United States and Europe (the last case to occur in this country was in 1949 in Hidalgo County, Texas). As recently as the mid-1960s, smallpox was still found in forty-four countries, and estimates of cases ran to 10 to 15 million. More recently the World Health Organization offered a finder's fee to anyone who reported a new case. After October 26, 1977, no one came forward. The vaccine had at last triumphed.

Yet the long and terrible history of smallpox did not quite end with public health service detectives and Ali Maow Maalin. Nearly a year after he had recovered, a medical photographer in Birmingham, England, developed strange symptoms, soon diagnosed as smallpox, and died of the disease. Shortly afterward her seventy-one-year-old mother came down with the illness but recovered. The source of the virus was vigorously sought, the search focusing on a laboratory where research into smallpox was going on—on a lower floor of the building where the photographer had her studio. Apparently the virus had been borne upward to her on the air.

As a result of this accident and the furor that ensued, controversy promptly arose in scientific circles, with some saying that all stocks of the virus should be destroyed and others insisting that making any form of life extinct runs counter to scientific philosophy. Would one save the tiger and not the virus? And might not the virus do some good after all, they asked? It might be needed in order to identify illnesses that look like smallpox but are not. In West and Central Africa in the early 1970s, seventeen patients were found to be suffering from symptoms that were identical to those of smallpox. Laboratory examination of specimens revealed a slightly different virus, a monkey pox that probably spread from animal to humans.

Even if smallpox is gone from the earth, the fear of disfigurement and death is so enduring that even after the Centers for Disease Control declared flatly in 1979 that "international travelers no longer have biological reasons for being vaccinated," 51 percent of countries in Africa, 31 percent of those in Asia, and Bolivia and Belize in the Americas were still requiring vaccination of anyone who would enter. And it was no longer possible to suggest that they "knew something" that we do not.

The last of the major diseases for which inoculation is required by many countries is yellow fever, which to most of us seems an exotic, historic disease. Its conquest is a part of medical mystique, where the heroic doctor researcher takes the ultimate risk. During the early years of this century the U.S. Army sent a Yellow Fever Commission to Cuba, because the disease was decimating the troops. A Cuban physician, Carlos A. Finlay, suggested that the fever was transmitted by an insect; investigating this theory, Dr. Jesse Lazaer, a member of the commission, was bitten by a mosquito, contracted the disease, and died. With the theory proven, mosquito control was followed by disease control. Only a few years later, however, the dread illness struck again in Panama, felling workers on the canal. A similar campaign against the mosquito halted the epidemic, and the building of the canal got under way again. But yellow fever has remained endemic in Panama, as well as in many countries of South America and South and Central Africa.

Recently cases began to show up in remote jungle regions of Panama. So few people live or work there that it did not seem likely that they could have infected enough mosquitoes to pass the disease. Two Smithsonian scientists, David Chalinor and G. G. Montgomery, then found that howler monkeys and, more surprisingly, sluggish tree sloths had yellow fever. They attached tiny radio transmitters to eleven two-toed and thirty three-toed sloths and followed them through the jungle. The disease also followed the trail. The insects which bit the monkeys and sloths then carried the infection to humans.

While poliomyelitis is not thought of as a tropical disease, it is so common there today and uncommon elsewhere—because of routine inoculations—that it might as well be. Plague, still a problem in many developing countries, is rarely much of a hazard for anyone staying on the tourist or businessman's route; only those who journey through remote rural regions where infected wild rodents abound need the vaccine today. Its effectiveness was proven during the Vietnam war, however, when very few cases of plague occurred among vaccinated soldiers at a time when several thousand cases were reported among the Vietnamese.

Until comparatively recently, it was assumed that anyone who traveled to a tropical region would contract disease and quite probably die of it. Those posted on business to the tropics would be told how in 1841 four British ships carrying 145 men journeyed up the Niger River to establish a farm. Within two months, 48 of the group were dead of tropical diseases. Becoming appointed a curator to the botanical gardens in Singapore was for some years akin to receiving a sentence of death. Three curators who arrived in Singapore from 1875 to 1889 died there of fever.

The fever that most often struck foreigners and natives alike in Asia and in Africa was malaria. In parts of tropical Africa, malaria is described as "stable," which is a euphemistic way of saying that there is no season when malaria is not being transmitted. This means, of course, that there is no season when the carrier Anopheles mosquito, perfectly adapted to heat and humidity, cannot function. This being so, a genetic adaptation offering some measure of protection evolved among native Africans—and is to be found among their American and African descendants. This adaptation, sickle-cell anemia, is a condition in which the red blood cells assume the distorted shape of a sickle. Since plasmodium malaria parasites cannot grow so well in cells of this shape, Africans subject to this disorder were the ones most likely to survive in areas with a high incidence of malaria, and they passed on the trait. Today, in the United States, sickle-cell anemia, affecting one in every 400 black Americans, presents much more of a health risk than does malaria.

Despite the frequency of sickle-cell anemia in many parts of Africa, malaria continues to be widespread. More than a million children die of the disease each year. "Everybody gets malaria here. I don't know anybody who doesn't have it." This statement does not date back to eighteenth- and nineteenth-century eras of exploration but was voiced recently by a worker on a rubber plantation in Acre, western Brazil. Like many of his co-workers, he had originally come into the town of Rio Branco seeking work. Unable to pay his hotel bill, he was enlisted by a labor foreman and taken into the jungle to clear the brush and slit the rubber trees for latex. Workers too sick with malaria to collect enough latex to pay for their food, he commented, became so burdened with debt that they were never able to improve their lot and leave the jungle labor gang.

To Americans, malaria has been one of the unwanted spoils of foreign wars and a matter of concern, as the carrier mosquito is found in this country as well as in the distant tropics. In 1952, thirty-five Camp Fire Girls in California came down with the illness after an outing in an area where a Marine veteran of the Korean war had camped out. The results of the Vietnam war in terms of bringing home malaria are also impressive: In 1969, 4,062 cases were reported in the United States and in 1970, 4,230. These figures compare to 616 for a typical peacetime year, such as 1978.

But typical can rapidly change to atypical, and a study of malaria statistics might almost serve as a study of world events. In 1980, more than 1,900 cases were reported. Why the sudden increase? The Centers for Disease Control had the answer: Starting in August 1979, the number of refugees from Southeast Asia entering this country rose to 14,000 a month. Most of the cases were among these refugees, with the largest single group being Vietnamese from refugee camps in Indonesia and elsewhere in the Far East.

In the United Kingdom, immigration from Africa and India accounted for the bulk of the 2,053 cases, highest in recent years, reported in 1979. The disease was also diagnosed in tourists, travelers on business, children going to see parents abroad, and military personnel. Five Britons who had contracted the illness on trips to Africa died.

Today, with malaria of epidemic proportions in sixty countries, it remains the most hazardous tropical disease to the traveler. Anyone who visits a country where malaria is endemic—and the Centers for Disease Control publishes a regularly updated list—is strongly urged to take a prophylactic drug, starting one week before the trip, continuing throughout the time spent in the foreign country, and for six full weeks after the return.

A merchant seaman suffered chills and fever, so on returning to the United States he went to a doctor, who diagnosed pneumonia. Feeling steadily worse, he entered a hospital, where the blood smear revealed malarial organisms. The ship's captain recalled that the seaman had gone into the countryside during a stopover on the Ivory Coast. Prophylactic medication stood on the tables in the crew's mess, but apparently he had not taken any.

A stranger-than-fiction series of events took place in California a few years ago. Every evening after dinner the woman in the case sat in her garden until darkness fell, disregarding the swarming mosquitoes. She suddenly became ill with malaria, although she had not traveled abroad. But health department investigators found a possible connection between her illness, a man living a quarter of a mile away, whom she had never met, and a fourteen-year-old recent immigrant from the Punjab in India. These two knew one another, and the Indian boy had been on a visit shortly before having a relapse of the malaria he had first caught in India. It was not long before his host developed malaria as well. The illness then struck a boy of eight who had been helping his father work a ranch just a mile away.

The link between the four cases appeared to be the mosquitoes which bred in a nearby gravel pit. They probably became infected first by biting the Indian, then by biting his host (who, being in the earthmoving business, often worked in the pit), moved on to the woman in her garden, and finally to the little boy on the ranch.

Another odd episode in American malaria annals began when a woman entered a small Georgia hospital for treatment of a bleeding ulcer. The ulcer improved, and she returned home. Ten days later she was back with chills and fever, and plasmodium parasites were found in her blood. The patient had not traveled abroad, and the only out of the ordinary thing that had happened to her was that she had received nine blood transfusions to replace the amount lost in surgery. The nine donors were tracked down, and one had served in Vietnam. The parasite had entered the woman's body with his blood.

When a malaria patient who was a heroin user was admitted to a hospital in Los Angeles, the troubled doctor asked whether the injection equipment had been shared with anyone during the previous month. Yes, replied the addict, with seven people, one a veteran of the Vietnam war. This young man was located and questioned. Yes, he had been ill with malaria overseas. Had he shared injection equipment with anyone besides the patient? Yes, he replied, with eight other persons.

Justice clearly is not done. The effects of the failure to take prophylaxis falls on others.

The most efficient way to stop malaria is to wipe out the Anopheles mosquito. In the 1940s, fields, stagnant ponds, and marshes where the mosquitoes come to breed were sprayed with DDT. Public health workers went through many tropical slums shack by shack, spraying the walls. They were not always welcome. In Oaxaca, Mexico, the exterminators were given the unflattering name of *los matagatos* (cat killers), because cats picked up the insecticide on their fur, licked it off, and died of it.

DDT was so effective that the eradication of malaria appeared to be at hand. The number of reported cases in India fell from 100 million in 1952 to 60,000 in 1962. But by the following decade the incidence was back up in the millions. And today, worldwide, malaria cases are estimated at 200 to 300 million a year. Enough mosquitoes learned to live with DDT to foil the efforts.

In order to stay a few jumps ahead of the rapidly mutating mosquitoes, new insecticides and methods of biological control have been developed. Male Anopheles mosquitoes are rendered sterile and released into their natural environment to compete with normal fertile males for the females.

Even though hopes that malaria would be wiped out by mid-century were dashed, there have been drastic cuts in its incidence and more than 800 million people now live in areas formerly malarial but currently malaria-free, says the World Health Organization, and as many or more are in regions where vigorous efforts at control are being made. Eradication, as with smallpox, may depend on development of the long-sought vaccine. A step toward this goal has been taken in the laboratories of Rockefeller University, where William Trager and James B. Jensen have succeeded in achieving continuous cultivation of the malaria parasites in human blood that was too old for transfusions. This readily available blood could free researchers from dependency on specimens taken from infected humans or owl monkeys, the most suitable animal host. The difficulty of obtaining this material has been a stumbling block to the making of a vaccine.

Conquest not only of malaria but of other tropical diseases as well has been slow in coming, because of the peculiar combination of stresses in the tropical environment. One might ask why malaria and so many other terrible and debilitating diseases are endemic to the tropics. What is there about these regions that encourages what have come to be known as "tropical" diseases?

Heat is the major factor, both directly and indirectly, and humidity, its companion in these areas, contributes greatly. Microbes, both pathogenic and harmless, and parasites of all kinds grow best in a hot, humid climate. To compound the problem, the many insect carriers of disease are stimulated to achieve new reproductive heights. In some regions they multiply at any time of year; in others they follow a seasonal pattern, as do the diseases they transmit.

The human population of the tropics is peculiarly vulnerable. For comfort at high temperature and humidity, clothing is wisely kept to a minimum. This helps to avoid heat injury, but it leaves the maximum area of skin uncovered and accessible to insect bites. Homes in regions where air conditioning is uncommon are also left open to insects. And added to all this is the fact that the native peoples are often ill fed, protein-deficient, and therefore susceptible to illness. Tropical diseases are to a large extent cultural as well as heat-related diseases, products of poverty, with its resultant poor sanitation, lack of medical care, and deprivations. Bellies are swollen with malnutrition or kwashiorkor or wasted with worms, cholera, or sprue. Sometimes confused with turista, sprue prevents the absorption of all but a small proportion of calories and nutrients. Because it does not kill, the presence of the disease often goes unrecognized. It is, after all, just one more of the weakening factors of life in the tropics.

"A child in a tropical country may be sick for one third of its life," says Kendall King of the Research Corporation, which sponsors investigation of some tropical diseases. Local customs may compound the nutritional problems of children. In parts of Africa, cattle serve the function of money, not food. The director of a hospital commented that when he visited homes of children suffering malnutrition, he sometimes found that while the parents owned thirty cows, the child had never received a cup of milk.

In addition to the estimated 1.4 billion people suffering from intestinal worms, there are 300 million with filariasis and 200 million with schistosomiasis. The skin of countless natives of Africa and the Americas is covered with the suppurating sores of yaws, blotched with gray or pinkish pinta, eaten away by leprosy or leishmaniasis. Legs, genitalia, arms, and breasts become elephantine when filaria worms block the lymphatic channels.

In some villages of Africa it is common to observe a chain of blind men, each holding the hand of the man in front, led by a small boy. This is the blindness of onchocerciasis, caused by worms that enter the body in the larval stage with the bite of the blackfly. Once inside, they grow into stringlike foot-long worms and produce tiny offspring which swim through the body, in time reaching the eyes. Medical field workers in Guatemala counted the blackflies landing on the bare legs of laborers on a coffee plantation. In November, admittedly a peak month, 45 flies an hour settled.

Dengue fever, also insect-borne, has been nicknamed "breakbone fever" because of the excruciating pain it produces. Agony of joints and muscles, a splitting headache, pain behind the eyes, a sore throat, and fever characterize this grim disease. Unaffected by antibiotics, it must run its course. The carrier mosquitoes, *Aedes aegypti* and *A. albopictus*, are among the greatest menaces of all those flourishing in tropical and subtropical heat, transmitting not only dengue but also yellow fever and other dread illnesses.

Dengue fever last appeared in Louisiana thirty-five years ago and remained, until recently, an exotic disease found in distant regions only. Just the occasional tourist venturing off the beaten track would pick up dengue. Then, in late August 1980, a case was diagnosed in Brownsville, Texas. Although the disease is present in Mexico, the patient, a five-year-old girl, had not traveled recently. When health officials performed a house-to-house survey, they learned of several cases of dengue-like illness in the previous month, most in the same neighborhood as the first patient. Knowing that the mosquitoes tend to breed near houses, the health workers searched the neighborhood where the first case had occurred. The mosquitoes were found breeding in containers with water in nearly one fourth of the houses. Within weeks the surveillance had turned up seven more cases in Brownsville and three in other Texas towns in the lower Rio Grande Valley. Dengue no longer seems so remote or exotic.

"My family brought me here when I became too tired to do any work," a peasant told a nurse in a hospital in Recife, Brazil. He was suffering from Chagas' disease, caused by a trypanosome protozoan and affecting an estimated 8 million or more South and Central Americans (as well as an unknown number of armadillos). Chagas' is the reason that Brazil has been called the "land of sudden death"; victims sometimes drop dead of heart failure in midlife without ever knowing they had the disease. The bloodsucking insect vector, called the "kissing bug" or the "shaving bug," often bites the face, favoring the eyelids when closed in sleep.

While Chagas' is accepted as a disease of Central and South America, animals infected with the protozoan have been found in the United States, and two human cases were reported in Texas. Blood tests taken in that state were positive in more than 1 percent of individuals with no known history of the disease, suggesting that the illness may go unrecognized.

Millions of Africans and Latin Americans are exposed to the tsetse fly, the carrier of the dread sleeping sickness parasite, a trypanosome related to the one causing Chagas' disease. The tsetse, brownish, bristly, and similar in size to the housefly, has but one food requirement: human or animal blood, obtained by piercing the skin or hide with its long thin snout. The fly injects trypanosome-containing saliva into the wound to keep the blood liquid. Although trypanosomiasis is curable, in the remote regions of Africa it often proceeds to its acute or sleeping phase. Outside of Africa, it is so uncommon that several Americans who became infected while on safari were treated for cancer because of their baffling symptoms.

The civil wars raging in Africa during the 1970s disrupted spraying operations. Undeterred by chemicals and encouraged by heat, by the end of the decade the tsetses had expanded their boundaries, and with the insects went the disease, afflicting animals as well as humans. "The wild game in Africa appears to be resistant to the tsetse, while commercial or domestic animals are not," states Lowell Hardin of the Ford Foundation. "Many parts of Africa have been destined to hoe agriculture, because the farmers could not keep a work animal such as a horse or buffalo alive."

"Typanosomiasis is the most formidable deterrent to the raising of cattle in an area of 4.5 million square miles of savannah in Central Africa," observed Roger O. Drummond of the U.S. Livestock Insects Laboratory. Efforts to control the disease include using insecticide sprays, clearing the brush, developing cattle that are tolerant to the parasite, and breeding tsetse flies that are sterile.

Sleeping sickness is but one of the frightening diseases common in hot climates. Around the turn of the century a British hunter was making his way through the rice paddies along the Yangtze River in China. In his notebook he jotted down the observation that the paddies were filled with snails. Soon afterward he was aware of a mild prickly sensation on his skin and then became sick with diarrhea, headache, and a cough. This hunter was one of the first Westerners to contract snail fever, or schistosomiasis, a disease seen throughout the tropical world. The snails, favoring warm-water habitats, are invaded by tiny parasitic worms, the schistosomes. So ubiquitous are these snails that they infiltrate even bowls of water intended for cleanliness. In Yemen, infected snails have been found in the fonts inside mosques where the religious wash before praying.

Where Chagas' disease has given Brazil the title "land of sudden death," Egypt was named by Napoleon Bonaparte as the "land of menstruating men," because of the bloody urine that often accompanies schistosomiasis. It has been estimated that about half of Egypt's population is infected.

In tropical regions where latrines, sinks, and showers are all but unknown, peasants infested with schistosomes relieve themselves in ponds, rivers, and canals, and the eggs pass into the water with the urine and feces. Large numbers of eggs survive in the comfortable heat of the stream and hatch. The free-swimming larvae must find and infest a certain freshwater snail of the type seen by the British hunter. If they fail to do so within twenty-six hours, they will die. Otherwise, once inside the snail, the larvae multiply by the thousands, flowing out of the snail's body and boring through the skin into the body of the next human to step into the water. So well adapted are the snails to their tropical environment that when conditions are not optimal, they aestivate.

Schistosomiasis can be prevented by eradicating snails or by using latrines and sinks or showers. It can be treated and cured with drugs. In the developing countries none of these measures is common. "This illness has little to do with doctors and drugs," remarked Otavio Clementino de Albuquerque, health director of the regional planning agency in northeastern Brazil. Fewer than half the people in the area he serves make as much as $60 a month. "People that poor cannot afford to invest in sanitary facilities."

Paradoxically, economic development is associated with an increase in schistosomiasis. As infected individuals move from their isolated rural villages to places where there are greater opportunities for making money, they carry the worm with them. When the Aswan Dam in Egypt made it possible for farmers in the region to irrigate their fields all year around, the increase in the amount of water was accompanied by increases in the number of snails and in the numbers of people with snail fever.

Although primarily a disease of poverty, schistosomiasis is so widespread that not all the affluent are spared. In 1977, Abdel Halim Hafez, a popular Egyptian singer, died at forty-six from complications of schistosomiasis. Tourists also have picked up the parasite while vacationing in exotic spots. The Parasitic Disease Drug Service of the Centers for Disease Control received 206 calls for drugs to treat the illness during the early 1970s. Many times this number of cases, it is believed, go unreported, brought into this country by immigrants from tropical countries. A physician with New York City's Health Department estimated in 1961 that there were 50,000 to 75,000 individuals with this disease in the city.

The belief that travel to tropical regions is dangerous is reinforced from time to time by the sudden appearance of a disease of strange and terrifying quality, particularly in Africa—a disease previously unknown to medical science, often lethal in effect, and without a cure. And so it was that in the fall of 1976 a native from the southern Sudan ran a high fever and headache and came to the hospital in Maridi, a remote primitive village that is, nonetheless, the regional center. He began to cough, to vomit, and to hemorrhage, and within a couple of days he was dead. His family came to claim the body, and two of them sickened as well and died. Soon the fever struck a Roman Catholic mission, and four Belgian medical missionaries died. The death toll quickly passed 300. Flights to the region were canceled, sections along the Zaire border were closed, and soldiers with submachine guns were stationed at the Kenya–Sudan border to check all those who would pass.

Diseases easily become established in the tropics. But by isolating the infected people and regions, authorities kept this illness from spreading. Epidemiologists entered 17,000 homes in 301 villages in Zaire alone to discover cases, hunt for rodents suspected of being carriers, and institute strict quarantine measures. The virus causing the swift and relentless fever was identified as a form of the Marburg virus, another terrifying tropical disease which bears the name of the town in West Germany where it struck laboratory workers handling infected African green monkeys and killed seven.

The most famous of the "killer" fevers, Lassa, made its first known appearance in 1969 at a mission in Nigeria. Doctors, nurses, missionaries, and researchers have been stricken since then. There is no vaccine, but some patients have been helped by a serum obtained from others who survived the disease.

Certainly no place on earth is completely safe from tropical diseases. New South Wales would seem to be a place where one could count on being free of the most exotic of illnesses. Yet a dock worker there became ill with a form of encephalitis and some years later had a stiff arm and then an onset of Parkinsonism. Doctors in the local hospitals were baffled by the combination of symptoms. After every other possibility had been ruled out, a test for Le Dantec virus was run and came out positive. This rare virus had never been identified outside of West Africa, and the worker had never been there. However, a few days before he first became ill, he had been unloading goods from a ship from West Africa, and had presumably been bitten by an insect hidden in the cargo.

While most of the "killer" fevers have raged across Africa, a number of strange temperature-linked diseases have arisen in the Americas. One of the most unusual was first described in the late summer of 1871, when a railroad being built from Callao to La Oroya in Peru reached a town 5,000 feet up in the Andes. An epidemic struck the workers, with fever, severe bone, muscle, and joint pain, jaundice, and anemia so total as to make dark-skinned men look white, reports Centers of Disease Control epidemiologist Schultz, a student of this illness. Others had another kind of sickness, with repulsive blood-filled tumors on the skin; many of them died.

A few years later a Peruvian medical student, Daniel Carrión, in an effort to learn more about how the disease developed, had himself injected with blood taken from the skin tumor of a fourteen-year-old patient. When he then showed the symptoms of fever and anemia, he realized that these and the skin tumors were different stages of the same illness. Carrión died of the disease, which was then given his name. (The colleague who had performed the injection was accused of homicide, but the charges were later dropped.)

Carrión's disease occurs only in valleys in the Andes that are positioned at right angles to the prevailing winds and are no lower than 2,500 feet above sea level or higher than 8,000 feet. "Even within this region, one can acquire the disease only from twilight to several hours thereafter," notes Schultz, because this disease is transmitted by the bite of tiny sandflies blown about by the wind. These flies cannot endure the dryness of altitudes lower than 2,500 feet or the cold temperatures at altitudes higher than 8,000 feet. Inactive during the day, they forage for food and are most likely to bite at dusk.

Sometimes, a link with temperature cannot be found, and yet it seems some link must exist. Multiple sclerosis appears to have a temperature-dependent range which has yet to be explained. This disease occurs much less frequently in tropical than in temperate climates. When natives of tropical countries move to the United States or Europe before adolescence, they increase their risk of getting multiple sclerosis. Conversely, if Americans or natives of northern Europe move to the tropics before the age of about fifteen, they reduce their risk considerably. However, those who emigrate after adolescence retain the risk of the place they came from.

The where, when, and how of many other illnesses are often determined by the life-style of the vector, and this is in large part determined by temperature. Rocky Mountain spotted fever, seen more often in the Southeast than in the Rockies, occurs only in warm weather, because the ticks which carry the infecting organisms to humans are active when it is warm and go out in search of food during the spring and summer only.

Babeosis is a tropical disease, similar to malaria and carried by a tick. In 1979 a patient was admitted to Massachusetts General Hospital with strange symptoms, and a laboratory technician who had served in Vietnam spotted babeosis parasites in the blood sample. Even so, the patient was not asked if he had traveled in Asia, Africa, or other regions where most people assume babeosis would be found. Instead, he was questioned as to whether he had been in Nantucket or Martha's Vineyard. In this country, the disease was given the nickname of Nantucket fever when, between 1969 and 1977, fourteen people on the island were stricken. Other cases showed up on Martha's Vineyard. The patient had never been in either place. He had, however, received blood transfusions, and one donor had been a summer resident on Nantucket.

The donor and most other victims, it was learned, had timed their stay on the island for the very months it is hot and the ticks are most active. Even in America, babeosis follows the pattern typical of tropical diseases.

14

The Many Faces of Fever

In early childhood we learn that fever is bad; it is a lesson never forgotten. Associated with our most severe discomforts, with malaise, nausea, dizziness, chills, headaches, and muscular aches and pains, it keeps us in bed, taking medicine by mouth or injection. Fever is the proof that one is really sick, a reason for staying home from school or work, missing appointments and parties, calling the doctor. When the temperature falls to normal, we are on the way to being well.

What is the point of fever? Many people believe its function is simply to give warning that a person is ill and needs care. It is essential to health in the same sense that feeling pain when touching a hot iron is essential. The fever itself, if not high enough to be dangerous, is an unpleasant byproduct or side effect of infection. Some scientists, however, are not satisfied with this simple explanation and suggest that fever has a second even more important function: Far from making us worse, fever helps us to fight off the pathogenic organisms that have invaded our systems. In other words, fever is good for us. Historical precedent for this view can be found in the attitude of the seventeenth-century British physician Thomas Sydenham: "Fever itself is nature's instrument."

Fever could be an evolutionary advantage, a theory in sharp contrast to the view that it is a weakness, but not so devastating as to cause humanity to die out. In seeking evidence of why such an uncomfortable manifestation should be good rather than bad, Matthew J. Kluger of the University of Michigan selected lizards of the species *Dipsosaurus dorsalis* to serve as models and infected them with bacteria. Being poikilothermic—cold-blooded—lizards do not run fevers as humans do, so temperature rises were achieved by warming their cages and observing the effects of different body temperatures on the course of their infections.

Within just twenty-four hours, half the lizards whose temperatures (and cages) were kept at 100.4 degrees were dead of the infection. However, only 14 percent of a group at 104 degrees were dead, and not a single lizard with a 107.2-degree temperature had perished. In sharp contrast to their feverish counterparts, lizards at a chilly 93.2 degrees were quickly consumed by the disease. In a week's time, every one of them was dead.

Severely burned human patients in the University of Michigan Hospital responded to fever in much the same way as the lizards, stated Kluger. Burn victims are very susceptible to bacterial infections, and these are often the cause of death. More of the patients who developed a mild fever survived infection, he noted, than those whose temperatures remained normal.

Certainly, there is no question that very high temperatures are dangerous. Hardly anyone has survived 113 degrees Fahrenheit for long. Any fever above 107.6 degrees (rectal) carries some risk of death. Few infections, however, produce fevers higher than 104 or 105 degrees, and by far the most common are in the 100- to 103-degree range.

Fever is a response to invasion by bacteria, viruses, or their endotoxins. The white blood cells release a small protein, the pyrogen, that increases the production of prostaglandins, the lipid substances found in many body tissues. These circulate to the temperature-regulating portion of the hypothalamus, which then dictates fever. Antipyretic drugs, such as aspirin, inhibit the release of the prostaglandins. They also increase sweating, which cools the feverish body just as it does the overheated athlete.

The chills when the fever is up, on the other hand, represent the body's effort to stay hot. The thermostat in the hypothalamus has been set a higher temperature, and all temperature-regulating mechanisms work to maintain that. The person with fever is so much hotter than the surrounding air that shivering, the involuntary exercise of warming, is begun.

As the body temperature rises, the basal metabolism rises with it— about 7 percent for each degree Fahrenheit. This speeds the heart, blood flow, and respiration. Extreme nervousness is usually present when the fever reaches 102 degrees; these patients are typically irritable. Another degree brings confusion, and one or two more can produce delirium. Children are particularly prone to high fever, and almost everyone has experienced the delirium it brings during an illness early in life. For years afterward at odd moments one can recapture that strange feeling of mingled horror and elation at the way everyday objects were altered. The ceiling was turning to a thick oozy custard dripping down onto the bed; moving figures lurked in the gloom of the room. Very young children may have convulsions when their temperatures rise suddenly.

While responses to fever are unpleasant to the patient, they set off reactions that are unpleasant for the pathogen too. At 107.2 degrees, a number of bacteria are so affected as to cease growing altogether, and they are damaged by temperatures considerably lower than that.

The secret of the benefit conferred by fever lies in the way it encourages the body to starve the pathogen, suggest scientists Ivan Kochan of Ohio's Miami University and Eugene D. Weinberg of Indiana University, Indiana. Bacteria require iron in order to grow and must obtain this from the tissues of the human or animal they have entered. As long as a person is well, the iron is tightly attached to the tissues by means of proteins. However, the invading bacteria release toxins that weaken the bonds holding the iron and produce compounds to carry that freed iron through the body. The bacteria then consume the iron. But fever changes all this. As the temperature rises, the ability of the bacteria to produce the compounds is reduced and they are foiled in their effort to get extra iron for growth and reproduction.

Not only is the amount of available iron reduced, but this happens at the very moment when the pathogen requires iron most. The *Salmonella typhimurium* organism responsible for food poisoning, for example, needs ten times as much iron at 104.5 degrees as at normal temperature.

Patients with protein-deficiency kwashiorkor are short of a key iron-binding protein and so have more free iron than is normal. These people are exceptionally vulnerable to infections and often die of them.

Fever also calls into play another protein that moves iron, zinc, and other metals out of the blood to the liver. Patients with viral hepatitis and liver damage are less well able to do this, and fever advocates attribute the long duration of hepatitis to this failure.

Deprived of these metals, the pathogens are less efficient in producing toxins and other harmful products. And at the same time, says Weinberg, the temperature itself can limit toxin production. Temperatures not high enough to prevent the microbes from growing render them impotent.

But before praising fever too fulsomely, it is well to recognize that aspirin given routinely to bring down fever does not appear either to prolong or to shorten an illness. More significant, some individuals who have good resistance run low fevers or none at all, at least for the more common infections, and they recover the most rapidly.

Those who see fever as good for you offer as a possible explanation that when the average person gets sick, there is an immediate drop in iron in the blood. Then comes the fever, accompanied by a second, bigger drop. But perhaps someone with an extremely effective immune system can fight off the microbial invader on just that first decline, while the less resistant individual needs all the additional help that fever would bring.

No matter how much harm it may be doing the infectious microorganism, no one suffers a fever gladly, and it is customary to seek to bring it down with antibiotics, aspirin, and alcohol rubs. The standard advice to drink a lot is sound, because of the heightened metabolism induced by fever and the copious sweating. "I myself can remember the Time when many Physicians would hardly allow their Patients a little Small-beer (much less Water) to cool their Tongues in a Fever," said an incredulous John Hancocke, rector of St. Margaret of Canterbury and chaplain to the Duke of Bedford, in 1722. Hancocke's opinion did not carry the day. In 1768, Surgeon Archibald Maxwell was moved to publish a work revealing the error of "the Use of cold Water in extinguishing FEVERS."

Indeed [wrote Maxwell], many ill effects are the consequence when it is administered rashly. . . . That navigator would be universally censured, who in delineating his chart should neglect to lay down the rocks and shallows: but alas such are the influences and predeterminations of vanity that in medical disquisitions, similar if not equally criminal omissions are frequently found.

Criminal or no, the water theory eventually won out, except in parts of the Far East, where rhinoceros horn is used both as a love potion—which might be expected to raise temperatures—and to reduce fever.

With or without rhinoceros horn, fever usually "runs its course," following the pattern of the specific disease. The final fall most often occurs overnight; the fever "breaks" and one awakens drenched in sweat, weak, feeling better, and much more prepared to give credence to the view that the fever was healthy, after all.

The view that fever is healthy has produced a rather odd corollary—that inducing fever is a sound means of therapy for a totally unrelated disorder. This practice, known as hyperthermia, has recently gained respectability in cancer therapy. However, for many years it was used almost randomly, sometimes producing discomfort greater than the conditions it was intended to cure. The caliph Watek Billah of a century or more ago, suffering some nameless disease, was heated in a warm oven so often and for such long periods that it is said he died of heatstroke rather than his original ailment.

Over the years a few luxurious touches were added. Rich tuberculosis victims of the 1880s were able to enter heating cabinets made to their measure. By the next decade, lupus, epilepsy, and arthritis patients were being treated with hyperthermia. At the Chicago Exposition of 1893, a cabinet heated with forty lamps and reflectors was displayed. The patient was to enter the cabinet nude and sit there with only the head outside. Light Institutes using this device were opened in many cities here and abroad; promotional material declared that the gout of King Edward of England was relieved by the light cabinet and that Kaiser Wilhelm had also been helped.

The idea of producing a fever in persons suffering from nonfebrile diseases by infecting them with a febrile disease instead of placing them in a heating cabinet came so naturally that in 1891 Professor Julius Wager-Jaurega was infecting the mentally ill with tubercular fevers. Objections were promptly raised, but as has occurred with many unpleasant treatments designed for psychotics, scientists of the time insisted that it was very helpful. Permanent cures, however, were rare.

It was not long before patients with arthritis, angina, and a host of other disorders were being given such devastating illnesses as malaria and dengue fever, which one would normally go to great lengths to avoid. (Dengue, it will be recalled, is the disease known as "breakbone fever" because of the excruciating pains it produces.)

Fever came into its own in the treatment of syphilis and gonorrhea before penicillin came into wide use. "Therapeutic" malaria was standard for syphilis, in particular, although some physicians preferred to use typhoid. This extreme treatment began with the injection of blood containing the malarial organisms into the frontal lobes of the brain, along with tetanus antitoxins. The fever that resulted reached 105.8 degrees, on the average, and lasted seven or eight days. The malaria was then treated with quinine. When the International Conference on Fever Therapy met in 1937, the result of such treatment of 435 patients with syphilitic paresis and paralysis was described and a cure rate of 81 percent claimed. In reviewing the medical literature of the 1920s, 1930s, and 1940s, physicians today will comment that hyperthermia did work for venereal disease, though the mechanism of action is not known.

The heating chamber did not go out of favor either. Diathermy, which produces local, not whole-body, high temperature, was used more often than malaria for gonorrhea. Electrodes were placed in the vagina of women so treated, and the temperature there raised to 105.5 to 106.5 degrees, occasionally to 109 or 110, maintained for twelve hours, and in many cases repeated twice. The physicians at the conference declared 113 of 121 women treated in this way had been cured and suggested that the gonococci were destroyed by the high temperatures. Similarly, when the genitals of male gonorrhea patients received local heating to about 107 degrees for five-hour stretches, with the treatment given every third day until symptoms disappeared, success was reported for 72.7 percent.

As fever therapy became more widely used, it was evident that a number of patients, particularly those over forty, did not tolerate it well, and some unpleasant side effects, occasionally even heatstroke, resulted. The advent of penicillin made malaria and typhoid out of date for syphilis and gonorrhea. But by then the potential of hyperthermia for cancer had been discovered.

The epidemiology of this disease suggested to some scientists that heat might be a protective factor. Many forms of cancer are less common in Finland and Japan than in most other countries, says Helen Coley Nauts of the Cancer Research Institute, and she points to the custom of sauna baths in Finland and the Japanese habit of taking daily baths in water heated to 110 to 120 degrees.

The era of cancer hyperthermia began a hundred years ago when the British medical journal *Lancet* reported the startling news that a patient with cancer of the lower lip, who had been struck but not killed by lightning, recovered not only from the shock but from the cancer. Then in Germany a patient with a cancer of the face caught erysipelas, a disease accompanied by a long-lasting high fever. By the time the erysipelas had gone away, the cancer had gone too.

In 1891 an American physician, W. B. Coley, had been amazed to see the reduction in size of an inoperable neck sarcoma after his patient became ill with erysipelas. It seemed only good sense to him then to infect other cancer victims with erysipelas and see what would happen. Coley did so for carcinomas of the breast, penis, head, and neck. Ten of 34 patients with inoperable cancers had remissions of their disease for one to seven years.

Infection is but one way of heating the body; there are others easier to control. In the mid-1960s, while searching through the basement of the University of New Mexico, Dr. Sterling W. Edwards came upon an abandoned iron lung. It was simple to pump it full of hot air with a hair drier and make it moist with a humidifier so that the patient's sweat would not evaporate and cool the body. The first five patients who tried it reported relief of their severe pain.

Seeking to improve his method, Edwards investigated further and learned that Dr. Robert T. Pettigrew, at the Western General Hospital of the University of Edinburgh in Scotland, had devised a most effective technique. After studying 82 patients, Pettigrew concluded that 108.5 degrees Fahrenheit was the highest temperature that was safe even in a hospital. It takes 280,000 to 300,000 calories of heat to raise the temperature of an average-sized man (154 pounds) to this point. The fever can be achieved by placing the patient in two polyethylene bags and then immersing him in a bath of molten wax. Some medical centers use the even simpler technique of circulating hot water through plastic blankets. And a more sophisticated method, an adaptation of the one used in open-heart surgery, raises the patient's temperature by carrying blood out of the body, heating it, and then returning it to the circulation. However achieved, the fever must be maintained for a number of hours and the treatment is usually repeated several times.

Pettigrew reported that the best results were obtained for cancers of the gastrointestinal tract, with eight of thirteen patients improving. Many more commented on freedom from pain and a sense of well-being.

Physicians came to hyperthermia via a number of routes. A stray cat with a sarcoma on its face was brought into the physics laboratory at Los Alamos where Dr. James M. Larkin was working. The physicists treated it with a radio-frequency generator, and the sarcoma disappeared. Impressed, Larkin subsequently used hyperthermia on cancer patients at the University of New Mexico. He found that, of forty patients, 43 percent had their cancers reduced in size and another 20 percent felt better. The best results were obtained for melanoma, gastrointestinal adenocarcinoma, and soft-tissue sarcoma.

Because hyperthermia is a new technique for cancer, patients treated in this way have usually first been treated by surgery, radiation, chemotherapy, or a combination of these—often repeatedly. And so, despite its many failures, Dr. John A. Dickson of England's Royal Victoria Infirmary remarked at a 1975 international symposium that hyperthermia's results for advanced malignancy have "never been surpassed." He warned, however, that systemic heating increases the metabolism of normal tissues and might render them more susceptible to cancer invasion.

While hyperthermia is beneficial in many ways, it is hard on the patient. Some suffer cardiac irregularities, with excessive increases in heart rate and rises in blood pressure. There may be a restless delirium or gastric upset and vomiting. At the end of treatment a great fatigue is felt, comparable to that at the end of a febrile disease. Administration of continuous anesthesia during the heat treatment and for hours afterward has been found to prevent these effects to some degree. Fever blisters and, in a few cases, superficial burns have been observed too. Children seem to endure fever therapy rather well.

Many of the problems attending hyperthermia can be circumvented by heating just the cancer, rather than the entire body, a method that works best for those that lie relatively near the skin surface. There is some evidence that local heating may stimulate a better immune response than is aroused by whole-body heating. When dealing with just the tumor, it is possible to kill the cells outright by cauterizing them with an electrical current, hot iron, or boiling liquid. Most widely used to destroy small cancers of the cervix, this technique has also been used to treat invasive cancers of the rectum otherwise removed by surgery. When the cancer is destroyed by heat, it crumbles and can be wiped away. Of 62 patients treated in this manner at the

Cleveland Clinic, 42 were still alive five years later, even though most of them were in their late sixties when the procedure was carried out.

Cautery kills the abnormal tissue. But it is also possible to damage tumor cells with lesser degrees of heat, achieved with hot water, hot air, ultrasound, microwaves, and diathermy. Just the part of the body where the tumor is located can be warmed by taking out blood, heating it, and then returning it to that area. This is a simpler version of whole body heating. In this case, the rest of the body remains at a normal temperature, while the tumor is brought to between 107.6 and 109.4 degrees, sometimes higher. The upper limit for local hyperthermia, however, is just about the same as for fever—about 113 degrees. At or above that point, normal as well as cancerous tissues are injured. And the success of both local and whole-body heating depends on using the temperature range that damages malignant cells only and leaves the healthy cells nearby unharmed.

As Dr. J. S. Stehlin of the Stehlin Foundation in Houston reports, "Every single cancer cell that has been checked in our laboratory in tissue culture is more sensitive to the lethal effects of heat than is the normal non-neoplastic [non-cancerous] cell from which it is derived." And, according to Drs. D. B. Leeper and K. J. Henle of Thomas Jefferson University, "The selective susceptibility of cancer cell metabolism to heat may be the agent that the therapist has been seeking for many years."

Why does this happen? Temperatures in the range of 105.8 to 107.6 degrees affect the DNA, RNA, and protein synthesis. The cytoplasm and nucleus shrink and other cell elements are destroyed. Changes that are transient in normal cells are lasting in cancer cells. Adding just a little more heat—107.6 to 109.4 degrees Fahrenheit for one to two hours—permanently impairs the ability of tumor cells to take in oxygen. In contrast, normal cells recover and perform respiration properly once the heat is removed. All cells are more heat-sensitive during the growth phase, when synthesizing DNA, than when resting. Since neoplastic cells tend to proliferate wildly, they are in a growth period more of the time than are normal ones.

A study that was to have considerable impact on cancer therapy was carried out in the early 1960s by Dr. George Crile, Jr., of the Cleveland Clinic. He implanted tumors on the feet of laboratory mice and exposed them to radiation; the tumors remained. Then he tried heating them; still the tumors remained. But when he both irradiated and heated the feet, the tumors were totally destroyed.

Crile then checked the records of all patients with sarcomas of the bone treated with conventional methods at the clinic from 1942 to 1962. Only one person had survived for five years. With such poor results for the standard therapies, it seemed worth trying something different. One of the patients who was brought to him was a girl of seven who was threatened with amputation after radiation had failed. The child's leg was first heated in a hot-water bath and then exposed to radiation. Three months later, the bone had recovered. Although the leg never grew to a normal length, it was still free of the sarcoma at a checkup six and a half years later.

A medical version of the one-two boxing punch is set into motion by combining radiation and heat in a variety of ways. The cancer cells are injured by the first procedure and then are prevented by the second from repairing this damage. The effectiveness of the radiotherapy is increased by 40 to 60 percent when combined with hyperthermia, and the X-ray dose can be lessened. After treating twenty patients with skin cancers, a German physician, K. Woeber, reported that when he added heat he was able to cut the radiation by 40 percent.

Dr. Max L. M. Boone of the University of Arizona Medical School went one step further in treating a woman with a painful vaginal cancer. The tumor was heated to 109.4 degrees, radioactive iridium was implanted, then removed, and the tumor heated again; then the patient was given chemotherapy. The tumor shrank to one tenth its previous size.

Hyperthermia prevents cells from repairing the damage done by anticancer drugs much as it does that by radiation. The chemical reaction rates within cells are speeded, which makes the drug more active. The heat increases the permeability of cell membranes, so greater amounts of the drug can get in. For these reasons, doctors say, it is possible to reduce the dose. Researchers report that the anticancer antibiotic Adriamycin is more effective in cells at 107.6 degrees Fahrenheit than at 105.8 degrees. One experimenter found that cells heated by ultrasound were damaged by half the quantity of nitrogen mustard required by tumors at their normal temperature.

For ten years, reported Stehlin, he had treated patients with malignant melanoma of the extremities with a powerful anticancer drug. About a third improved. Then he raised the temperature in the extremity by heating the blood carrying the drug, and eight of ten patients were helped. Fewer amputations were necessary. In the future, perhaps, local heating, whole-body hyperthermia, radiation, and chemotherapy may all be combined, suggests Boone, to act synergistically.

Heat is not a cure-all. Not every patient—or cancer—responds well to heat, whether given alone or with chemotherapy and/or radiation. Some do not improve at all; some very briefly, and some have side effects. Nor is hyperthermia completely risk-free, though a number of medical centers reported no injuries of any kind in large series of patients. Even with all precautions, some deaths have occurred.

Still, the results of initial trials are promising. As Dr. F. Dietzel of the University of Giessen, Germany, put it, "On the one hand, hyperthermia increases resistance of the body against cancer, on the other hand, heat damages the tumor directly."

Certainly, heat has not replaced more conventional cancer treatments. Use of hyperthermia is still at a comparatively early stage, and no one can predict how far it will go. But many physicians would probably agree with Dr. Donald L. Mott, Chief of Oncology at the University of Southern California, as quoted in a medical publication: "Hyperthermia is the hottest news in cancer therapy."

The fact that cancers are damaged by heat is surprising when one considers that heat is the normal state for a cancer to be in. One of the ways of diagnosing cancer is by measuring the temperature of cells or tissues. This diagnostic tool, thermography, is based on the fact that cancerous tissues metabolize more rapidly than normal ones and so are supplied with more blood and throw off more heat.

All parts of the body give off infrared radiation, and the warmer the tissue, the more intense the energy it emits. The thermograph records the various intensities in the form of a heat picture. In black-and-white thermography, the white patches are the hottest; when color is used, red is the hottest, orange is still hot, yellow moderately so. The thermogram does not actually show the cancer; what it does show is the presence of an area of high temperature and increased blood flow. Additional tests are needed to prove that a malignancy is the cause.

Thermography was most widely publicized as a breast-cancer screening method. Because it has not lived up to the hopes it aroused initially, many have become disenchanted with the technique altogether. Detractors point to the results obtained in twenty-seven screening centers where a variety of diagnostic tests were used. Half the tumors ultimately discovered by other means were in women with thermograms interpreted as normal. However, results varied widely from one center to the next, suggesting that greater or lesser expertise in reading the thermogram may have been the cause.

The cancers that could not be detected in thermograms may well have been cooler than the ones producing a clearly abnormal pattern. They may therefore have been developing more slowly, points out Dr. Herman I. Lipshitz of the M. D. Anderson Hospital and Tumor Institute. And, indeed, these cancers responded better to treatment than those which gave abnormal heat pictures. In addition, unlike radiation, thermography is harmless, an advantage in screening women without symptoms under the age of fifty, who are advised against any but the most essential diagnostic radiation exposure. Mammography would then be reserved for those with strongly abnormal thermograms. Pendulous or dense breasts which do not reveal much in mammograms present a characteristic heat pattern in thermograms.

Tissue temperature also points to a number of problems other than cancer. The thermogram can reveal when the blood flow through the carotid arteries to the brain is decreasing. This is most often due to a blockage within that artery and is a common cause of stroke. The blood volume of the carotid artery on each side of the forehead sets the skin temperature, and in a healthy person the whole forehead is almost the same in temperature. If the difference between the two sides is greater than 1 degree, a dark area will reveal the cool spot that lacks a proper blood supply. Unlike the breast thermogram, in which heat stands for trouble, in the thermogram of blood flow to the brain, cold stands for trouble. Similarly, blockages in the veins characteristic of impending phlebitis, or embolism, can be diagnosed by the cold dark patches on the heat pattern.

Thermograms may also reveal the exact site of pain by displaying, in patches of brightness and darkness, the heat of swelling and inflammation or the coolness of areas with a poor blood supply. They are, therefore, coming into wide use at pain clinics to determine the often elusive causes of chronic pain. One young patient at Mississippi Rehabilitation Center kept complaining that his wrist hurt, though no source of the pain could be found with standard diagnostic techniques; a thermogram displayed an area that was 3.6 degrees warmer than the rest of the boy's arm. When a surgeon opened the wrist at that point, an embedded rose thorn was discovered.

Even greater diagnostic puzzles have been solved by thermography. A workman hurt his knee in an accident on a construction site; long after the injury had apparently healed, the pain remained. Because the original swelling and inflammation had disappeared, the temperature of the knee should have returned to normal, but the thermogram showed a cold spot. In this case the injury to the area had caused the blood vessels to constrict, cool, and damage the tissues sufficiently to produce pain.

Once the source of pain is recognized by the heat picture, it can often be alleviated by heat. Many cancer patients have remarked on the pain relief brought by hyperthermia; simpler treatments, the hot-water bottle or electric heating pad, have soothed literally millions of aching joints, bruises, and cramps.

In Oriental medicine, the pain-relieving technique of acupuncture is traditionally accompanied by heat. Some practitioners do not use needles but rely on "moxabustion" alone, holding a lighted pellet of "moxa" to the acupuncture points. Any plant substance can be "moxa," a common one being mugwort, which contains a high concentration of plant oils and burns slowly and evenly.

The medicine man of the Cherokee Indians would warm his thumb and press it firmly against a tribesman's painful tooth. In a South African tribal practice, recorded some years ago, a man with chest pains went to the witch doctor with a friend. They waited while a metal hoe was heated until it was glowing. The friend then put out his foot, its sole nearly as hard as leather from a lifetime of going barefoot, and the witch doctor rubbed it with leaves that had been chewed and mixed with grease. The glowing hoe was placed against the sole of the foot and held there long enough to transfer its heat. The man then raised his hot foot and planted it firmly on the chest of his friend.

Poultices made of heated mud and leaves or hot mashed millet are traditional folk medicine. In Parnü, Estonia, thick black mud from the Baltic beaches is heated to 104 to 108 degrees, and each visitor to the Tervis Sanitarium there lies in the mud for fifteen to twenty minutes a day. "The mud encourages the organism to correct itself, to heal itself," states Robert Trink, who specializes in giving the mud treatments. The sanitarium is a cross between a hotel, in that it is a vacation spot, and a hospital, in that admission is by doctor's order. The bill is shared by the Soviet citizen and his trade union. Nervous disorders, insomnia, arthritis, rheumatism, convalescence after heart attacks, and just "to feel better" are the reasons for going there.

In the nineteenth century, hot sand baths, given the impressive name of psammotherapy, became extremely popular along the French and Italian Riviera. Vacationer patients lay on the beach entirely covered with sand, except for the head.

Bladud, the father of King Lear, so goes the story, was in 863 B.C. cured of leprosy by being covered with hot mud taken from the springs of what was to become the famous spa and resort city of Bath, 105 miles southwest of London. The Romans later built a system of baths, making use of the mineral waters that ran at a temperature of 114 to 120 degrees. To this day the British and other Europeans go to "take the waters" at Bath. Research into hydrotherapy has gone on there, and the Bath Orthopaedic Hospital was established to treat cripples.

Warm baths are universally used for pain relief. Pain is often due to the decreased blood flow resulting from injury or obstruction, and heat improves the circulation. The muscle cramp is relaxed by heat. Because the effect of hot water in soothing discomfort is enhanced by having the water move over the body, a motor installed in tub or pool creates whirlpools. According to medical historian Sidney Licht, the whirlpool was limited to "female complaints" until World War I, when it was adopted for use by wounded soldiers.

Warm waters flow from Pine Mountain in Georgia to a spring, and it was there that Franklin Delano Roosevelt frequently went to bathe and relieve limbs paralyzed by poliomyelitis. The health-giving qualities of the Warm Springs waters had been known to the Indians. A resort had been on the site since 1830, and Roosevelt, who went there frequently over the years both before and during his presidency, established a foundation for other victims of poliomyelitis.

Warm baths and whirlpools are obviously too enjoyable to be limited to the ill, and whirling devices have been installed in many home bathtubs and "hot tubs." Bursting into popularity in the late 1970s, the hot tub can accommodate one, two, five, eleven, or more people, as they rest comfortably on submerged lounges, sofas, or chairs, contoured to fit the body. The tub, which may be placed outdoors or indoors, costs thousands of dollars, is usually made of a high-quality wood, such as redwood, and comes in a wide variety of sizes. (One manufacturer offers tubs 29 to 60 inches deep, 4 to 12 feet in diameter, and 6 to 15 feet long. The size selected, he remarks, depends on whether the purchaser has a "large family" or "entertains a good deal.")

The recommended water temperature is 105 degrees for a few minutes, 102 degrees for longer immersion, but many are tempted to protracted stays at higher temperatures. Water in an ordinary bathtub is usually just as hot at the start, but it cools off, while the heating device in the hot tub maintains the high temperature even outside on a cool day. So interesting a "toy" as the hot tub is easily misused, and several deaths have been reported. The high temperatures can increase the stress on the heart. Alcohol and drugs do not mix well with hot-tub use, and some physicians are warning pregnant women to avoid staying in too long, citing the rise in body temperature that begins after immersion of just 15 minutes at 102 degrees as a possible cause of birth defects.

Such an attitude would stun the women of the ancient walled city of Zaria in Nigeria; they believe that baths hotter than the American hot tub are essential to health. From finding warmth good to declaring cold bad is but a short step, after all. Among many primitive peoples of tropical regions, cold is held to be at the root of all illnesses, and efforts to overcome it are extreme. Consider the young Nigerian mother who has just given birth and refuses to take the steaming hot bath that was ordered. The midwives of the tribe force her into the scalding water and splash it over her again and again with a bundle of leaves. She is required to take two baths a day for forty days and spend the rest of the time in a hut heated with glowing embers, lying on a dried mud bed that retains the warmth. After a few days she comes to accept the necessity of the baths.

The women of Zaria are noted throughout the region for their strictness in carrying out postpartum hot baths; when natives of neighboring cities adopt this custom, they are described as being "like the women of Zaria." The duration of the hot-bath regimen is never less than forty days and may be extended to four months among the most fervent believers. Unfortunately, the exposure to this extreme heat places such stress on the heart that cardiac failure in the first two months after giving birth is extremely common. Each new mother, however, undergoes this risk under the conviction that heat will protect her and her infant from all illnesses brought on by cold, or "sanyi."

The concept that changing cold to warm is healthful is current among some practitioners in the United States, who use this as the basis for biofeedback treatment of migraine headaches. The idea is that if the migraine sufferer, who usually has cold hands, learns to warm them, the headache will abate. Theoretically, when the blood vessels in the hand dilate, the painfully dilated vessels in the head constrict.

Biofeedback has been used with some success in helping people gain control over customarily involuntary reactions. The finding that warm hands may help migraine was made by serendipity when physicians at the Menninger Psychophysiology Laboratory were teaching biofeedback to patients seeking to lower their blood pressure and heart rates. Among them were some individuals with migraine, which from time to time coincided with the biofeedback training. Occasionally during the session, the migraine lifted just when the blood flow to the fingertips increased and temperature rose.

In the training, electrodes taped to the skin send a signal to electronic equipment, which "feeds back" an indication, usually a clicking sound, when the person is not relaxing muscles or warming hands. The goal is to make the clicking sound stop. In time many individuals become able to warm their hands or slow the heart without help from the equipment.

Finger-warming techniques may relieve other psychosomatic ailments triggered by stress, note members of the Department of Psychiatry at the University of Texas Health Science Center at San Antonio. A drop in finger temperature accompanies almost any startling or emotion-packed situation, they say. Even just the ring of the telephone will make the temperature of the fingertips fall a degree or so. Those people who develop physical symptoms when under stress tend to have cold hands and feet whenever they are tense, and warm ones when they feel comfortable.

This scientific observation fits in remarkably well with the principle behind the "mood rings" that come into style every few years. These rings turn color when the wearer is happy, go the advertising claims. The rings contain a chemical that changes color along with changes in finger temperature. Happiness in this case means warm.

15

Of Fire: Arson, Witchcraft, Volcanoes, and Cookery

"Do you get a thrill from it? Does it give you the sexual satisfaction you're not getting elsewhere?" a detective asks a suspect at the scene of a fire.

The heat and brilliance of a fire may arouse an emotion akin to that of sexual excitement. The thrusts of the flame are suggestive of the movements of the penis during intercourse. The "licking" flames are comparable to the flicks of the tongue. Thus, Freud described the sexual implications of fire. Viewing a fire and the setting of fires, therefore, can represent a desire to obtain sexual stimulation and fulfillment.

The pyromaniac feels forced to set fires out of an irresistible urge, an impulse with no apparent reason. To be sure, there is a motive, but it is one not readily recognized by the normal person.

Arson for gain or profit is far more common than arson out of pyromania. The owner of a building or business may find that he would collect more money from fire insurance than from rents or sales, so he sets the fire himself or hires a professional arsonist to do it for him. Malicious mischief, the desire to conceal other crimes, and the wish to defraud insurance companies are also frequent causes of arson. Insurance payments each year cover a good proportion of the $1.4 billion of property losses due to arson, noted by the National Fire

Incident Reporting System, as well as some of the indirect losses, which are estimated at anywhere from $10 to $15 billion.

The pyromaniac, unlike the criminal or profiteer, stands to gain nothing but enjoyment and release of tension. Most often, pyromania represents a distorted way of obtaining sensual pleasure. The fire fetishist has almost invariably been rejected, both socially and sexually. This type of arsonist has sexual problems even when he has a partner, but usually at the time the fire is set has no outlet for his sexual urges.

Fire is the ultimate sex symbol. Arsonists often dream of fire—pleasant, erotic dreams culminating in orgasm. Later comes the wish to experience awake what was felt asleep, and it seems clear that only the heat of a fire and the leaping of the brilliant red gold-flames can be sufficiently arousing for sexual gratification. Fire-setting may serve as a substitute for masturbation in individuals who believe such behavior to be damaging to health, sinful, and forbidden. In contrast, arson does not seem wrong and is satisfaction enough. Other pyromaniacs masturbate to climax, stimulated by the sight of the flames.

When there is a motive besides sensual pleasure, it is most often jealousy and/or revenge. The bed, clothing, or home of the lover who abandoned or deceived is ignited. One young farm worker set fire to his employer's barn, killing three horses and twenty cows, in revenge for being given leftovers for his lunch. Suicide by self-immolation is occasionally a motive, with five fires in Dade County, Florida, one year being set (successfully) for this purpose.

An arsonist imprisoned for repeated crimes explained to the psychiatrist that his obsession began when he was a soldier in Vietnam. He had received a letter from his fiancée telling him that she was going to marry someone else. As he looked up, the village before him was struck by an incendiary bomb and was consumed by flames. It seemed to him that he was seeing the body of his faithless lover being destroyed. Years passed, and on the surface he led a normal life. Yet whenever he was angered or felt rejected, he would set a fire to recapture the feeling that he was destroying a person who had wronged him.

Children are frequent fire setters, usually as a result of playing with matches but occasionally out of anger at some member of the family. These youngsters often describe a rich fantasy life in which they are in control of adults. Similarly, when women arsonists in a British prison were interviewed, many said that fire was their only means of attaining power over others.

In the nineteenth century it was accepted that fire setters were most likely to be pubescent females, an unstable lot. However, the statistics of arson do not bear that out. When the results of a study of 1,145 fire setters by N.D.C. Lewis and H. Yarnell were released in 1951, they revealed that the largest number were adolescent males, with the peak at age seventeen. More than two thirds were men of sixteen or over, and only 13 percent were adult women. The majority were below normal in intelligence. (This conclusion, however, may be unfair to the mental capacities of fire setters, because most arsonists are never caught.) Among adolescents from eleven to fifteen years of age, fire setting was often a gang activity. There were a few geriatric arsonists, most of them senile or psychotic.

About 40 percent of the adult males in the classic Lewis-Yarnell study fitted the pyromaniac definition, behaving out of blind impulse. Another 30 percent set fires for revenge or out of jealousy, and another 5 percent did so with the desire to put out the flames and so call attention to themselves as heroes. (This type of behavior has been noted from time to time in volunteer fire fighters and is behind the unfounded claim that firemen are arsonists.)

The young Zen priest protagonist of Yukio Mishima's novel *The Temple of the Golden Pavilion* (Alfred A. Knopf, 1959) uses mosquito netting to set the blaze that destroys the magnificent Kinkakuji temple. As a child, the priest had watched mosquito netting billowing over his mother's body as she engaged in sexual intercourse. This fictional incident rang so true to psychiatrist Jacob A. Arlow that he cited it in a Freud Anniversary Lecture as a valid example of fire as an instrument of revenge for having been forced or allowed to watch parental intercourse.

Individuals who become arsonists are most likely to have had childhoods lacking in stability and support. Typically, they were in difficulties in school early, failed at most endeavors, and were picked up by the police repeatedly for crimes involving cheating, lying, stealing, and destroying property. The history of 67 convicted arsonists in England revealed that more than half had previous convictions, most for crimes against property, not people. Fire setting may not only bring immediate sexual release but also satisfy sadistic and other aggressive tendencies. The arsonist lacks the self-confidence to be overtly aggressive; rape is not an arsonist's crime.

Many of the qualities characteristic of arsonists were evidenced by a man who came to the psychiatric clinic of a London hospital seeking help for depression, says Dr. Donald Scott, consultant in charge. The patient's face was disfigured by a burn. He admitted to being a heavy drinker and user of drugs, arrested several times for burglary, often fired from jobs, and frequently quarreling bitterly with his family. Arson was not mentioned by the patient until he was well into therapy for his depression. Only then did he confess that when he felt really desperate, he set fires, and this act brought him relief from all his tensions for a time.

Facial disfigurement was surprisingly common among the arsonists Scott observed, as, less surprisingly, was alcoholism. These individuals were more likely to be single than married; if married, conflict was frequent, as was separation or divorce.

It does not take much in the way of frustration to put an arsonist into a state of unbearable tension and restlessness. A quarrel with the family or trouble at work or in school can bring on a bout of fire setting, sometimes many fires in a single night; afterwards the arsonist goes home and sleeps peacefully for the first time in weeks.

Fire has always been a symbol for our most basic emotions. In recent times this has meant associating it with sex. In an earlier era, with different attitudes and modes of expression, fire was linked to the heart and soul. In different countries and over the course of many centuries, the brilliance of external fire has been described as analogous to the internal fires. The heart is to the body as fire and the sun are to the earth, said the ancient Egyptians. Life itself follows the changes of fire in sleeping and waking, being born and dying, observed Heraclitus of Ephesis about 500 B.C.

To Aristotle, "the innate heat of the heart is treated as the source of life and of all its powers," and "the soul is, as it were, set aglow with fire." Galen of Pergamon in the second century A.D. thought the "vital flame" of the body should be compared to the oil in a lantern. And in the 1620s René Descartes wrote that "so long as we live, there is a continual fire in our heart . . . the fire that is the basis of all the movements of our parts."

Whatever its symbolism and whatever its cause, fire holds a strange fascination for all people. As Mishima wrote to his mentor Shimizu, when fires were raging in Tokyo as World War II drew to an end, it was like watching the light of a distant bonfire at "a great banquet of extravagant death and destruction."

It is held to be the prerogative of a city's mayor to have the joy of riding the fire engine to the scene of the flames. Crowds are drawn to the scene of disaster, often overlooking the tragedy in the excitement.

More than 2.5 million fires are reported each year, notes the National Fire Data Center. The magnitude of the damage done by these fires is of staggering proportions. The National Research Council's Committee on Fire Research has estimated that arson is responsible for 35 to 45 percent of losses due to fire from all causes.

Incendiarism and fires of suspicious origin are fourth in the center's list of the eight most common factors in residential fires. Smoking in bed is the most frequently reported cause of death in the home, with cooking fires next. Death and injury also often result from fires started by electrical malfunctions or faulty heating equipment, children's playing with matches, and adults' carelessness with fires. Outside the home, forest fires are the major cause of property loss and injury.

A unique weapon against fire was brought forth during the 1906 San Francisco earthquake, which was accompanied by widespread fires. A number of Italian families carried their barrels of red wine up from the cellar and poured the wine onto the flames. A far more sophisticated weapon, cloud seeding, has been employed to make rain and extinguish forest fires.

"If a catastrophe is defined as an event that causes five or more deaths at one time, fire is the catastrophe that occurs most frequently in this country," declared the center. About 1,000 deaths and 10,000 injuries result from arson each year, and fire from all causes kills and injures many times that number. Each year 110,000 injuries, most serious enough to require hospital treatment, are reported, and at least another 200,000 of comparable severity are not reported. If lesser injuries are figured in, an estimate of 2 million burns a year seems most moderate.

First-degree burns which damage only the superficial cells of the epidermis heal within a few days, while second-degree burns go through the upper level of the dermis, take about a month to heal, and may leave scars. Worst are the third-degree burns, so-called because all three layers of the skin are destroyed, the entire epidermis and dermis along with some of the subcutaneous fat and muscle. While first- and second-degree burns are very painful, the much more dangerous third-degree burns are not, because the sensory nerves are destroyed.

Small wonder, then, that fire has been a favored weapon since the time primitive man hurled firebrands at enemies. Archimedes, during the second Punic War, placed a burnished mirror so that it would catch the sun's rays and set fire to the Roman ships in the harbor at Syracuse; in ancient China a woman who had attempted to kill her husband, or, worse yet, assault her mother-in-law, was pierced through the breast with a hot iron; convicted arsonists in Rome were put to death by burning; medieval knights poured boiling oil over their castle walls onto the recoiling bodies of those who would break in; and today's flamethrowers and incendiary bombs bring flaming ruin.

The fear and fascination fire holds for us is intensified by our knowledge of the terrible havoc wreaked by the natural fires beneath the earth, an attitude stemming from the very first mentions of Vesuvius and Pompeii in school. Indeed, if one were to ask the average person to name a volcanic disaster, there is little question that the answer would be the eruption of August 23, A.D. 79, which buried the entire towns of Pompeii, Herculaneum, and Stabiae under a heavy burden of ash. Pliny the Elder, hearing of the catastrophe, rushed to the rescue of survivors, got as far as Stabiae, and died there, suffocated by the poisonous fumes.

In August of 1883, the huge volcano of the very small island of Krakatoa, which lies in the strait between Java and Sumatra, erupted, giving forth explosions that could be heard more than 2,000 miles away. At least 36,000 deaths are believed to have been caused by lava and by the tumultuous sea aroused by the shock waves. The ash drifted around the world three times, and enough remained in the upper atmosphere to produce sunsets of incredible coloration and beauty for the next five years.

Another volcanic explosion, which occurred in May 1902 on Mount Pelée on the island of Martinique, was so catastrophic that the most violent phase of eruption ever since has been known by its name— pelean. The smell of sulfur had been heavy over St. Pierre at the base of the volcano during the whole month of April. In early May a drifting of ash appeared on streets and windowsills. Residents became nervous, and there was talk of taking all one could carry and fleeing; however, a government-appointed commission gave reassurance. (Later some said that the commission's report was colored by a need to have a full electorate for an impending vote.) Mud began to flow down the sides of Mount Pelée on May 5, and three days later came the first of a series of explosions. Gas-charged lava and superheated steam rushed down the side of the mountain at a speed of 100 miles an hour. Within two minutes, St. Pierre was covered with lava, trees were uprooted, and ships lying offshore were sunk. Estimates of the dead ranged from 30,000 to 40,000, most consumed by fire; only four people survived in St. Pierre.

When Kilauea of Hawaii erupted in 1952, the lava flow, measured with thermocouples to a temperature of 2,084 degrees Fahrenheit, blistered the earth and wiped out all living things in its path.

Even so, "Nobody in the United States took volcanoes seriously until Mount St. Helens," remarked volcanologists. On Sunday, May 18, 1980, Dr. David A. Johnston of the U.S. Geological Survey was manning an observation post five miles from Mount St. Helens, Washington. His excited message, "Vancouver! Vancouver! This is it!" went to a listening post 35 miles away. No more was ever heard from him. The volcano exploded with such force that the top was blown off the mountain and a column of steam and ash sent 12 miles up. Volcanic ash settled on towns 500 miles away, and clouds swept across the continent. By Tuesday, volcanic dust had reached New York and on Wednesday was blowing out across the Atlantic and beginning its rise to the upper atmosphere. Searches over the next few weeks turned up thirty-one bodies, while thirty-three others were missing and assumed to be dead. Immediate damages were placed at more than $2.5 billion.

The devastation wrought by volcanic fires may have been the original source of the belief held by many peoples that the world would end in fire. The patristic theologians of the first centuries A.D. had it that a river of fire would consume everything and then a new heaven and earth would be created. Later came the concept that fire would burn up the world but that the righteous would hide in caves and be saved. Before purgatory was established as a doctrine, it was believed that, at the last judgment, souls passed through a river of fire, which did not harm the virtuous.

A similar concept of ordeal by fire exists in many cultures. The most successful outcome was experienced by Shadrach, Meshach, and Abednego, who were thrown into a fiery furnace by Nebuchadnezzar and rescued by an angel when, despite their plight, they praised the Lord. Among the ancient Hindus, a person accused of wrongdoing was first given the opportunity to pray to the fire god. Then his hands were wrapped in leaves and he was required to pick up a heated iron ball and carry it through eight concentric circles. Should he drop the ball, he had to pick it up again and start over at the first circle. If his hands were not burned by the end of the eighth circle, he was declared innocent.

A different type of ordeal by fire, so goes the legend, was willingly undertaken by the knights of the Middle Ages who faced the horrific mythical creature, the winged dragon. Its breath scorched the earth and threatened the knight with a fiery death. "Slaying the dragon" came to be the phrase standing for overcoming a great obstacle. The most famous of all dragon slayers, Saint George, who was to become patron saint of England, soldiers, and boy scouts, rescued a maiden by his act, but it did not save him from torture and beheading and martyrdom.

An explorer in French Guinea in 1704 wrote of his horror at seeing the trial of a native accused of breaking a tribal taboo. The priest heated a copper bangle until it glowed red and then rubbed it three times over the tongue of the accused man. If the tongue did not blister, he was innocent. From the reactions of the onlookers, the explorer gathered that all accused of a crime turned out to be guilty.

In primitive societies, the fear of fire was such that the victim of either natural or man-made flames could not hope for help. A traveler to South Africa in the early years of this century watched the burial of a man struck by lightning. The fear that his body would hold the lightning and cause it to strike again was so great that the victim was not returned to his native village for the traditional rites but, instead, was buried on the spot where he fell. And no one would so much as touch an animal struck by lightning, even in times of famine.

In what used to be called the French Congo, death by lightning was believed to be due to a violation of tribal taboo by the victim. The body was hurriedly carried into the woods and buried under an ant heap to be eaten. Even the skull was not placed with those of the victim's ancestors, so that the memory that he had ever existed would be lost. On one occasion a house was struck by lightning and small children were trapped within. Although their screams could be clearly heard by their parents and neighbors a short distance away, no one dared to come to the rescue. Not a single person approached the house until it had collapsed into a heap of ashes.

But to consider only the harm done by fire is to overlook the fact that humanity's ability to range over the entire globe is possible only because of fire. Its discovery by our ancestors was the greatest step forward in human development. On a field trip to Ethiopia, J. Desmond Clark, Professor of Anthropology at the University of California in Berkeley, explored the areas above the prehistoric sites of Omo, Hadar, and East Turkana. "We have found evidence of a human settlement in this mountainous area that probably began one million years ago," he stated. "By this time our evidence indicates that man appears to have been using fire systematically and we have a record of movement between the plateau and the rift."

For thousands, even millions of years, fire was not essential to survival, because warm-blooded primates evolved in the kindly tropical climates of Africa, Asia, and Eurasia. But even there, fires enhanced the quality of our ancestors' lives, for some nights were cool, and the fires scared away the fierce jungle beasts. Soon hunters learned to use fire more aggressively, to drive game to an area where it could easily be captured.

The first fires must have occurred naturally as a result of volcanic activity, lightning, or spontaneous combustion. But in time humans learned to rub two pieces of wood together or to make a flint. Among some primitive peoples it became the custom to bury a flint, along with a stone on which to strike it in the next world, beside the body of the deceased. Anthropologists cite the conscious use of fire as a key difference between humans and all other animals.

Gradually humans spread over much of the world and eventually Europe and other regions grew colder. Nonetheless, the human race, spawned in the tropics, became able to adapt to these environments in part physically, in part by obtaining external warmth from fires.

Over the millennia, additional uses for fire were found. Because fire possesses the capacity of utterly consuming whatever it touches, it has been a basic method for disposing of the dead. Although the Egyptian practice of mummification has attracted the most attention, cremation was more customary among ancient peoples. In India it was the custom to place the body of the male deceased on a funeral pyre and set it aflame. Then came suttee, from the Sanskrit word *sati,* meaning true or faithful wife, in which the still-living wife was given the privilege of being faithful enough to be burned.

Cremation is being widely practiced today. With space for burial growing scarce in twentieth-century Tokyo, a locker cinerarium contains 3,950 compartments to hold the ashes of the dead. The number of cremations in the United States also has increased, so markedly that hundreds of funeral homes have gone out of business.

Although consuming and consumed, fire, like the mythical phoenix, has the ability to renew itself. This fabled bird, sacred to the sun, has played a role in epics dating from the fifth century B.C. Large and with gloriously colored plumage, the phoenix in its initial incarnation was held to be very long-lived, its exact longevity varying from one myth to the other from a maximum of 12,954 years to a mere 500. Always a male, the beautiful phoenix built a nest out of the twigs of spice trees. When the time had come for the bird to die, it set the nest on fire and burned itself alive. From the ashes of its body arose another phoenix.

Fire is but the rapid chemical combustion of oxygen with carbon and other organic substances producing light, heat, and flames. But humans have always given it more than this chemistry definition. On its very simplest level, fire itself has been worshipped. Divination by pyromancy takes the noises of combustion to represent the voice of the fire spirit, which must be consulted before any important action is undertaken.

Virtually all ancient religions had a fire god as a central figure. Ahura Mazda, the Persian god of fire, was also viewed as the god of goodness and light, all three apparently synonymous. He fought for humanity against Ahriman, the spirit of evil and darkness, again synonymous. Amen was the fire god of the Egyptians, Baal of the Chaldeans and Phoenicians, Agni of the Aryan Hindus, and Gibil of the Assyrians. The names of these gods were to have a long linguistic heritage. Agni lives again in the Latin word for fire, *ignis*, with its many derivations in the Romance languages and English, and Mazda lives on as a light bulb.

The myths of every culture must explain the wonder of fire. The most familiar of all is the Greek legend in which Zeus hid fire from man but Prometheus stole it and brought it to earth. For this crime, Prometheus was chained to a mountain rock where an eagle devoured his liver during the day. Each night, however, the organ was regenerated. Prometheus endured this punishment until he was freed at last by Hercules.

The Persian hero Hushenk hurled a stone, thinking to kill a snake lying on a rock. The reptile slithered away and the stone hit the rock, giving forth sparks that burst into flame. Among the North American

Indians it was the buffalo of the prairies whose hooves hit the barren rock and forced out sparks. For the Cook Islanders it was the Polynesian hero Maui who made the perilous journey to hell, where he learned that two sticks rubbed together generate a spark and managed to survive to bring this valuable information to his people.

In the Bible, fire is presented as miraculous and also paradoxically as terrible. "And the angel of the Lord appeared to him in a flame of fire out of the midst of a bush; and he looked, and lo, the bush was burning, yet it was not consumed. And . . . God called to him out of the bush, 'Moses, Moses!' " (Exodus 3:2, 4 RSV). In contrast to this glory is the Book of Revelation: "If any one worships the beast and its image . . . he shall be tormented with fire and brimstone" (14:9–10, RSV) and "the devil who had deceived them was thrown into the lake of fire and brimstone where the beast and the false prophet were, and they will be tormented day and night for ever and ever" (20:10, RSV).

Nor is burning hell limited to Christian theology; the Buddhist cosmogeny has a series of eight hot hells, eight cold hells, a weeping hell, and a heating hell, and Buddhist philosophers warned of the great burning hell of Majjhima, where those who would break away from the faith suffered for an "age of the world." The ancient Greeks placed the underworld in Tartarus, the abyss under the volcano where Zeus had imprisoned the earlier gods, the Titans. The relationship between the fires of hell and the fires of volcanoes appeared so obvious that by the Middle Ages it was generally believed that volcanoes were located at the entrances to hell, and the sounds of lava boiling within were taken to be the moans of souls burning in torment.

Giordano Bruno was burned at the stake in 1600 for heresy, having espoused the unspeakable theory that volcanic eruptions were due to the interactions of ocean water and the hot interior of the earth and had nothing to do with the Lord's plans for humanity. The punishment was a classic one. Until comparatively recent times, burning was considered the only way to completely destroy heretics or witches and free the world of their evil. The most famous of all those tried for heresy and witchcraft was Joan of Arc, burned at the stake for insisting that she heard the voices of Saints Michael, Catherine, and Margaret and thus was divinely inspired. During the Spanish Inquisition, as many as a hundred heretics were burned in a day of carnival activities.

Malleus maleficarum ("the witches' hammer"), written a few years earlier by Johann Sprenger and Heinrich Kraemer, expounded the theory that burning was the best way to overcome the devil in that it destroyed his host, the witch. Women were more likely to be witches than were men, because of their "carnal lust."

"Lying with the devil" has for centuries been accepted as valid grounds for burning. Sylvanie de la Plaine, in 1616, before being burned as a witch, declared that the devil's penis was cold as ice and ejaculated streams of frigid sperm. As he withdrew, however, she felt the semen turn hot, as if warmed by hellfire.

The peasants of eastern Europe held the belief that vampires and fiends could be kept at bay by a fire barrier.

Because flames are both evanescent and essential to our lives, the everlasting flame figures as a symbol in many of the world's religions. The most revered virgins of ancient Rome tended the fires of the hearth goddess Vesta and kept them burning all year around. Among the Indians of Peru, before the coming of the Spanish conquerors, a fire was kindled each year at the autumnal equinox by focusing the sun's rays on a burnished mirror. Virgins tended the flames and never let them go out. If a maiden broke her vow of chastity and someone learned of her lewd action, she was buried alive.

In 165 B.C., Judah Maccabbee and a Jewish army retook the city of Jerusalem from the Syrians. When the rabbis prepared to rededicate the temple, profaned by the religious rites of the Syrians, they could find only one cruse of oil which still bore the unbroken seal placed there before the conquest. It contained enough oil for only one day, but it burned for the eight days it took for new holy oil to be prepared.

The concept of the eternal flame is everlasting. In ancient Greece the Olympic games were given in honor of Zeus and the flaming torch had a religious meaning. This connotation has been lost, and yet still today the Olympic torch has a mystique. Before the 1980 Olympic winter games in Lake Placid, New York, a torch was lit in Olympia, Greece, site of the ancient games, and brought by airplane to Langley Air Force Base in Virginia. Then relays of fifty-two runners carried the torch across the countryside to Lake Placid, where it lit the flame that burned until the games ended.

The Greeks used the hearth fire to keep the flame of their civilization aglow. Whenever a new colony was founded, a brand was brought from Athens and used to kindle the hearth fires. Fire had such significance as a life force that the Greek midwife would hold her hands briefly over an open flame, pick up the newborn infant, and run with it around the hearth.

The marriage fire has symbolized union in many widely divergent cultures. Among the Mongolian Yakut tribe, for example, the bride approaches the fire from the north, carrying three sticks that she has brought from the hearth of her own "yurta." She throws in the sticks, adding a lump of butter to make the flames leap. As they do so, she declares that now she is to be the mistress ruling the hearth.

Fire is given whatever specific power would do most to improve the conditions of life in a given region. And so there was a long tradition among European farmers that fire from the hearth, the "need fire," could cure the illness of their animals. The custom originated before the Middle Ages and continued well into the nineteenth century, even, in a few isolated areas, into the twentieth. Whenever cattle and other farm animals were attacked by an epidemic disease, the ritual was carried out: All fires out of doors and all hearth fires were extinguished. The "need fire" was then kindled, according to local practice, by chaste young men, or by twin brothers, or married men, or a pre-adolescent boy and girl, or by first-begotten sons. When the flames died down, the sick animals were driven over the glowing embers, with the pigs going first. Then embers were taken home to rekindle the all-important hearth fires.

As every home must have a hearth fire, it is hardly surprising that levying a hearth tax seemed an excellent idea to rulers. During Anglo-Saxon days the king demanded the hated "fumage," from the French word for smoke, a tax on each hearth sending forth smoke. In 1662 the sum of two shillings per hearth was ordered, a tax so bitterly opposed that it was lifted after twenty-two years.

The word "hearth" has an emotional overlay; it is often used as a synonym for home. It represents the family gathering place, the source of psychological and physical warmth, and in an earlier day the heat for cooking food.

For all the psychological, sexual, and religious aspects of fire, its mundane use in cooking remains central. Tamed in stoves or in the backyard, fire allows us to boil, bake, broil, charcoal-broil, steam, poach, fry, barbecue, sauté, roast, toast, pressure-cook, braise, simmer, stew, scald, blanch, flame, deep-fat-fry, smoke, brown, grill, and sear.

Broiling takes a heat of 550 degrees Fahrenheit, scalding 185 degrees, simmering 130 to 160 degrees, and boiling 212 degrees—at sea level.

In the mountains, 10,000 feet up, 194 degrees will bring water to a boil, and atop a 30,000-foot peak, only 158 degrees.

Our very appearance has been influenced by these many cooking practices. The evolution of the face from that of prehistoric humans to ours took a forward step when fire and food were brought together. Whatever the technique, cooking softens food and makes it tender.

When the heavy jaws and huge sharp teeth essential to rending raw animal flesh ceased to be an evolutionary advantage, they disappeared and were replaced by the face we see in the mirror.

Glossary

Acclimatize: To adapt to a changing environment, here used in the context of adapting to heat.

Aestivate: To be in a state of dormancy or torpor during a period of excessively high temperature and/or acute water shortage; analogous but not identical to hibernate.

Autoclave: To apply steam under pressure.

Burn: The distinction between the three degrees of burns is as follows: a third-degree burn is the most severe, with destruction of epidermis, dermis, subcutaneous fat, muscle, and sensory nerves; a second-degree burn involves the epidermis and dermis; a first-degree involves the epidermis only.

Clostridia: Common, spore-forming bacteria, with some species capable of producing powerful toxins remarkable for heat-resistance.

Diathermy: The raising of temperature within body tissue produced by passing high-frequency electric currents through the tissues.

Ectotherm: An animal that obtains body heat from external sources; a cold-blooded animal.

Endotherm: An animal with an internal temperature-regulating mechanism; a warm-blooded animal.

Estrus: A state of sexual excitability when the female is receptive to the male and can be impregnated; in heat.

Fahrenheit: The temperature scale with freezing at 32 degrees and boiling at 212 degrees, still the most common measurement in the

United States and used here for that reason. Conversion: (F minus 32) 5/9 = Celsius.

Fight or flight reaction: The coordinated physiological response to exposure, extreme heat, cold, or emotion.

Heatstroke: The most serious of heat injuries, occurring when the temperature-regulating mechanism of the body breaks down.

Heliothermy: Gaining heat from the sun.

Homeotherm, also spelled Homoiotherm: An animal with a relatively constant body temperature maintained independently of the environment; a warm-blooded animal.

Hyperthermia: Abnormally elevated body temperature, either due to illness or induced artificially; fever.

Hypothalamus: Portion of brain which controls many sympathetic nervous system activities, here used for its heat-regulating function.

Hypothermia: Subnormal body temperature, either occurring accidentally or induced artificially.

Melanin: Black or brown pigment in skin, hair, or eyes that gives them color and offers protection from sunburn; present in larger amounts in skin of natives of hot than of cold climates.

Poikilotherm: An animal with a body temperature that fluctuates with changes in the external temperature; a cold-blooded animal.

Rete mirabile: Latin for wonderful net; a network of arteries and veins which in certain animals is arranged in such a way as to prevent blood from becoming dangerously overheated (or cooled).

Schistosomiasis: One of the most common tropical diseases, caused by parasitic schistosomes or blood flukes which spend part of their life cycle in the body of snails; also known as snail fever and bilharziasis.

Stomata: Tiny pores on plant leaves that open and close for gas exchange and for the entry or exclusion of water and sunlight; significant to heat and drought tolerance.

Superheated: The state of being liquid at temperatures at or above the boiling point.

Temperature-humidity index (THI): An index figure based on both temperature and humidity and reflecting comfort or discomfort more accurately than either reading alone. The formula used to compute the index is: THI = 0.4 (dry-bulb temperature F plus wet-bulb temperature F) plus 15.

Thermography: The technique of using an instrument to make a visual record (thermogram) of variations in heat given off by body tissues.

Thermophile: Literally, heat lover; used to refer to an organism that grows best at high temperatures.

Thigmothermy: Gaining heat by contact with a hot substance.

Vector: Carrier of a pathogen or parasite, frequently an insect.

Bibliography

Adolph, E. F., et al. *Physiology of Man in the Desert.* New York: Interscience Publications, 1947; reprinted, New York and London: Hafner Publishing Co., 1969.

Air Training Command. *Afoot in the Desert,* rev. ed. Maxwell Air Force Base, Ala.: 3636th Combat Crew Training Wing, Environmental Information Division, June 1974.

_____. *Plant Sources of Water in Southeast Asia,* rev. ed. Maxwell Air Force Base, Ala.: 3636th Combat Crew Training Wing, Environmental Information Division, April 1972.

American College of Sports Medicine. *Prevention of Heat Injuries During Distance Running,* position statement. Madison, Wis., May 1975.

Andrews, Robin, and A. Stanley Rand. "Reproductive Effort in Anoline Lizards," *Ecology,* Autumn 1974.

Ansbacher, Rudi, moderator. "Forum: Management of Infertility," *The Female Patient,* August 1979.

Apple, J. Lawrence. "Plant Pathogens and Losses in World Food." American Association for the Advancement of Science, meeting, Denver, Feb. 20–25, 1977.

Arlow, Jacob A. "Pyromania and the Primal Scene: A Psychoanalytic Comment on the Work of Yukio Mishima," *Psychoanalytic Quarterly* vol. 47, no. 1 (1978).

Bachelard, Gaston. *The Psychoanalysis of Fire,* trans. Alan C. M. Ross. Boston: Beacon Press, 1964.

Baron, Robert A. "Aggression and Heat: The 'Long Hot Summer' Revisited," in A. Baum and S. Valins, eds., *Advances in Environmental Research,* vol. 1. Hillsdale, N.J.: Lawrence Erlbaum Associates, 1978.

————, and Paul A. Bell. "Aggression and Heat: The Influence of Ambient Temperature, Negative Affect, and a Cooling Drink on Physical Aggression," *Journal of Personality and Social Psychology*, vol. 33, no. 3 (1976).

————. "Aggression and Heat: Mediating Effects of Prior Provocation and Exposure to an Aggressive Model," *Journal of Personality and Social Psychology*, vol. 31, no. 5 (1975).

Barrau, Jacques, ed. *Plants and the Migrations of Pacific Peoples.* Tenth Pacific Science Congress Symposium. Honolulu, Hawaii: Bishop Museum Press, 1963.

Barrett, Alan H., and Philip C. Myers. "Subcutaneous Temperatures: A Method of Noninvasive Screening," *Science*, Nov. 14, 1975.

Barrett-Connor, Elizabeth. "Advice to Travelers," *Western Journal of Medicine*, July 1975.

Bastian, Hartmut. *And Then Came Man*, trans. Desmond I. Vesey. New York: Viking Press, 1964.

Beisel, William R., Ralph F. Goldman, and Robert J. T. Joy. "Metabolic Balance Studies During Induced Hyperthermia in Man," *Journal of Applied Physiology*, Jan. 1968.

Bernoulli, C., et al. "Danger of Accidental Person-to-Person Transmission of Creutzfeldt-Jakob Disease by Surgery," *The Lancet*, Feb. 26, 1979.

Blatteis, Clark M. "Influence of Body Weight and Temperature on the Pyrogenic Effect of Endotoxin in Guinea Pigs," *Toxicology and Applied Pharmacology*, no. 29 (1974).

Blum, Harold F. "Does the Melanin Pigment of Human Skin Have Adaptive Value?" *Quarterly Review of Biology*, vol. 36 (1961).

Bramwell, C. D., and P. B. Fellgett. "Thermal Regulation in Sail Lizards," *Nature*, March 16, 1973.

Branda, Richard F., and John W. Eaton. "Skin Color and Nutrient Photolysis: An Evolutionary Hypothesis," *Science*, Aug. 18, 1978.

Breeland, Samuel G., Geoffrey M. Jeffery, Clifford S. Lofgren, and Donald E. Weidhaas. "Release of Chemosterilized Males for the Control of *Anopheles albimanus* in El Salvador: I. Characteristics of the Test Site and the Natural Population; III. Field Methods and Population Control," *American Journal of Tropical Medicine and Hygiene*, March 1974.

Brinton, Daniel G. *The Basis of Social Relations.* New York: G. P. Putnam's Sons, 1902.

Brock, Thomas D. "High Temperature Systems," *Annual Review of Ecology and Systematics*, Vol. 1 (1970).

————. *Predicting the Ecological Consequences of Thermal Pollution from Observations on Geothermal Habitats.* Vienna: *International Atomic Energy Agency, 1975.*

———, and M. Louise Brock. Recovery of a Hot Spring Community from a Catastrophe," *Journal of Phycology*, vol. 5, no. 1 (1969).

———, Gary K. Darland. "Limits of Microbiological Existence: Temperature and pH," *Science*, Sept. 25, 1960.

Brown, A. W. A., T. C. Byerly, M. Gibbs, and A. San Pietro. *Crop Productivity-Research Imperatives*. International conference sponsored by Michigan State University and Charles F. Kettering Foundation. Yellow Springs, Ohio; Waverly Press, 1976.

Brown, E. S. "Armyworm Control." *PANS* (Pest Articles and News Summaries), Centre for Overseas Pest Research, London, June 1972.

Bruce-Chwatt, Leonard J. "Endemic Diseases, Demography and Socioeconomic Development of Tropical Africa" *Canadian Journal of Public Health*, Feb. 1975.

Bueding, Ernest. "Dissociation of Mutagenic and Other Toxic Properties from Schistosomicides," *Journal of Toxicology and Environmental Health*, 1975.

Bull, James J. "Sex Determination in Reptiles," *Quarterly Review of Biology*, March 1980.

Bull, Joan M., and Paul B. Chretien. "Heat as Cancer Therapy," *Journal of the American Medical Association*, May 17, 1976.

———, and R. C. Vogt. *"Temperature Dependent Sex Determination in Turtles,"* *Science*, Dec. 7, 1979.

Burcombe, J. V., and M. J. Hollinsworth. "The Relationship Between Developmental Temperature and Longevity in *Drosophila,"* *Gerontologia*, 1970.

Buskirk, Elsworth R., and David E. Bass. *Climate and Exercise*. Natick, Mass.: Quartermaster Research and Engineering Center, July 1957.

Butler, Robert N. "Energy and Aging," testimony before the U.S. Senate Special Committee on Aging, April 5, 1971, National Institute on Aging.

Cabanac, Michel. "Temperature Regulation," *Annual Review of Physiology*, Comroe, Julius H., Jr.; Sonnenschein, Ralph R., Edelman, I. S., eds., Palo Alto, Calif., vol. 37, 1975.

Calderon, O. H., R. S. Hutton, and E. E. Staffeldt. "Deposition of Microorganisms on Missiles and Related Equipment Exposed to Tropical Environments," *Developments in Industrial Microbiology*, vol. 90. Washington, D.C.: American Institute of Biological Sciences, 1968.

Caldwell, Martyn M. "Physiology of Desert Halophytes," *Ecology of Halophytes*. New York and London: Academic Press, 1974.

———. "Solar Ultraviolet Radiation and the Growth and Development of Higher Plants," *Photophysiology*, vol. 6. New York and London: Academic Press, 1971.

Calloway, Nathaniel O. "Body Temperature: Thermodynamics of Homeothermism," *Journal of Theoretical Biology*, 1976.

_____. "Heat Production and Senescence," *Journal of the American Geriatrics Society*, April 1974.

Calorie Requirements Committee. *Calorie Requirements*, second report. Rome: FAO, 1957.

Cancer Therapy by Hyperthermia and Radiation, International Symposium. *Proceedings.* Sponsored by the National Cancer Institute and the American College of Radiology in cooperation with University of Maryland School of Medicine. Washington, D.C.: April 28–30, 1975.

Cannon, Walter B. *Bodily Changes in Pain, Hunger, Fear, and Rage*, 2nd ed. New York: Harper & Brothers, 1929.

Carter, Richard, and David H. Chen. "Malaria Transmission Blocked by Immunisation with Gametes of the Malaria Parasite," *Nature*, Sept. 2, 1976.

Census, Bureau of the, *World Population*. Washington, D.C.: U.S. Dept. of Commerce, 1977.

Centers for Disease Control, *Health Information for International Travel.* Atlanta, Ga.: Quarantine Division, Bureau of Epidemiology, 1979.

_____. *Malaria Surveillance*, annual report. Atlanta, Ga.: Quarantine Division, Bureau of Epidemiology, 1971–78.

_____. *Morbidity and Mortality Weekly Report*, Atlanta, Ga.: Quarantine Division, Bureau of Epidemiology, Oct. 26, 1979; Sept. 19, 1980; Oct. 10, 1980; Oct. 17, 1980; Jan. 9, 1981.

_____. *Trichinosis Surveillance.* Atlanta, Ga.: Quarantine Division, Bureau of Epidemiology, 1977.

Centro Internacional de Agricultura Tropical. *Annual Report.* Cali, Colombia: 1975.

Clarke, Jean M., and J. Maynard Smith. "Two Phases of Aging in *Drosophila subobscura, Journal of Experimental Biology*, Sept. 1961.

Clarke, John F. "Some Effects of the Urban Structure on Heat Mortality," Irving J. Selikoff, ed., *Environmental Research*, vol. 5. New York: Academic Press, 1972.

Clyde, David F., et al. "Immunization of Men Against Sporozoite-induced Falciparum Malaria," *American Journal of Medical Sciences*, 1973.

Cobley, Leslie. *An Introduction to the Botany of Tropical Crops.* London: Longmans, Green & Co., 1956.

Collins, Margaret S., et al. "High-Temperature Tolerance in Two Species of Subterranean Termites from the Sonoran Desert in Arizona," *Environmental Entomology*, Dec. 1973.

Colquhoun, W. P., and Ralph F. Goldman. "Vigilance Under Induced Hyperthermia" (U.S. Army Natick Laboratories), *Ergonomics*, 1972.

Commission on International Relations, *Guayule*, Report of an Ad Hoc Panel of the Board on Agriculture and Renewable Resources. Washington, D.C.: National Academy of Sciences, 1977.

_____, *More Water for Arid Lands*, Report of an Ad Hoc Panel of the Advisory Committee on Technology Innovation. Washington, D.C.: National Academy of Sciences, 1974.

_____, *The Winged Bean*, Report of an Ad Hoc Panel of the Advisory Committee on Technology Innovation. Washington, D.C.: National Academy of Sciences, 1975.

Connor, W. G., et al. "Prospects for Hyperthermia in Human Cancer Therapy," *Radiology*, May 1977.

Cooney, Donald G., and Ralph Emerson. *Thermophilic Fungi*. San Francisco: W. H. Freeman & Co., 1964.

Crile, George, Jr. "Heat as an Adjunct to the Treatment of Cancer," Cleveland Clinic Quarterly, April 1961.

_____, and Rupert B. Turnbull, Jr. "The Role of Electrocoagulation in the Treatment of Carcinoma of the Rectum," *Surgery, Gynecology & Obstetrics*, Sept. 1972.

Cross, F. L., and E. A. Livingstone. *The Oxford Dictionary of the Christian Church*, New York: Oxford University Press, 1974.

Davidson, N. McD., Lorna Crevitt, and E. H. P. Parry. "Peripartum Cardiac Failure in Nigeria," *Bulletin of the World Health Organization*, vol. 51, no. 2 (1970).

DeLaney, R. G., and A. P. Fishman. "Analysis of Lung Ventilation in the Aestivating Lungfish *Protopterus aethiopicus,*" *American Journal of Physiology*, 1977.

Drinkwater, B. L., et al. "Aerobic Power as a Factor in Women's Response to Work in Hot Environments," *Journal of Applied Physiology*, Dec. 1976.

_____, et al. "Response of Prepubertal Girls and College Women to Work in the Heat," *Journal of Applied Physiology*, 1977.

Drummond, Roger O. "Animal Pests and World Food Production." AAAS meeting, Denver, Feb. 20–25, 1977.

Dubos, René. *Man Adapting*. New Haven: Yale University Press, 1965.

Eckholm, Erik P. "Desertification: A World Problem." AAAS meeting, Boston, Feb. 18–24, 1976.

Edmonson, Charles Howard. *Bernice P. Bishop Museum*. Honolulu: 1928; reprinted, Millwood, N.Y.: Kraus Reprint Co., 1974.

Edney, E. B. "The Body Temperature of Tenebrionid Beetles in the Namib Desert of Southern Africa," *Journal of Experimental Biology*, 1971.

_____. "The Effect of Parental Temperature upon Filial Egg Period in *Drosophila melanogaster,*" *Physiological Zoology*, July 1969.

Edwards, George A., and William L. Nutting. "The Influence of Temperature upon the Respiration and Heart Activity of Thermobia and Grylloblatta," *Psyche*, June 1950.

Ellis, F. P. "Mortality from Heat Illness and Heat Aggravated Illness in the U.S., in Irving J. Selikoff, ed., *Environmental Research*. vol. 5, New York: Academic Press, 1972.

Environmental Fund. *World Population Estimates*, Washington, D.C.: 1975, 1976, 1977, 1978, 1979, 1980.

Fage, J. D., and R. A. Oliver, eds. *Papers in African Prehistory*, London: Cambridge University Press, 1970.

Farrar, W. V. "Tecuitlatl: A Glimpse of Aztec Food Technology," *Nature*, July 23, 1966.

Finkelstein, Richard A. "Cholera," *Critical Reviews in Microbiology*, vol. 2, no. 4 (1973).

_____. "Immunology of Cholera," *Current Topics in Microbiology and Immunology*, vol. 69. Berlin: Springer-Verlag, 1975.

_____. "Possibilities of Immunization Against Cholera and Related Enterotoxic Enteropathies," 14th Congress of the International Association of Biological Standardization, Douglas, Isle of Man, 1975. *Devel. Biol. Stand.*, vol. 33. Basel: S. Karger, 1976.

Foege, W. B., J. D. Millar, and D. A. Henderson. "Smallpox Eradication in West and Central Africa," *WHO Bulletin*, vol. 52, no. 2 (1975).

Food & Agriculture Organization/WHO Joint Ad Hoc Expert Committee, Report of, *Energy and Protein Requirements*, FAO of the United Nations, Rome, 1973.

Force, Roland W. "Health-Related Effects, Consequences, and Results of Social Change in the Pacific," *American Journal of Tropical Medicine and Hygiene*, Sept. 1975.

Fox, Robert W., and Jerrold W. Huguet. *Population and Urban Trends in Central America and Panama*. Washington, D.C.: Inter-American Development Bank, 1977.

Frazer, Sir James George. *The Golden Bough*. New York: Macmillan Co., 1942.

Freud, Sigmund. "The Acquisition of Power over Fire," *International Journal of Psychoanalysis*, October 1932.

Friedman, Jacob, Zippora Stein, and Amotz Dafni. "The Rose of Jericho," *Biblical Archaeology Review*, Sept. 10, 1980.

Frith, H. J. "Incubator Birds," *Scientific American*, Aug. 1959.

Furtick, William R. "Weeds and World Food Production." AAAS meeting, Denver, Feb. 20–25, 1977.

Gaarder, Kenneth R., and Penelope S. Montgomery. *Clinical Biofeedback*. Baltimore: Williams and Wilkins Co., 1977.

Gangarosa, Eugene J., and William H. Barker. "Cholera: Implications in the U.S.," *Journal of the American Medical Association*, Jan. 14, 1974.

Gajdusek, D. Carleton. "Unconventional Viruses and the Origin and Disappearance of Kuru," *Science*, Sept. 2, 1977.

————. *Unconventional Viruses in Human Diseases Caused by Viruses: Recent Developments* (H. Rothschild, F. Allison, and C. Howe, eds), New York: Oxford University Press, 1978.

————, et al. "Precautions in Medical Care of and in Handling Materials from Patients with Transmissible Virus Dementia (Creutzfeldt-Jakob Disease)," *New England Journal of Medicine*, Dec. 8, 1977.

Gavin, James D., and John A. Dixon. "India: A Perspective on the Food Situation," *Science*, May 9, 1975.

George, Uwe. *In the Deserts of this Earth.* New York: Harcourt Brace Jovanovich, 1976.

Givoni, B., and Ralph F. Goldman. "Predicting Rectal Temperature Response to Work, Environment, and Clothing," *Journal of Applied Physiology*, June 1972.

Goldman, Ralph F. "Environmental Limits, Their Prescription and Proscription," *International Journal of Environmental Studies*, 1973.

————. "Physiological Costs of Body Armor," *Military Medicine*, March, 1969.

————, Edward B. Green, and P. F. Iampietro. "Tolerance of Hot, Wet Environments by Resting Men," *Journal of Applied Physiology*, March 1965.

Graham, Jeffrey B. "Low-Temperature Acclimation and the Seasonal Temperature Sensitivity of Some Tropical Marine Fishes," *Physiological Zoology*, Jan. 1972.

————, I. Rubinoff, and M. K. Hecht. "Temperature Physiology of the Sea Snake *Pelamis platurus,*" *Proceedings of the National Academy of Science*, June 1971.

Greenberg, Gary. "The Effects of Ambient Temperature and Population Density on Two Inbred Strains of Mice, *Mus musculus,*" *Behaviour*, 1972.

————. "An Ethogram of the Blue Spiny Lizard, *Sceloporus cyanogenys,*" *Journal of Herpetology*, 1977.

————. *Physiological and Behavioral Thermoregulation in Living Reptiles.* AAAS meeting, Washington, D.C., Feb. 12–17, 1978.

————, and Paul D. MacLean, eds. "Behavior and Neurology of Lizards," National Institute of Mental Health, Rockville, Md., 1978.

Griffitt, William. "Environmental Effects on Interpersonal Affective Behavior: Ambient Effective Temperature and Attraction," *Journal of Personality and Social Psychology*, 1970.

————, and Russell Veitch. "Hot and Crowded: Influence of Population Density and Temperature on Interpersonal Affective Behavior," *Journal of Personality and Social Psychology*, 1971.

Gutheim, Frederick. *The Livable Winter City Today.* International Conference on the Livable Winter City, Minnesota, March 19–21, 1978.

Guyana, National Research Council of and National Academy of Science.

U.S.A. Workshop on Aquatic Weed Management and Utilization. *Some Prospects for Aquatic Weed Management in Guyana.* Georgetown, Guyana, Mar. 15–17, 1973.

Haisman, M. F., and R. F. Goldman. "Physiological Evaluations of Armored Vests in Hot-Wet and Hot-Dry Climates," *Ergonomics,* 1974.

Hale, Henry B., James P. Ellis, Jr., and Edgar W. Williams. "Climatologic Aspects of Obesity and Therapeutic Semistarvation," *Aviation, Space, and Environmental Medicine,* Feb. 1975.

Hancocke, John. *Febrifugum Magnum: or, common water the best cure for fevers, and probably for the plague.* London: 1722, printed for R. Halsey in St. Michael's Church-Porch, Cornhill: And Sold by J. Roberts, near the Oxford-Arms in Warwick Lane.

Hardin, Garrett. *Beyond 1976: Can Americans Be Well Nourished in a Starving World?* New York Academy of Science meeting, Philadelphia, Dec. 1, 1976.

Hartman, J. Ted, and George Crile, Jr. "Heat Treatment of Osteogenic Sarcoma," *Clinical Orthopaedics.* Philadelphia: J. B. Lippincott Company, 1968.

Haskell, P. T. "The Hungry Locust," *Science Journal,* Jan. 1970.

Hastings, James, with John A. Selbie. *Encyclopaedia of Religion and Ethics.* New York: Charles Scribner's Sons, 1912.

Hastings, Robert C., R. R. Jacobson, and John R. Trautman. "Long term Clinical Toxicity Studies with Clofazimine (B663) in Leprosy," *International Journal of Leprosy,* Sept. 1976.

Hawkes, Jacquetta. *Man and the Sun.* New York: Random House, 1962.

Heinrich, Walter. *Vegetation of the Earth in Relation to Climate and the Ecology,* trans. Joy Wieser. London: English Universities Press, 1973.

Hemming, C. F. *The Locust Menace.* London: Centre for Overseas Pest Research, 1974.

Henwood, Kenneth. "Infrared Transmittance as an Alternative Thermal Strategy in the Desert Beetle, *Onymacris plana,"* *Science,* Sept. 19, 1975.

Holm, Erik, and E. B. Edney. "Daily Activity of Namib Desert Arthropods in Relation to Climate," *Ecology,* Winter 1973.

Horvath, Steven M., ed. in chief. *Standards for Occupational Exposures to Hot Environments,* Proc. Symposium, Pittsburgh, Feb. 27–28, 1973. Cincinnati: National Institute for Occupational Safety and Health, Jan. 1976.

Hough, Walter. *Fire as an Agent in Human Culture.* Washington, D.C.: Smithsonian Institution, 1926.

Howard, Richard A. *Sun, Sand and Survival,* Air Training Command, 3636th Combat Crew Training Wing, Environmental Information Div., Maxwell Air Force Base, ALA 1953.

Hutton, R. S., and Calderon O. H. Staffeldt. "Aerial Spora and Surface Deposits on Microorganisms in a Deciduous Forest in the Canal Zone," *Developments in Industrial Microbiology,* Am. Inst. of Biolog. Scis. Washington, D.C. 1968.

Iampietro, P. F., et al. "Exposure to Heat: Comparison of Responses of Dog and Man," *International Journal of Biometeorology,* vol. 10, no. 2 (1966).

———, and Ralph R. Goldman. "Tolerance of Men Working in Hot Humid Environments," *Journal of Applied Physiology,* Jan. 1965.

International Agricultural Research, Consultative Group on. *International Research in Agriculture.* New York: 1974.

International Rice Research Institute. *Research Highlights for 1975,* Los Baños, Philippines: 1976; *for 1979,* 1980.

———. *Rice, Science and Man.* 10th anniversary celebration of IRRI, Los Baños, April 20–21, 1972.

Ireland, Alleyne. *Tropical Colonization.* New York: Macmillan Co., 1899.

Jacobson, Elliot R., and Walter G. Whitford. "Physiological Responses to Temperature in the Patch-Nosed Snake, *Salvadora hexalepsis,"* *Herpetologica,* Sept. 1971.

Jordan, Peter. "Schistosomiasis, Research to Control," joint meeting, American Society of Tropical Medicine and Hygiene and Royal Society of Tropical Medicine and Hygiene, Philadelphia, Nov. 3–5, 1976.

Kamon, Eliezer. "Acclimation Processes by Daily Exercise Stints at Temperate-Conditions Followed by Short Heat Exposures," *Aviation Space and Environmental Medicine,* Jan. 1976.

Kerr, James W., Conf. Chairman, *Incendiarism,* a Report on a Conference on Arson and Incendiarism, July 29–30, 1975, Washington, D.C. National Academy of Sciences. Committee on Fire Research.

Key, Marcus M., et al., eds., *Occupational Diseases,* rev. ed. National Institute for Occupational Safety and Health, June, 1977.

Kibler, Hudson H., and Harold D. Johnson. "Temperature and Longevity in Male Rats," *Journal of Gerontology,* Jan. 1966.

Klipstein, Frederick A., et al. "Enterotoxigenic Intestinal Bacteria in Tropical Sprue," *Annals of Internal Medicine,* Nov. 1973.

———. "Nutritional Status and Intestinal Function among Rural Populations of the West Indies," *Gastroenterology,* vol. 63 (1972).

Kluger, Matthew J., Daniel H. Ringler, and Miriam R. Anver. "Fever and Survival," *Science,* April 11, 1975.

Kochan, Ivan. *Role of Iron in Regulation of Nutritional Immunity,* American Chemical Society meeting, New York, 1976.

Kuhlemeier, K. V., et al. *Assessment of Deep Body Temperature of Workers in Hot Jobs.* Cincinnati: National Institute for Occupational Safety and Health, Aug. 1976.

Landsberg, Helmut E. *Weather and Health.* Garden City, N.Y.: Doubleday & Co., 1969.

Latham, Michael C. "Nutrition and Infection in Natural Development," *Science*, May 9, 1975.

Lechowich, Richard V., chairman, *Nitrites in Meat Curing*, Council for Agricultural Science and Technology, Ames, Iowa, March 6, 1978.

Lee, Douglas H. K. "Biological Consequences of Environmental Control through Housing," *Environment Health Perspectives*, 1975.

———. "Human Adaptations to Arid Environments," *Desert Biology*, vol. 1. New York: Academic Press, 1968.

———. "Large Mammals in the Desert," *Physiological Adaptations to Desert and Mountain*. New York: Academic Press, 1972.

LeVeen, Harry N., et al. "Tumor Eradication by Radiofrequency Therapy," *Journal of the American Medical Association*, May 17, 1976.

Levine, Richard J. "Epidemic Faintness and Syncope in a School Marching Band," *Journal of the American Medical Association*, Nov. 28, 1977.

Levitt, J. *Responses of Plants to Environmental Stress*. New York: Academic Press, 1972.

Libshitz, Herman I. "Thermography of the Breast," *Journal of the American Medical Association*, Oct. 31, 1977.

Licht, Sidney, ed. *Medical Climatology*, New Haven: Elizabeth Licht, 1964.

———. *Therapeutic Heat & Cold*. New Haven, Elizabeth Licht, 1965.

Lind, A. R., et al. "Influence of Age and Daily Duration of Exposure on Responses of Men to Work in Heat," *Journal of Applied Physiology*, Jan. 1970.

Liu, Robert K., and Roy L. Walford. "Mid-Life Temperature-Transfer Effects on Life-Span of Annual Fish," *Journal of Gerontology*, 1975.

Lugo, Ariel E., and Gilberto Cintrón. *The Mangrove Forests of Puerto Rico and their Management*, Proceedings of the International Symposium on Biology and Management of Mangroves, University of Florida, Gainesville, 1975.

Luk, Kenneth H., Michael R. Hulse, and Theodore L. Phillips. "Hyperthermia in Cancer Therapy," *Western Journal of Medicine*, March 1980.

———, and Theodore L. Phillips, "Thermal Dosimetry and Clinical Requirements," *Cancer Research*, June 1979.

MacDonald, Gordon A. *Volcanoes*. Englewood Cliffs, N.J.: Prentice-Hall, 1972.

MacPherson, R. K., and F. Ofner. "Heat and the Survival of the Aged and Chronically Ill," *Medical Journal of Australia*, Feb. 27, 1965.

Malaria Research, *Symposium*, Rabat, Maroc, April 1–5, 1974.

Marmor, Michael. "Heat-Wave Mortality in N.Y.C., 1949 to 1970," *Archives of Environmental Health*, March 1975.

Masefield, G. B. *A History of the Colonial Agricultural Service*, Oxford: Clarendon Press, 1972.

Mata, Leonardo, J. "Malnutrition-infection Interactions in the Tropics," *American Journal of Tropical Medicine*, July 1975.

Mavromatis, Mary, and John R. Lion. "A Primer on Pyromania," *Diseases of the Nervous System*, Nov. 1977.

Maxwell, Archibald. *An Answer to Mr. Kirkland's Essay, Towards an Improvement in the Cure of those Diseases which are the Cause of Fevers, wherin is shown, The Error of his Arguments for the Use of cold Water in extinguishing FEVERS*. London: 1768; sold by T. Beckett and P. A. De Hondt, in the Strand.

May, Herbert G., and Bruce M. Metzger, eds. The Oxford, Bible annotated with the Apocrypha, rev. standard version. New York: New York Oxford University Press, 1965.

Mayer, Jean. "Toward a Non-Malthusian Population Policy," *Columbia Forum*, Summer 1969.

Mendelsohn, Everett. *Heat and Life, the Development of the Theory of Animal Heat*. Cambridge, Mass.: Harvard University Press, 1964.

Mills, Clarence A. *Medical Climatology*. Springfield, Ill.: Charles C. Thomas, 1939.

Milner, Max. *Post-Harvest Losses*. AAAS meeting, Denver, Feb. 20–25, 1977.

Minard, David. "Hazards of Heat and Cold," *Practice of Medicine*, rev. ed. New York: Harper & Row, 1975.

Momiyama-Sakamoto, Masako, and Kunie Katayama. "Recent Changes in Seasonal Variation of Senile Mortality," *Meteorology & Geophysics* (Japan), Dec. 1975.

———, Juichiro Takeuchi, and Kunie Katayama. "Signs Seen in Japan of Deseasonality in Human Mortality," *Papers in Meteorology and Geophysics*, June 1975.

Morton, Eugene S. "The Adaptive Significance of Dull Coloration in Yellow Warblers," *The Condor*, Autumn, 1976.

———. "Food and Migration Habits of the Eastern Kingbird in Panama," *The Auk*, Oct. 12, 1971.

Mosser, Jerry L., and Thomas D. Brock. "Effect of Wide Temperature Fluctuation on the Blue Green Algae of Bead Geyser, Yellowstone National Park," *Limnology & Oceanography*, July 1971.

National Academy of Sciences. *Underexploited Tropical Plants with Promising Economic Value*, rev. ed. Washington, D.C.: International Development Committee on International Relations, 1978.

———. *Food Science in Developing Countries*. Washington, D.C.: 1974.

National Institute on Aging, *Special Report on Aging 1980*, August 1980.

Newburgh, L. H. *Physiology of Heat Regulation and the Science of Clothing*. New York: Hafner Publishing Co., 1968.

New York City Police Department. Crime Comparison Reports, May, June, July 1977.

Nisbet, Robert A., and Duncan T. Patten. "Seasonal Temperature Acclimation of a Prickly-Pear Cactus in South Central Arizona," *Oecologia*, vol. 15 (1974).

Office of Technology Assessment. *OTA Priorities*. Washington, D.C.: 1979.

Ostrom, John H. "The Evidence for Endothermy in Dinosaurs," AAAS meeting, Washington, D.C., Feb. 12–17, 1978.

Parry, E. S., and I. S. Lister. "Sunlight and Hypercalciuria," *Lancet*, May 10, 1975.

Passmore, R., B. M. Nicol, and E. M. De Mayer. *Handbook on Human Nutrition Requirements*, Rome: FAO of the UN, 1974.

Peters, Wallace. "Malaria." *New England Journal of Medicine*, Dec. 8, 1977.

Peterson, William. "Effects of Government Policies on the Fertility of Less Developed Countries," AAAS meeting, Washington, D.C., Feb. 12–17, 1978.

Porteus, Stanley D. *The Psychology of a Primitive People*. New York: Longmans, Green; London: Edward Arnold & Co., 1931.

Precht, H., et al. *Temperature and Life*. Berlin: Springer-Verlag, 1973.

Prieto, Andrew A., Jr., and Walter G. Whitford. "Physiological Responses to Temperature in the Horned Lizards," *Phrynosoma cornutum* and *Phrynosoma douglassii, Copeia*, no. 3, 1971.

Provins, K. A., and C. R. Bell. "Effects of Heat Stress on the Performance of Two Tasks Running Concurrently," *Journal of Experimental Psychology*, vol. 85, no. 1 (1970).

Quagliato, R., et al. "Bacteriological Status (Point, Prevalence) of Lepromatous Outpatients Under Sulfone Treatment," *WHO Bulletin*, vol. 52 (1975).

Rockefeller Foundation. *The Role of Animals in the World Food Situation*, A Conference, Dec. 1975.

Rohles, Frederick H., Jr. *Thermal Comfort in Sedentary Man*. Copenhagen: 5th International Congress for Heating, Ventilation, and Air Conditioning, 1971.

———, and M. A. Johnson. "Thermal Comfort in the Elderly," *ASHRAE Transactions*, vol. 78 (1972).

———, J. E. Woods, and R. G. Nevins. "The Influence of Clothing and Temperature on Sedentary Comfort." ASHRAE Spring Conference, Regina, Saskatchewan, Canada, May 16–18, 1973.

Roth, Jan J. "The Parietal-Pineal Complex Among Paleovertebrates: Evidence for Temperature Regulation." AAAS meeting, Washington, D.C., Feb. 12–17, 1978.

Rue, de la, Hubert, François Bourliére, and Jean-Paul Harroy. *The Tropics*. New York: Alfred A. Knopf, 1957.

Ruebush, T., and D. Juranek. "Epidemiology of Human Babeosis on Nantucket Island, Mass.," USPHS Professional Association meeting, Atlanta, March 27–30, 1978.

Russell, Stephen M. "Regulation of Egg Temperature by Incubating White-Winged Doves," in C. C. Hoff and M. L. Riedesel, eds., *Physiological Systems in Semiarid Environments*. Albuquerque: University of New Mexico Press, 1969.

Sabol, Paul, and Don R. Dickson. *The Effect of Temperature on Birth Rates in the Southern U.S.* Conference on Urban Environment and 2nd Conference on Biometeorology, Nov. 2, 1972, Philadelphia, Pa.; Boston: AMS.

Sanchez, P. A., and S. W. Buol, "Soils of the Tropics and the World Food Crisis," *Science*, May 9, 1975.

Sands, W. A. "Termites as Pests of Tropical Food Crops." PANS (Pest Articles and News Summaries), June 1973, Centre for Overseas Pest Research, London.

Schechter, Joel, "Desert Research in Israel," *Kidma-Israel Journal of Development*, vol. 1, no. 1 (1973).

Schmidt-Nielsen, Knut. *Desert Animals—Physiological Problems of Heat and Water*. New York: Oxford University Press, 1964.

Schultz, Myron G. "Daniel Carrión's Experiment," *New England Journal of Medicine*, June 13, 1968.

_____. "Parasitic Diseases and Public Health Problems in the Developing World." Atlanta Symposium, Albert Schweitzer Centenery, April 7–12, 1975.

_____. "The Surveillance of Parasitic Diseases in the U.S.," *Journal of Tropical Medicine and Hygiene*, vol. 23, no. 4 (1974).

_____. "Imported Malaria," *WHO Bulletin*, no. 50 (1974).

Schuman, Stanley H. "Patterns of Urban Heat Wave Deaths and Implications for Prevention," in Irving J. Selikoff, ed., *Environmental Research*, vol. 5. New York: Academic Press, 1972.

_____, and George W. Williams. "Biochemical Profiles During a Michigan Heat Wave," *Ecology of Food and Nutrition*, vol. 3 (1974).

Scientific Research and Technology, Academy of, Cairo, Egypt. "Arid Lands Irrigation in Developing Countries," Proceedings of a Symposium, Alexandria, Egypt, Feb. 16–21, 1976.

Scott, Donald. "Malicious Fire Raising," *The Practitioner*, June, 1977.

Scotto, Joseph, Thomas R. Fears, and Gio B. Gori. *Measurements of Ultraviolet Radiations in the U.S. and Comparisons with Skin Cancer Data*, NCI, Nov. 1975.

Shookhoff, Howard B. "Clinical Aspects of Manson's Schistosomiasis," *New York State Journal of Medicine*, Nov. 15, 1961.

Simpson, Walter M., chairman. *Fever Therapy*. First International Conference, March 29–31, 1937, New York: Harper & Bros., 1937.

Slayter, R. O., and R. A. Perry, eds. *Arid Lands of Australia*. Proceedings of a Symposium. Canberra: Australian National University Press, 1969.

Smart, Grover C., Jr., and V. G. Perry. "Tropical Nematology," Society of Nematologists meeting, Daytona Beach, Florida., August 1966.

Smith, Ray F. "Insect Pest Losses and the Dimensions of the World Food Problem," AAAS meeting, Denver, Feb. 20–25, 1977.

Spencer, J. E., and W. L. Thomas. *Asia, East by South: A Cultural Geography,* 2nd ed. New York: John Wiley & Sons, 1971.

Spickard, Anderson, and Joe Worden. "How to Prevent Heat Stroke in Football Players," *Journal of the National Athletic Trainers Association,* Fall 1968.

Stein, Jane. *Water: Life or Death.* Washington, D.C.: International Institution for Environment and Development, 1977.

Stein, Philip L., and Bruce M. Rowe. *Physical Anthropology.* New York: McGraw-Hill, 1974.

Streeter, Carroll P. *Colombia.* New York: Rockefeller Foundation, Sept. 1972.

———. *India.* New York: Rockefeller Foundation, Dec. 1969.

Sturrock, R. F. "Distribution of the snail *Biomphalaria glabra,* intermediate host of *Schistosoma mansoni* within a St. Lucian field habitat," *WHO Bulletin,* vol. 52, no. 3 (1975).

Takeuchi, J., and M. Momiyama-Sakimoto. "Seasonal Variation of Infant Mortality," *Journal of the Meteorlogical Society of Japan,* Dec. 28, 1973, and Aug. 28, 1975.

Tansey, Michael R., and Thomas D. Brock. "The Upper Temperature Limit for Eukaryotic Organisms," *Proceedings of the National Academy of Sciences,* Sept. 1972.

Taylor, M. G. "Immunisation of Baboons Against *Schistosoma mansoni* using irradiated *S. mansoni* cercariae and schistosomula and nonirradiated *Sodhaini* cercariae," *Journal of Helminthology,* 1976.

Terhune, Elinor. "Plants as Indicators of Desertification," AAAS meeting, Washington, D.C., Feb. 12–17, 1978.

Thompson, K. V. A., and R. Holliday. "Effect of Temperature on the Longevity of Human Fibroblasts in Culture," *Experimental Cell Research,* Aug. 1973.

Torre-Bueno, José. "Thermoregulatory Adjustments to Flight in Birds." Doctoral thesis, Rockefeller University, New York, April 7, 1975.

Trager, William, and James B. Jensen. "Human Malaria Parasites in Continuous Culture," *Science,* Aug. 20, 1976.

Tromp, S. W., in cooperation with twenty-six contributors. *Medical Biometeorology: Weather, Climate, and the Living Organism.* Amsterdam: Elsevier Publishing Co., 1963.

———, ed. *Progress in Biometeorology, Micro- and Macro-Environments in the Atmosphere and their Effects on Basic Physiological Mechanisms of Man.* Amsterdam: Swetz & Zeitlinger, B. V., 1974.

UNESCO, Programme on Man and the Biosphere. *Ecological Effects of In-*

creasing *Human Activities on Tropical and Subtropical Forest Ecosystem*, Paris, Sept. 3, 1974.

————. *Impact of Human Activities and Land Use Practices on Grazing Lands: Savanna, Grassland*, Paris, April 1975.

————. *Integrated Ecological Research and Training Needs in South Eastern Asian Region*, Regional Meeting. Kuala Lumpur, Aug. 19–22, 1974. Paris, April 1975.

U.S. Department of Agriculture. *Climate and Man*. Washington, D.C.: Yearbook of Agriculture, 1941.

U.S. International Biological Program. *Desert Biome, Ecosystem Analysis Studies*, Proposal for 1974–76 Ecology Center, Utah State University, Logan, Utah, Aug. 1973.

Unrau, G. O. "Individual Water Supplies as a Control Measure Against *Schistosoma mansoni*," *WHO Bull.*, vol. 52, no. 1 (1975).

Urbach, Frederick, ed. *The Biologic Effects of Ultraviolet Radiation*, Proceedings of the First International Conference. Oxford: Pergamon Press, 1969.

Valiente, Doreen. *An ABC of Witchcraft Past and Present*. New York: St. Martin, 1973.

Vreeland, R. G., and M. B. Waller. *The Psychology of Firesetting*, Center for Fire Research, National Bureau of Standards, Washington, D.C., Dec. 1978.

Wagner, J. A., et al. "Heat Tolerance and Acclimatization to Work in the Heat in Relation to Age," *Journal of Applied Physiology*, Nov. 1972.

Ward, P. *A New Strategy for the Control of Damage by Queleas*, PANS (Pest Articles and News Summaries), March 1973, Centre for Overseas Pest Research, London.

Warner, Robert R. "The Adaptive Significance of Sequential Hermaphroditism in Animals," *American Naturalist*, Jan–Feb. 1975.

Weathers, Wesley W. "Contribution of Gular Flutter to Evaporative Cooling in the Heat Stressed Quail," *Federal Proceedings*, 34, 472, 1975.

Weber, Fred R., tech. consult. "Reforestation in Arid Lands," Action/Peace Corps, Vita, 1977.

Weinberg, Eugene D. "Metal Starvation of Pathogens by Hosts," *Bioscience*, May 1975.

————. "Secondary Metabolism: Raison d'Etre," *Perspectives in Biology and Medicine*, Summer 1971.

————. "Trace Elements Metabolism in Animals," in W. G. Hoekstra, et al., eds., *Roles of Temperature and Trace Metal Metabolism in Host Pathogen Interactions*. Baltimore: University Park Press, 1974.

Weissman, Jack B., et al. "A Case of Cholera in Texas," *American Journal of Epidemiology*, vol. 100, no. 6 (1975).

Whitford, Walter G. "The Effects of Temperature on Respiration in the Amphibia," *American Zoology*, 13 (1973).

Wickstrom, Conrad E., and Richard W. Castenholz. "Thermophilic Ostracod: Aquatic Metazoan with the Highest Known Temperature Tolerance," *Science*, Sept. 14, 1973.

Wilbert, Charles G. "Physiological Regulations and the Origin of Human Types," *Human Biology*, 1957.

Wilson, C. M. *Ambassadors in White, the Story of American Tropical Medicine.* New York: Henry Holt & Co., 1942.

Wistreich, George A., and Max D. Lechtman. *Microbiology and Human Disease.* New York: Glencoe Press, 1973.

Wolf, Isabel D., and Edmund A. Zottola. *Home Canning, Fruits, Vegetables and Meats*, Agricultural Extension Service, U. of Minn. St Paul. rev. Sept. 1978.

Wolstenholm, G.E.W., ed. *Pyrogens and Fever*, a CIBA Foundation Symposium. Edinburgh & London: Churchill Livingstone, 1971.

Wrigley, Gordon. *Tropical Agriculture*, New York: Frederick A. Praeger, 1969.

Yoshimura, H., and S. Kobayashi. *Effect of Thermal Living Environment on Thermal Adaptability.* Japanese Commentary for the International Biology Program. Tokyo: U of Tokyo Press, 1975.

Yousef, Mohamed K., Steven M. Horvath, and Robert W. Bullard, eds. *Physiological Adaptations, Desert and Mountain*, New York: Academic Press, 1972.

Zottola, Edmund A., et al. "Home Canning of Food: Evaluation of Current Recommended Methods," *Journal of Food Science*, vol. 43 (1978).

Index